Expert Systems 85

THE BRITISH COMPUTER SOCIETY WORKSHOP SERIES

EDITOR: P. HAMMERSLEY

The BCS Workshop Series aims to report developments of an advanced technical standard undertaken by members of The British Computer Society through the Society's study groups and conference organisation. The Series should be compulsive reading for all whose work or interest involves computing technology and for both undergraduate and post-graduate students. Volumes in this Series will mirror the quality of papers published in the BCS's technical periodical *The Computer Journal* and range widely across topics in computer hardware, software, applications and management.

Some current titles:

Data Bases: Proceedings of the International Conference 1980
Ed. S. M. Deen and P. Hammersley

Minis, Micros and Terminals for Libraries and Information Services
Ed. Alan Gilchrist

Information Technology for the Eighties BCS '81
Ed. R. D. Parslow

Second International Conference on Databases 1983
Ed. S. M. Deen and P. Hammersley

Research and Development in Information Retrieval
Ed. C. J. van Rijsbergen

Proceedings of the Third British National Conference on Databases (BNCOD 3)
Ed. J. Longstaff

Research and Development in Expert Systems
Ed. M. A. Bramer

Proceedings of the Fourth British National Conference on Databases (BNCOD 4)
Ed. A. F. Grundy

People and Computers: Designing the Interface
Ed. P. Johnson and S. Cook

Expert Systems 85
Ed. M. Merry

Expert Systems 85

Proceedings of the Fifth Technical
Conference of the British Computer Society
Specialist Group on Expert Systems

University of Warwick, 17–19 December 1985

MARTIN MERRY
Hewlett Packard Laboratories

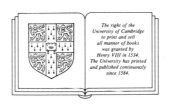

The right of the
University of Cambridge
to print and sell
all manner of books
was granted by
Henry VIII in 1534.
The University has printed
and published continuously
since 1584.

CAMBRIDGE UNIVERSITY PRESS
Cambridge
London   New York   New Rochelle
Melbourne   Sydney

Published by the Press Syndicate of the University of Cambridge
The Pitt Building, Trumpington Street, Cambridge CB2 1RP
32 East 57th Street, New York, NY 10022, USA
10 Stamford Road, Oakleigh, Melbourne 3166, Australia

© British Informatics Society Ltd   1985

First published 1985

Printed in Great Britain at the University Press, Cambridge

Library of Congress cataloguing data available

British Library cataloguing in publication data

British Computer Society:*Specialist Group on
Expert Systems. Technical Conference (5th: 1985:
University of Warwick)*
Expert systems 85: proceedings of the Fifth
Technical Conference of the British Computer
Society Specialist Group on Expert Systems,
University of Warwick, 17–19 December 1985.—
(The British Computer Society Workshop series)

1. Expert Systems (Computer science)
I. Title   II. Merry, Martin   III. Series
006.3'3   QA76.9.E96

ISBN 0-521-32596-X

Unless Recalled Earlier

Date Due

MAR 1 8 1988		
AUG 1 9 1988		
AUG 1 9 1988		
DEC - 2 1988		
JUN 2 1989		
JUN - 1 1990		

Contents

Organising Committee

General Chairman: Bernard Kelly   *Deputy chairman*: Tom Addis

Programme committee

Martin Merry (Chairman)
Richard Young (Deputy Chairman)
Max Bramer
Julie Gadsden
Alison Kidd
Tim O'Shea
Peter Ross

John Lumley (Applications Stream)
Keith Clark
Jim Hunter
Ken MacCallum
Kevin Poulter
Robert Worden

Referees

Tom Addis
Max Bramer
Bill Clocksin
Robert Corlett
Peter Hammond
Jim Hunter
Caroline Knight
Ken MacCallum
Tim O'Shea
Allan Ramsay
Bill Sharpe
Sam Steel
Robert Worden

Peter Alvey
Keith Clark
Derek Colemen
Julie Gadsden
Graham Higgins
Alison Kidd
John Lumley
Jo Marks
Kevin Poulter
Peter Ross
Karen Sparck Jones
Steve Todd

Preface

This volume is the Proceedings of the Fifth Annual Conference of the British Computer Society Specialist Group on Expert Systems, held at the University of Warwick in December 1985. Following the precedent set in 1984, it includes an introductory paper written by the programme chairman.

The proceedings include all the refereed papers which were presented at the conference, together with the invited papers by Austin Tate and Abe Mamdani; papers from the other invited speakers were not available at the time of going to press.

I would like to thank all those concerned for their work in putting together the programme for this conference: in particular the members of the Programme Committee, and all those who refereed papers.

Martin Merry
Programme Chairman

EXPERT SYSTEMS - SOME PROBLEMS AND OPPORTUNITIES

Martin Merry
Hewlett-Packard Research Laboratories
Bristol

INTRODUCTION

We are constantly being told that we are living in an electronic age; that we are undergoing the second industrial revolution; and that the information technology era is now upon us. Journalists describe the latest advances in computing in tones usually reserved for slow motion pictures of the Wonders of Nature or close up views of Halley's Comet.

Despite all this reverence, however, computer science is very young. It has roots in a number of different disciplines (engineering, mathematics, psychology, neurophysiology,...) and still forms a rather uneasy synthesis of ideas from these areas. Unsurprisingly, therefore, progress has been much greater in some areas than in others.

As far as hardware performance goes, exaggeration is scarcely needed. The last 30 years have seen 6 orders of magnitude improvement in hardware performance/cost. Expected lifetimes for new hardware products decrease constantly (as anyone who has bought a micro knows - if only you'd waited 6 months you'd have been able to buy something substantially better and cheaper).

In other areas of computing, however, progress has been rather less meteoric. This is due in part to the difficulty of the many problems that need to be solved, but is also due to delays in technology transfer from laboratories to general use. For example, think how long it took Pascal to emerge from universities into widespread use: even now, FORTRAN and COBOL still have a strangle-hold over many sectors of computing. Other examples now reaching a wider audience include: object oriented programming; logic programming; and the "overlapping windows" user interface paradigm. The typical gestation period for new ideas, languages, etc. appears to be between 10 and 15 years.

Expert systems are no exception. The well-known early expert systems, DENDRAL and MYCIN date from the late 60's and early 70's (Buchanan et al 69; Shortliffe 74), and yet the expert systems "boom" has really only appeared over the last two or three years. Most current applications work involves very few substantive new ideas over these early systems. Arguably, the most noticeable advances in current application systems are inherited directly from advances in the underlying hardware - systems can now be developed on reasonably sized hardware and run relatively quickly.

While all this is rather depressing from the point of view of wanting to see new ideas taken up quickly, it should at least make it somewhat easier to predict what's likely to happen in the next few years. In this paper we have a quick glance at three particular topics currently being explored in research laboratories: knowledge-based planning, new architectures for expert systems, and qualitative reasoning. This will hopefully show us what is likely to come into public view in the near future.

KNOWLEDGE-BASED PLANNING SYSTEMS

Most existing expert systems work in *analytic* domains, where problem-solving consists of identifying the correct solution from a pre-specified finite list of potential answers e.g. fault diagnosis is concerned with identifying which potential fault is actually present. Many possible application domains, however, do not have this restriction: these domains are *synthetic* - problem-solving involves actually synthesizing a new solution. This is substantially more complex.

Over the past few years there has been increasing interest in building expert systems in these sort of domains, drawing on techniques from AI planning and expert systems. AI planning systems actually pre-date expert systems - significant work was being done in the mid 60's (e.g Doran & Michie 1966) - but the convergence of the two streams is relatively recent. Expert systems applied to synthetic domains necessarily use planning techniques; modern planning systems use significant amounts of knowledge from the application domain to help formulate their plans. A survey of knowledge-based planning techniques will be found in the review paper by Austin Tate (Tate 86) in this volume.

It is not only in synthetic domains that the techniques of knowledge-based planning are important for expert systems. The control of expert systems themselves is in itself a real-time planning task (Lesser 1984). This will arguably be the dominant use of these techniques as larger and larger expert systems are built.

In my own work on expert systems I have found that the large majority of problems that people have brought to me, looking for expert system solutions, have required knowledge-based planning techniques; I have regretfully sent most of these people away again because the necessary techniques just did not exist or were not sufficiently robust. This is slowly changing. More and more experimental systems are being built to tackle these sort of problems; the number of people working in these areas is steadily increasing. For example, the Special Interest Group on Planning, formed as part of the Alvey Expert Systems Research Theme, has gone from strength to strength over the last two years and now holds regular workshops. In this volume there are more papers on these sorts of systems than in any of the earlier proceedings of BCS Expert Systems conferences; we expect this number to increase again next year.

NEW ARCHITECTURES FOR EXPERT SYSTEMS

The traditional expert system architecture, consisting of a single *knowledge base* and an *inference engine*, is well-known. Within this framework there are many variations - different flavours of knowledge representation, uncertain reasoning, control strategies etc. - for a good analysis of a number of traditional expert systems see Johnson and Keravnou 1985.

Whilst a lot has been achieved within this framework, as more complex problems have been tackled, it has been found to be inadequate, and a number of variations have emerged. Probably the best known is the *blackboard* architecture, where the expert system has a number of distinct knowledge bases, each of which contribute to problem-solving by writing hypotheses etc. about the problem to be solved on a common "blackboard". This architecture was originally developed for the speech understanding system HEARSAY-II (Erman et al 1980).

In general, frameworks like the blackboard architecture are needed when different types of knowledge are used in an expert system, which may need, for example, different forms of knowledge representation. This leads to partitions in the knowledge base and then to different means of drawing inferences from the different types of knowledge. A number of systems tackling such problems have been built, leading to a host of different architectures (many of these are called blackboard architectures but have many differing features; others, like MOLGEN mentioned earlier, use rather different techniques). Different architectures have also been developed for many other reasons e.g. to cluster related pieces of knowledge (Aikins 83).

I have been involved in a number of feasibility studies for systems with the requirement to handle varying kinds of knowledge. Many problems fall into this category; these are not solved by simply putting knowledge into a conventional shell. Something more flexible is needed - today's toolkits are a short term response to the problem.

Like knowledge-based planning systems, we believe systems based round new architectures will become much more prominent over the next few years. However, many of these architectures are in a state of flux - it will probably be a long time before they stabilize. In many ways, this is because they lack any sort of formally defined semantics - they can be criticized as short term technical fixes to problems that need to be understood much better before longer term solutions can be found. The next topic we consider is one direction for research on such long term problems.

QUALITATIVE REASONING

The first two topics we have discussed both appear to be ideas whose time has come; work in both areas has acquired its own momentum and no great predictive skill is needed to see that these topics will become more and more influential. Qualitative reasoning, unfortunately, does not come into this category.

Most current expert systems only represent very shallow expert knowledge - a collection of fragments of compiled expertise. These, in general, form a small fragment of the problem-solving skills an expert brings to bear upon a problem. Typically, in addition to rules of thumb, the expert is able to reason about the deep structure of a problem. If the domain is sufficiently concrete, this reasoning may be completely quantitative e.g. the manipulation of particular mathematical formalisms. In general, however, much of this reasoning is qualitative, and is concerned, for example, with questions of causality.

We can illustrate this by means of a toy example. An expert system for fault diagnosis in a vending machine might have a rule like "IF you have inserted 10p AND a cup has come out AND there is no drink in the cup THEN hit the machine just to the left of the tea-no-sugar button". This rule is highly specific to a particular (model of) vending machine. If one wished to build an expert system to diagnose faults in an arbitrary vending machine, based round a model of the machine in question, it would need to be able to follow a chain of reasoning similar to "the coin is progressing through the machine...it has passed the mechanism which releases the cup...it has not reached the mechanism which releases the drink...it is therefore stuck at a certain place...this is immediately behind just to the left of the tea-no-sugar button...therefore hit the machine here".

Qualitative reasoning is concerned with capturing this kind of problem-solving skill. Slightly blurring the definition, it is concerned with all kinds of representation and manipulation of "deep" knowledge, and also "common-sense" reasoning. It is a problem that has been looked at throughout the whole of the history of Artificial Intelligence (e.g. see McCarthy 58).

Much work has been done; there are now expert systems based round qualitative models (Weiss et al 78; Mozetic et al 83). However, these systems were largely ad hoc; there is still no principled way of handling qualitative reasoning and many extremely hard problems remain to be solved (some argue that these problems are inherently insoluble e.g. see Dreyfus 1981).

Nevertheless, at least a partial solution to some of these problems needs to be found in order to realize many of the claims currently being made for expert systems. For example, one property of human experts is *graceful degradation* - if you ask an expert a question which is slightly outside his domain of expertise you tend to get an answer which is reasonable, if not completely correct; if you ask a similar question of an expert system you get garbage in response. [This of course is true of other computer systems - if you give a Pascal program to a FORTRAN compiler you don't expect it to produce almost working object code, but at least it produces a string of error messages - current expert systems don't "know what they know", and are as likely to produce wrong advice as no advice at all].

Qualitative reasoning, then, is an area in which much work is needed. We do not expect to see many application papers presented at Expert Systems conferences in the near future which are built round qualitative models - we do hope, however, to see more papers on theoretical work in this area.

CONCLUSION

In this paper we have briefly looked at some of the current work on expert systems which is likely to make itself widely felt in the near future. The first two topics, knowledge-based planning systems, and systems which use differing types of knowledge already have many exemplars and are likely to become of great commercial significance relatively quickly. The third topic, qualitative reasoning, is already making itself felt: it is conspicuous by its absence.

In the introduction to the paper we pointed out that a slow rate of perceived progress can be attributed to two things: the time taken for technology transfer, and the difficulty of many of the problems to be solved. While most of this paper has been motivated by the first of these reasons one must <u>not</u> underestimate the second. Qualitative reasoning is but one example of an extremely hard problem area where major theoretical breakthroughs are needed before we will see significant progress (others include: reasoning about time, a *good* way of handling uncertainty, reasoning with defaults, learning from mistakes, etc.).

One advantage of the expert systems boom is that these problems are receiving far more publicity than ever before, and that hopefully therefore more effort is being expended on them; a disadvantage is that expectations have been raised which will need some of these problems to be solved before they can be met. We must be careful not to assume that mere publicity is sufficient to solve these problems; mounting large scale projects which require unsolved research questions to be answered before they can be completed is rather unwise. Raising unjustifiable expectations in the early 70's led, amongst other things to the removal of much of the funding for work on AI in the UK - we must not let this happen again.

ACKNOWLEDGEMENTS

I would like to thank John Lumley, Bill Sharpe and Steve Todd for their constructive comments on earlier drafts of this paper.

REFERENCES

Aikins, J. S. 1983. Prototypical knowledge for expert systems. *Artificial Intelligence* 20 pp 163 - 210.

Buchanan, B.G., Sutherland, G.L. and Feigenbaum, E.A. 1969. Heuristic DENDRAL: A program for generating explanatory hypotheses in organic chemistry. In Meltzer, B. and Michie, D. (eds) *Machine Intelligence 4*. Edinburgh University Press.

Doran, J. E. and Michie, D. 1966. Experiments with the graph traverser program. *Proc Royal Society A*, pp 235 - 259.

Dreyfus, H.L. 1981 From micro-worlds to knowledge representation: AI at an impasse. In Haugeland, J. (ed.) *Mind Design* Bradford Books.

Erman, L. D., Hayes-Roth, F, Lesser, V. and Reddy, D. 1980. The HEARSAY-II speech-understanding system: Integrating knowledge to resolve uncertainty. *Computing Surveys* 12, pp 213 - 253.

Johnson, L. and Keravnou, E.T. 1985 *Expert Systems Technology: a guide*. Abacus Press.

Lesser, V. 1984. Control in complex knowledge-based systems. Tutorial presented at *First Conference on Artificial Intelligence Applications*, Denver.

McCarthy, J. 1958. Programs with common sense. *Mechanization of thought processes, Proc Symp Nat Phys Lab* vol 1 pp 78 - 84 London : HMSO. Reprinted in Minsky, M. (ed.) *Semantic Information Processing* MIT Press 1968.

Mozetic, I., Bratko, I. and Navrao, L. 1983 An experiment in Automatic Synthesis of Expert Knowledge through Qualitative Modelling. *Proc Logic Programming Workshop 1983* Algarve, Portugal.

Shortliffe E.A. 1974. MYCIN: a rule-based computer program for advising physicians regarding antimicrobial therapy selection. Ph.D. dissertation, Stanford University.

Stefik, M. J. 1981a. Planning with constraints. *Artificial Intelligence* 16 pp 111 - 140.

Stefik, M. J. 1981b. Planning and meta-planning. *Artificial Intelligence* 16 pp 141 - 169.

Tate, A. 1986. A Review of Knowledge-Based planning techniques. This volume.

Weiss, S. M., Kulikowski, C.A., Amarel, S. and Safir, A. 1978. A model-based method for computer-aided medical decision making. *Artificial Intelligence* 11 pp 145 - 172.

WHAT DO USERS ASK? - SOME THOUGHTS ON DIAGNOSTIC ADVICE

A L Kidd
British Telecom Research Laboratories, Martlesham Heath,
Ipswich, Suffolk IP5 7RE

Abstract   The paper addresses the problem of what types of
advice users actually require in a diagnostic task domain and
how some of these requirements might be met in an expert
system. An analysis of human expert consultations suggests
that (i) users are much more concerned with the potential
remedies than they are with identification of a fault and
(ii) they approach the task with their own intentions,
expectations and constraints, which significantly affect the
choice of an appropriate remedy by the expert. The
implications which these findings have on the type of
knowledge which is represented within a diagnostic system are
discussed.

1 INTRODUCTION

Diagnostic expert systems are primarily designed to provide
advice to users on the following two questions: 'What is the fault?' and
'What is the appropriate remedy?' with trace-style explanations provided
if the user should want to know 'how' or 'why' the system reached its
conclusion (e.g. Hayes-Roth et al, 1983). A few more recent systems are
now branching out to tackle questions in the form 'What would happen
if..?' (e.g. Chandrasekaran, 1983) and the intelligibility of
explanations is improving all the time (e.g. Clancey, 1983). However, are
any of these questions the critical ones on which users actually require
advice in diagnostic task domains? If not, then our current expert
systems, however powerful at solving problems, will never provide
effective decision support to their users.

In the absence of any well-articulated theory of diagnostic
advice, the first part of this paper describes a study of naturally
occurring consultations between human experts and 'users' in diagnostic
task domains in order to discover what kinds of advice the latter
actually request. The findings are: (i) that users are much more
concerned with the potential remedies (i.e. what they can do about the
situation) than they are with the identification of the fault and (ii)
that they approach the task with their own intentions, expectations and
constraints which significantly affect the choice of an appropriate
remedy by the expert. The latter part of the paper discusses some of the
implications of these findings on the type of knowledge which is
represented within a diagnostic expert system. It is concluded that

future expert systems must be able to represent and reason about classes of diagnostic remedies in order to support the kind of advice giving which users actually require.

2 WHAT ADVICE DO USERS WANT? - A STUDY OF EXPERT CONSULTATIONS

Over the past year, we have recorded naturally occurring consultations between experts and their 'users' in a variety of domains. At the outset of the study, we recorded a number of radio 'phone-in' programs where experts in domains such as: spring cleaning, health and cooking were consulted by callers with particular problems. More recently, we have recorded consultations between engineers and technicians trouble-shooting electronic equipment over the 'phone. The results of these studies and their implications for the dialogue design of expert systems is more fully discussed in Kidd (1985).

For the purpose of the present paper, we concentrate on some of the different categories of advice which users commonly sought from the expert. These are described below:-

2.1 Negotiation of Appropriate Remedy

In most of the dialogues we analysed, the users seemed happy to accept the expert's diagnosis of the fault without much argument or even interest. However, when it came to deciding on an appropriate remedy, the users took an active role in the problem solving process. Each user approached the problem with his own set of constraints on what constituted an appropriate remedy, e.g. 'It must be quick', or 'It mustn't affect X'. He volunteered these to the expert at an early stage in the consultation. In contrast to current expert systems, where the answer is provided at the end of the dialogue with little comeback possible from the user, our experts usually generated 'first-stab' answers from an early stage in the consultation. The expert and user then engaged in a negotiating dialogue aimed at finding which remedy was best tailored to the user's particular needs and convincing the user of the validity of this advice (see Pollack et al, 1982; Coombs & Alty, 1984). Once an initial remedy had been presented, this negotiation process consisted of the following activities:

- The user checked that his constraints had been taken into account, e.g. 'Are you sure that will be quick enough?'.
- The user rejected the remedy because he had already tried it without success or because it failed to meet some constraint, e.g. 'That won't work because.....'.
- The user requested provision or evaluation of alternative remedies, e.g. 'Isn't X as effective?' or 'What else will work?'

Even in the dialogues where the user did not volunteer constraints etc., the expert still tended to describe the space of possible remedies, setting out the pros and cons of the various alternatives, e.g. 'If the machine has been behaving like that for a long time then X is probably the only thing that will work, but it might be worth giving Y a try first as long as you're sure that the switching unit works.....'. In this way, the initiative for deciding which remedy to try was always left with the user.

2.2 Evaluate Remedy Proposed by User

In many instances, the user actually approached the expert
with a specific proposal about what the remedy for his problem might be
or what he wanted it to be. He then asked the expert to evaluate this
proposal, e.g. 'Is X the right remedy?' or 'Is it a good idea to do Y?'.
If his proposal was wrong then he wanted to know why as well as be given
a convincing alternative. In some instances, the user was aware of a
number of possible remedies and he wanted the expert to evaluate and
compare them, e.g. 'Which is the best remedy: X, Y or Z?'.

This kind of approach to expert advice giving has recently
been dubbed the 'critiquing' approach and has been explored in the domain
of medical management by Langlotz and Shortliffe (1983) and Miller
(1984). Given a set of patient data, the user proposes his own plan of
action to the system. The system then analyses and critiques the user's
plan, discussing the pros and cons of the proposed approach as compared
to alternatives which might be reasonable or preferred. The results of
our own study clearly endorse the importance of developing the critiquing
approach for expert systems. However, in the work cited above, the users
of the critiquing systems were themselves experts in the task domain. A
surprising point which came out of our study was that even users who were
relatively inexperienced in the domain, still had their own ideas,
preferences and expectations about an appropriate kind of remedy for
their problem. This suggests that a critiquing approach to advice giving
may be applicable to a range of users.

2.3 Explain Remedy

e.g. 'Why did remedy X work?'. Questions of this type
were particularly common in equipment diagnosis applications where, at
the time the problem occurred, the user's prime goal was to get the
equipment working again as fast as possible (by fair means or foul!) and
identification of the fault was only of secondary interest. However,
after the event, when the user had time for reflection, he was usually
keen to understand what had happened in order to justify the successful
remedy (even if it was kicking the equipment!) and also to equip himself
better for a repeat occurence of the fault.

On further analysis, questions of this type actually break
down into two distinct categories which require different problem solving
processes on the part of the expert to answer them. In the first
category, the remedy for which the user is requesting an explanation is a
known or 'predictable' one, e.g. 'Why did spraying on WD40 get the engine
started?' and the expert can fairly readily trace the causal 'link'
between these two events. In the second category, the remedy is a
'surprise' one (to the expert as well as to the user), e.g. 'Why did
kicking the engine get it started?'. Here the expert is forced to
generate a new causal link between the two events by reasoning from first
principles (cf Davies, 1984). (It is worth mentioning briefly at this
point a third related category of question, i.e. 'Why **didn't** the expected
remedy work?', e.g. 'Why **didn't** spraying on WD40 get the engine
started?'. I am currently carrying out a study which compares the
different problem solving techniques experts employ in order to answer
these three questions.)

From the findings of the above study, we concluded the following:-

i In certain diagnostic task domains, users are much more concerned to receive advice about potential problem remedies (i.e. what they can do about the situation) than with detailed reasoning about the identification of the fault.

ii Most users wish to set their own constraints on what constitutes an acceptable remedy. Experts must be able to take these into account in their reasoning.

iii Often users have already thought out their own remedy for the problem and they only want the expert to evaluate and/or explain this for them. Further analysis of the recorded dialogues has revealed that ii and iii are directly governed by one or more of the following factors:-

a The user's intentions within the domain, i.e. what it is he is trying to do which the current 'fault' is preventing him from doing.

b The user's expectations about the domain, i.e. his own naive causal model of the domain.

c The user's knowledge of 'outside' factors relevant to the selection of a suitable remedy.

3 IMPLICATIONS FOR EXPERT REASONING ABOUT DIAGNOSTIC REMEDIES

The findings described above suggest a very different approach to expert advice giving from that currently adopted by expert systems. Unfortunately, a full implementation of these features is still many years away because it must involve the development of sophisticated mixed-initiative dialogues, intelligent inference of user goals and powerful explanation generators. In the meantime, I believe that a modest capability to reason about suitable remedies for the user's problem and answer some simple questions could be achieved by extending existing knowledge representations to include more explicit knowledge about the class of possible remedies in any diagnostic domain.

Evaluation of the first generation of diagnostic expert systems has revealed that representations based purely on 'if-then' empirical associations between faults and symptoms are effective only on a limited set of problems (Davis, 1982). A growing number of AI workers are now attempting to develop systems which represent and make use of a 'deeper' level structural and functional knowledge of the domain in order to carry out their diagnostic reasoning, create explanations and answer more interesting questions (e.g. Davies, 1983; 1984; Sembugamoorthy & Chandrasekaran, 1985) If, as our study suggests, experts need to reason about and explain remedies as well as fault finding strategies then I believe that systems are also going to require 'deeper' level knowledge about, for example, functional classes of remedies rather than merely empirical associations linking certain classes of faults and particular remedies. To clarify my use of terms here; by a 'functional class' of remedy I am referring to something like 'lubricator' or 'painkiller'. Specific instances within those remedy classes would then be 'oil' and 'aspirin' respectively.

Recent work by Kulikowski & Weiss (1982) on representing therapy information within their CASNET model is moving in this direction. However, the findings from our study help clarify two kinds of reasoning about remedies which the expert needs to engage in:-

1 The expert needs to be able to select a functional class of remedy which operates to clear the fault at the appropriate level within the domain, i.e. at the right level to to meet the user's requirements.

2 Having decided on an appropriate functional class of remedy the expert then needs to select the most appropriate instance of that class to match a given set of problem characteristics and user-imposed constraints.

3.1 Selecting a Functional Class of Remedy

A fault on a piece of equipment can be described at different levels; unfortunately these are not clearly distinguished across different domains or even different AI approaches. To keep it simple for the sake of our current discussion, I have chosen to talk about three levels only:-

SYMPTOM   - the top level perceivable evidence that 'something is wrong'
DISORDER - the mal-state of the system
CAUSE   - what initiated the mal-state.

The point I wish to make is that a fault can potentially be cleared at any one of these levels and the level at which it is cleared depends on which functional class of remedy is used **and this is of direct concern to the user.** Figure 1 shows a simple diagnostic example in the domain of spring cleaning taken directly from one of our recordings. An excerpt from the original dialogue is given below the diagram. Here the user had a problem of a "black deposit between the bathroom tiles". The expert first selected a functional remedy at the shallowest level, i.e. cleaning away the deposit (Line 8) but then later (Line 18) he dropped down a level to describe the cause of the problem, i.e. dampness and selected a functional remedy, ventilation (Line 21), to clear the fault at this level.

At the shallowest (i.e. symptom) level, a remedy will usually have the fastest effect but the least permanence. At the deepest (i.e. causal) level, a remedy will usually have the slowest effect but the greatest permanence. Negotiation between the expert and user is necessary in selecting the right level because the expert, we have found, usually reasons on the basis of maximising the permanence of effect whereas, the user, because of his higher-level goals, is often more concerned about the speed of effect and about clearing symptoms rather than underlying causes. From this point of view, the example shown in Figure 1 was in fact an exception. Here the user was actually concerned about the permanence of the remedy (Line 14) which is why the expert dropped down to that level to provide advice.

3.2 Finding the Appropriate Instance within a Remedy Class

Having selected a functional class of remedy (e.g. cleaning) the next step is for the expert to select the most appropriate remedy

FIGURE 1

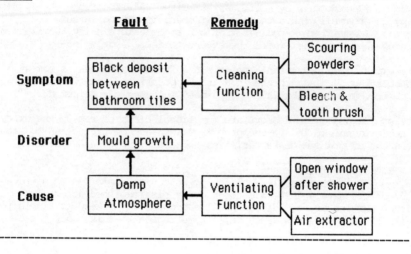

```
 1 USER:    My problem is in the shower room and it's the grouting
 2          between the tiles that gets a black deposit...
 3 EXPERT:  Oh yes, oh yes
 4 USER:    Now this is a shower we created; it's not over the bath, it's a
 5          separate area of the bathroom which we tiled and put in a shower
 6          tray at the bottom and it has a glass door, a folding glass door
 7          and there is space at the bottom to let the steam out
 8 EXPERT:  Have you tried bleach and a toothbrush?
 9 USER:    No, we have only tried the proprietary scouring powders or bath
10          cleaners
11 EXPERT:  Yes, I suggest bleach and a fine toothbrush and just scrub it
12 USER:    And that won't damage the tiles?
13 EXPERT:  Won't damage the tiles, no
14 USER:    I even had it regrouted once when I had the bathroom redecorated
15          but it has come back again
16 EXPERT:  The important thing to remember is this is a mould growth
17 USER:    Yes, that's what I thought...
18 EXPERT   And it's recurring because the room's damp so you have got to
19          cure the dampness to stop it recurring
20 USER:    Yes
21 EXPERT:  If the shower has got a folding glass door, make sure you fold
22          the door back immediately after a shower
23 USER:    Yes, it's not actually folding, it swings closed
24 EXPERT:  Oh yes, you need to prop it open after a shower. Have you got a
25          window in the room you could open?
26 USER:    Well, no...it's all part of the bathroom; in fact, it was a bit
```

```
27              of the landing which we incorporated into the bathroom
28 EXPERT:  What sort of ventilation have you got?
29 USER:    Um, well, just the bathroom window which I'm afraid in the
30              winter, we don't tend to open very much
31 EXPERT:  Well, unfortunately, the only cure for this problem is to
32              ventilate
33 USER:    To ventilate, yes...
34 EXPERT:  So, if you could get into the habit of opening the window just
35              for ten minutes after a shower and then closing it again, you
36              would stop the problem
37 USER:    Yes......and bleach and a toothbrush would get rid of..er..the
38              actual black?
39 EXPERT:  Yes, it should cure the mould growth you see
40 USER:    Yes
41 EXPERT:  OK?
42 USER  :  Thankyou very much indeed
```

(e.g. scouring powder or bleach and toothbrush etc) from within that class. On the basis of our dialogue analysis, I suggest that the following information needs to be represented about individual remedies within a class:

-   Pros and cons of each remedy in relation to particular fault
    characteristics (e.g. 'with an ink stain, if you act fast and get milk
    onto it, it will bring it out but if it's dried then you'll probably
    need a professional cleaner..... don't use salt in case the dye runs.
    If you have a greasy stain just quickly dust some talcum powder
    on....')
-   Pros and cons in relation to common user requirements and preferences.
    These include:-
    .   information about unwanted side effects of remedy
    .   information about cost (money, time and effort and user skills
        required to operate remedy)
    .   information about availability of remedy

Such a representation of the 'remedy space' could then be used to support the following reasoning by the expert system:-

i   **Evaluating and comparing** alternative remedies within a class.

ii   **Recommending an optimal remedy** on the basis of both the relevant
fault characteristics and the requirements and preferences of the user.

iii **Answering user question 'Is X the right remedy?'** (see section 2.2).
For example, the system would first check if X was listed within the
right functional class of remedies (e.g. lubricating agents) and check
its pros and cons within that class and then provide a critique based on
this information. If X was listed in another (unselected) functional
class, the system would explain why it wouldn't work e.g. 'Sorry, X is a
cleaning agent, a lubricating agent is required for this fault'. If X did
not appear at all, the system could at least answer 'A lubricating agent
is required for the fault, if X fulfils this function then OK'.

iv   **Answering user question 'Why did remedy X work?'** (see section 2.3).
In this case, the system would check to see if X was listed within the
right functional class of remedies. If it was, the system could provide
an explanation in functional terms, e.g. 'The fault required a
lubricating agent. X worked because X is a lubricating agent....' If X
was not listed then the system could at least ask: 'Could X act as a
lubricating agent? - If so then.....'

v   **Describing functional requirements of remedy.** In some instances (see
Figure 2), the user will not have access to any of the remedies proposed
by the expert system. With a traditional expert system, the user is stuck
at this point. However, with the kind of representation proposed in this
paper, the system could provide the user with a functional description of
the remedy needed. In the broken fan belt case shown in Figure 2, the
system would explain to the user that an agent was needed to connect the
engine and the waterpump. It could go further and give defining
characteristics of this connecting function, e.g. 'Must be: strong, long,

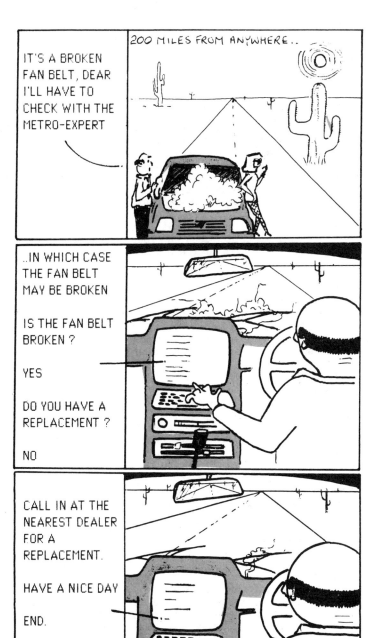

FIGURE 2

narrow, non-elastic'. Given this information, the user could use his own
initiative and generate some possible instances of this class (e.g. tie,
nylon stocking etc).

4 CONCLUSION
In agreement with the work of Pollack et al (1982), our study
of naturally occurring expert consultations in a range of diagnostic task
domains has demonstrated the importance of the expert and user
negotiating over the suitability of a remedy to clear a particular fault.
However, the sophisticated dialogue and goal inference processes
necessary to support adequately such a complex negotiation task will not
be achieved for some time yet; although work such as Webber & Finin
(1984) and Pollack et al (1984) represents a promising approach to these
problems. In the meantime, I propose that some of the users' advice
requirements might be met by an expert system which represents and makes
use of detailed knowledge about functional classes of remedies and about
the pros and cons of alternative remedies within these classes. We are
now exploring ways to implement this idea in order to evaluate its
usefulness in improving the utility of the advice offered to users in a
real application.

ACKNOWLEDGEMENTS
I would like to acknowledge many helpful comments made by my
colleagues at BTRL on the contents of this paper and, in particular, the
efforts of Dr Philip Stenton in providing the illustration for Figure 2.
Acknowledgement is made to the Director of Research, British Telecom
Research Laboratories for permission to publish this paper.

REFERENCES
Chandrasekaran, B. (1983). Towards a Taxonomy of Problem Solving Types.
      The AI Magazine, 4, no. 1, 9-17.
Clancey, W.J. (1983). The Epistemology of a Rule-based Expert System: a
      Framework for Explanation. Artificial Intelligence, 20,
      215-251.
Coombs, M. & Alty, J. (1984). Expert Systems: An Alternative Paradigm.
      Int. Journal of Man-Machine Studies, 20, 21-43.
Davis, R. (1983) Reasoning from First Principles in Electronic
      Troubleshooting. Int. Journal of Man-Machine Studies, 19,
      403-423.
Hayes-Roth, F. et al (1983). Building Expert Systems. Addison-Wesley,
      Reading, Massachusetts.
Kidd, A.L. (1985). The Consultative Role of an Expert System. In People
      and Computers: Designing the Interface, eds. P. Johnson & S.
      Cook, Cambridge University Press, Cambridge.
Kulikowski, C.A. & Weiss, S.M. (1982). Representation of Expert
      Knowledge for Consultation: the CASNET and EXPERT Projects.
      In Artificial Inteligence in Medicine, ed. P. Szolovits,
      Westview Press Inc, Colarado.
Langlotz, C.P. & Shortliffe, E.H. (1983). Adapting a Consultation System
      to Critique User Plans. Int. Journal of Man-Machine Studies,
      19, 479-496.

Miller, P.L. (1984). A Critiquing Approach to Expert Computer Advice: ATTENDING. Pitman Advanced Publishing Program, Boston.

Pollack, M.E. (1984). Good Answers to Bad Questions: Goal Inference in Expert Advice-Giving. Proceedings of 5th Biennial Conference of Canadian Society for Computational Studies of Intelligence, Ontario.

Pollack, M.E. et al (1982). User Participation in the Reasoning Process of Expert Systems. Proceedings of AAAI National Conference, 358-361.

Sembugamoorthy, V. & Chandrasekaran, B. (1985). Functional Representation of Devices and Compilation of Diagnostic Problem Solving System. Cognitive Science (in press).

Webber, B.L. & Finin, T. (1984). In Response: Next Steps in Natural Language Interaction. In Artificial Intelligence Applications in Business, ed. W. Reitman, Ablex Publishing Corp, Norwood, New Jersey.

RELEVANT CRITERIA FOR CHOOSING AN INFERENCE ENGINE
IN EXPERT SYSTEMS.

Han Reichgelt
Frank van Harmelen
Department of Artificial Intelligence
University of Edinburgh
Scotland

Abstract. Shells and high-level programming language environments suffer from a number of shortcomings as knowledge engineering tools. We conclude that a variety of knowledge representation formalisms, for which we use different logics, and control regimes are needed. In addition guidelines should be provided about when to choose which logical formalism and which control regime. In this paper, we give criteria which are relevant in this decision. We have not yet made a systematic attempt to correlate the criteria and different logics and control regimes. although we make some preliminary remarks throughout the paper.

Introduction.

Two types of tools are currently available for constructing expert systems, namely expert system shells and high level programming language environments. Both of these types of tool suffer from a number of shortcomings which limit their usefulness.

The first type of available tools, shells, are usually constructed by abstraction from a concrete expert system. One takes a concrete expert system and takes out the contents of the knowledge base which is specific to the problem at hand to arrive at a shell. A shell thus normally exists of an inference engine and an empty knowledge base and some usually rather primitive debugging and explanation facilities. Buyers of shells often believe, and manufacturers often claim, that the shell is appropriate for a number of tasks in a number of domains. However, a large number of people have expressed dissatisfaction with expert system shells. The two most frequently heard complaints about shells (e.g. Alvey, 1983) are that the view that the inference engine which was successful in one application will also be successful in other applications is unwarranted, and that the knowledge representation scheme often makes the expression of knowledge awkward if not impossible. Shells have proven too rigid. The idea that one inference engine and one knowledge representation scheme is appropriate for a large number of domains and tasks has turned out to be mistaken.

The conclusion is that the initial monistic position of one inference engine for every domain and every task has to be given up for a more pluralistic position. The proponents of high level language programming environments, such as KEE, ART (Williams, 1983) or LOOPS (Bobrow and Stefik, 1983), can be seen as taking an extremely pluralistic position:- instead of providing knowledge engineers with pre-fabricated inference engines, one does not provide them with any at all. Rather, one provides them with programming tools which should enable them to construct their own inference engines with a minimum of difficulty. Thus, the answer of the pluralists to the failure of shells can be regarded as totally giving up the idea that there are such things as domain-independent inference engines, and giving knowledge engineers every chance of creating their own inference engines.

Whilst we accept that systems such as KEE are useful as tools for program development, we would claim that they are less useful as tools for building expert systems. Their main problem is that they provide the knowledge engineer with a bewildering array of possibilities and little, if any, guidance under what circumstances which of these possibilities should be used. Unless used by experienced programmers, high level programming environments encourage an ad hoc programming style in which no attention is paid to a principled analysis of the problem at hand to see which strategy is best suited for its solution.

The conclusion we draw from the failure of shells and the problems associated with high level programming language environments is that there are a number of different 'models of rationality' and that different tasks and different domains require different inference engines to realise these models of rationality. When constructing expert systems, knowledge engineers have to decide which model of rationality is appropriate to the domain and the task at hand. It is our belief that it is possible to give some guidelines which should make this decision easier for the knowledge engineer.

We make a distinction between two aspects of any problem for which the knowledge engineer may want to construct an expert system. First, there is the domain which the knowledge to be embedded in the expert system is about. Thus, the domain of an expert system may be electronics, or internal medicine. Secondly, there is the task which the knowledge engineer wants the expert system to perform. Thus, the task of a system can be diagnosing a faulty electronic circuit or monitoring a circuit.

These two aspects of an expert system more or less directly correspond to the two problems associated with shells. The first complaint about shells concerns the expressiveness of the knowledge representation language. This clearly is related to the structure of the domain. The second complaint about shells concerns the rigidity of the inference engine. But, as pointed out by Chandrasekaran (1985), typical expert system tasks such as diagnosis, planning, monitoring etc. seem to be related to particular control regimes.

We propose to solve the problem of unexpressive knowledge representation schemes by making available a number of logical languages. Which logical language to choose depends on certain characteristics of the domain. For example, in time-dependent domains one would probably choose the language of some temporal logic as the representation language. The main advantage of using logical languages for expressing knowledge is the fact that logical languages have a well-understood semantics.

Although choosing a logical language (and a proof theory to go with it) as knowledge representation language also gives some machinery for doing inference, one still needs a control regime to transform the proof theory into a working inference engine. There are various ways in which this can be done. We suggest that the best way of choosing a control regime is on the basis of certain characteristics of the task which the expert system is intended to perform. So, we conjecture that by looking at certain characteristics of the task one can choose a particular problem-solving strategy, such as generate-and-test, constraint-propagation or means-end analysis. Choosing a problem-solving strategy in turn leads to a particular control regime for the logic whose language is used for the representation of the domain knowledge.

In this paper, we will formulate two sets of criteria which are relevant for choosing a control regime and a logic for a particular application respectively. Although we will make some suggestions about the correlation between the guidelines and different logics or problem-solving strategies, we have not yet looked at this correlation in a systematic way. This is one of the problems we are working on at the moment. The proper level at which to formulate the guidelines is the epistemological level in the sense of Breuker and Wielinga (1985). Generalizing work by Brachman (1979), they distinguish between five levels at which one can discuss the representation and manipulation of knowledge in expert systems: the linguistic, the conceptual, the epistemological, the logical and the implementational level. The linguistic level corresponds to simply representing what an expert reports on his knowledge. At the conceptual level, the question is addressed which primitives are needed to represent the knowledge formally. The analysis at the epistemological level uncovers structural properties of the knowledge expressed at the conceptual level, using types of concept and types of inference strategy. The logical level of analysis applies to the (logical) formalisms in which the knowledge and the inference strategies are expressed. At the implementational level, implementational mechanisms are uncovered on which higher levels are based.

Before we give the list of criteria, three more introductory remarks have to be made. First, the criteria we give are intended as guidelines rather than as prescriptions. Secondly, we shall assume that the different criteria which we give here are independent of each other. We realize that this is an idealization which may have to be given up later. For the time being, however, we will not make any attempt to relate the different criteria. A further idealization lies in the fact that we will present our criteria as being discrete, while in practice most of our criteria will represent continua in which many intermediate values exist in between the extremes. The third introductory remark is a terminological point. One can distinguish between two different types of information used in an expert system. First, there is the permanent knowledge encoded in the knowledge base. Secondly, there is session dependent information. We will call the first type of information 'knowledge' and the second type of information 'data'. The term 'information' will be used as the general term. Thus, both knowledge and data are special cases of information.

Classifications in the literature.

There have been a few initial attempts at classifying expert systems. Chandrasekaran and his associates have done some work in this area and their work is based on the same intuition underlying our work, namely that there are task specific models of rationality and that the inference engine and the knowledge representation which are most appropriate for a particular application, depend on the type of task at hand. (Cf Chandrasekaran, 1983, 1985). However, as far as we know, they have made no attempt to give a list of criteria on which this choice could be based. In this respect, we aim to go further than Chandrasekaran and his colleagues.

The most widely quoted classification in the literature is the one in Stefik, et al. (1982). This classification is based only on the way the system searches its solution space. Although this pre-occupation with search strategies is by no means unusual, it is for our purposes too limited. We would claim that the way the program searches its solution space is more of an implementation issue than an epistemological one. The pre-occupation with search thus leads to analyses which are at a lower level than the ones we are embarked upon. Whilst we acknowledge that the search strategy encoded in a program is of central importance, we are primarily interested in what properties of the domain and the task are relevant in determining which search strategy would be appropriate. Stefik et al. try initially to do just that:- starting off with a very simple domain for which a very simple search strategy is appropriate, they gradually relax the restrictions in the domain thus leading to more complex search strategies. However, when it comes to drawing fine distinctions, they soon give up the attempt to correlate domain features with search strategies, and base their distinctions on implementational issues.

Another classification in the literature is to be found in the introduction to the book *Building Expert Systems* (Hayes-Roth, et al., 1983, 13-16). They distinguish between ten different types of expert systems. Without going into this classification in too much detail, we claim that their classification of expert systems suffers from two basic shortcomings. Firstly, a number of the expert systems which are included in the classification are built up from more primitive expert systems. No reason is given why these systems are included whereas other possible combinations of 'primitive' expert systems are not included. Secondly, even if we ignore the first problem, we see that there are some hierarchical relations among the primitive expert system tasks. For a more detailed criticism of this classification the reader is referred to a longer version of this paper. (Reichgelt & van Harmelen, 1985).

Thus, the existing classifications in the literature all suffer from certain shortcomings. In the next section, we will give our own classification which we hope overcomes at least some of these problems.

Task related criteria.

We will now discuss two sets of criteria which we believe are important for choosing an appropriate control regime and the correct logic when constructing an expert system. We will first discuss three types of considerations which we believe to be important when choosing a control regime.

1. The structure of the task.

A first criterion which is relevant in the choice of the control regime is the type of task which the system is expected to perform. We distinguish between four types of task, namely classification/interpretation, monitoring, design and prediction. The list of tasks we propose is a rationalization of a similar list in Hayes-Roth et al. (1983). Some of the preliminary suggestions for control regimes are taken from Chandrasekaran (1985).

1.1. Classification.

In a classification or interpretation task, the expert system is expected to analyse some data to arrive at a higher-level description of the situation in which the data were observed. The system is asked to identify some data with a specific element in a pre-determined set of higher- level situation descriptions. It is important to point out that in classification tasks it is practical to enumerate the solution space in advance (Cf Clancey, 1984). Although for a number of existing expert systems a complete enumeration of the solution space would be possible in theory, the solution space is so large that enumeration is not practical. Such expert systems should therefore not be seen as performing classification, but rather as performing one of the other types of task mentioned below.

The "input" in a classification task is a number of data, some "low-level" descriptions of observed events. There is of course the question of how to define what counts as a "low-level" description of an observed event, and philosophers have discussed this question a lot. For our purposes, however, the precise definition of this notion is irrelevant. We can at least say that the notion is not an absolute one but is relative to a number of factors. Consider for example the speech domain. On a low level, the "low-level" descriptions of observed events are representations of the actual speech sounds produced by the speaker. The output of this module, i e. the higher level situation description, would be, say, a phoneme lattice. But, on a higher level, one can see the phoneme lattice as the low-level situation description and a word of English as the higher-level situation description. The moral is that what counts as a low-level description is task dependent. After all, in the speech understanding system the output of one stage of the problem solving process is a low level situation description for the next stage. However, in general, the data in a classification task always constitutes a description of the situation which is at a lower level than the situation description which is the output.

Given that the solution space can be completely enumerated in advance, and given the fact that often the solutions can be hierarchically ordered, we follow Chandrasekaran (1985) and suggest that an appropriate control regime for classification tasks might be top-down refinement or establish-refine:- each concept at a given level is tried to see if it explains the data. If it does then its subconcepts are tried until one fits the data, etc. If a concept does not fit the data, then it and all its subconcepts are rejected.

1.2. Monitoring.

In a monitoring task, an expert system iteratively observes the behaviour of some system to extract features that are crucial for successful execution. Often the features are potential flaws in the plan according to which the system is performing.

Monitoring tasks have some characteristics in common with classification tasks. In particular, in both cases the solution space can be completely enumerated in advance. The main difference between monitoring and straightforward classification is the fact that monitoring has an iterative aspect, and that the outcome on the nth iteration might depend on the outcome of the n-1th iteration.

The control regime for monitoring systems is likely to be bottom up:- incoming data are interpreted in order to determine if they correspond to possible problems for the performance of a system.

1.3. Design.

In design tasks, the expert system constructs a complex entity which satisfies certain conditions and constraints. The complex entity under construction can be of very many different kinds. In particular, if it is a configuration of actions, then we are dealing with what is normally called a planning system.

The conditions which a successful solution has to fit, fall into two categories. The first category are those conditions or constraints which describe the present situation, as the present situation may constrain what solutions are possible and acceptable. The second category describes some requirements which the solution has to satisfy, i.e. they may specify a number of conditions the user may wish the solution to meet. Thus, in a planning system we would specify both the present situation and the desired situation.

The main difference with classification and monitoring systems lies in the fact that the solution has to be constructed and cannot be found in some pre-determined set of possible solutions. It is not always the case that the solution space cannot in principle be enumerated. Often enumaration is in principle possible, but the solution space is so large that enumeration is impractical.

1.4. Simulation.

Another task which an expert system can be asked to perform is simulation or prediction. In tasks of this kind, the expert system is given a state of some system and a change in it, and asked to infer whatever other changes will happen or can be expected to happen. In simulation systems, as in design systems, it is usually impractical or impossible to enumerate the space of possible solutions completely inadvance.

The control regime which is to be used in simulation systems is likely to be bottom up:- changes in state of the system are interpreted as changes in the behaviour of sub-systems, and this information can then be used to predict other changes in the behaviour of the overall system.

2. The role of the system in the interaction.

A second factor which is important in the selection of a control regime is the role the expert system is to play in the interaction with the user and the status of the solution of the problem posed to it by the user.

2.1. Advisory expert systems.

In advisory expert systems, the system puts forward possible solutions for the problem at hand. The user is then asked whether he or she accepts the conclusion in question. If the solution is accepted, then the particular problem is considered to be solved. If the user rejects the solution, then the system goes back and tries to find another solution. In advisory expert systems then, the user is the final authority on the acceptability of the solution put forward by the system. Users may reject the advice the system puts forward because they do not agree with the rules the system uses or because they do not agree with the facts the system assumes to hold.

2.2. Dictatorial expert systems.

In dictatorial expert systems, the system itself is the final authority on the acceptability of the solution. The system works on the assumption that the solution it puts forward is the only correct solution. It therefore does not try to find an alternative solution if the user rejects a particular solution the system has come up with. An example of a dictatorial system would be a system monitoring a power plant in a closed loop.

2.3. Criticizing expert systems.

Another role the system can play in the interaction with the user is that of critic. In systems of this type, the user presents the system with a problem and a solution. The system then analyses and comments on the proposed solution. An example of a system of this type is ATTENDING (Miller, 1983) in which plans for anaesthetic management are critically commented upon by the expert system.

3. Time limitation in the task.

Another factor which we include here, even though it is almost certain that it will interact with some of the earlier criteria mentioned before is whether the problem solving process is time dependent or not. We can make a distinction between time critical applications, where the system has to come up with a certain solution within a certain time-limit, and non time critical applications.

Domain related criteria.

In this section we will discuss a number of domain-related criteria. The criteria mentioned here are expected to be relevant in the selection of an appropriate logic as knowledge representation language.

1. Nature of the knowledge in the system.

A first domain related criterion is the nature of the knowledge encoded in the knowledge base. One can distinguish between a model of the domain based on empirical associations, and a causal model of the domain. The terms 'shallow' versus 'deep' models have been used (Hart, 1982).

1.1. Systems with shallow models.

Systems with shallow models rely for their inference rules on empirical associations which have been observed between certain phenomena. Since the nature of the link between the phenomenon described in the antecedent and the one described in the consequent is usually unclear, because there is no complete theory of the domain, these systems often have to reason with uncertainty as well.

1.2. Systems with deep models.

In systems with deep models, the inference rules are based on some causal model of the domain. The phenomenon described in the antecedent causes the phenomenon described in the consequent. Systems of this type may explicitly want to reason about causal relations. Since one could see causality as a necessary connection between cause and effect, systems of this type may require modal logics.

2. The temporary nature of the data.

Another criterion which is important in determining the nature of the problem, is the temporary nature of the data. In the introduction data were defined as the session dependent knowledge the system is equipped with. If the data are completely determined before a session with the system, and the user could in principle give the system all the potentially relevant data before the expert system draws any inference, then we have a static problem. Otherwise, we have a dynamic problem.

2.1. Static problems.

In static problems all the constraints which the solution has to meet can be specified before a session with the system. It is assumed that the problem at hand does not change during the session. The data which is potentially relevant for the solution, is known beforehand by the user, who can supply the system with the relevant information as and when requested.

2.2. Dynamic problems.

In dynamic problems one cannot specify all the constraints beforehand. They may change as time goes on, as in monitoring systems such as VM (Fagan, 1980). An expert system dealing with dynamic problems may need to be able to reason explicitly about time, and it is therefore likely that we need temporal logics for this type of problem. We distinguish between two possibilities.

2.2.1. Predictable changes.

The changes in the constraints on the solution might be predictable. Thus, given that we have all the information we need at time t, we can predict with certainty what the situation at time t + n will be. Thus, although the constraints change over time, we are still able to predict what the constraints are going to be at some later stage if we know the constraints at an earlier time.

2.2.2. Unpredictable changes.

A second possibility is that the constraints which hold at a later time cannot be completely reliably predicted from the information available at an earlier moment in time. We have two possiblities here.

2.2.2.1. More information.

It is possible that as time goes on more information becomes available. Moreover, the new information is not predictable at an earlier stage. The problem then is the decision if it is worthwhile to wait for more information. Is there enough information available to draw a reliable conclusion or would waiting for more information pay off? Decisions of this kind become very important in real-time applications. The crucial feature is that the amount of information increases monotonically, i.e. no previously acquired information becomes false because of more recently acquired information.

2.2.2.2. Different information.

A second type of unpredictable changes in the constraints on the solution is the possibility that the constraints change during the session with the expert system. The system will thus have to be able to react quickly and efficiently in the data it is using to arrive at its conclusion. VM is a system of this kind. It is important to point out that the new information may invalidate previous information. We are therefore dealing with non-monotonic increases in information and we probably need a non-monotonic logic.

3. Certainty of the information.

The certainty of the information is bound to play an important role as well. One can distinguish between perfect and imperfect information. There is probably a strong correlation between this criterion and the nature of the knowledge in the system, i.e. between this and the first domain related criterion.

3.1. Perfect information.

Perfect knowledge is information which can be assumed to be true without qualifications.

3.2. Imperfect information.

Imperfect information is information which cannot be assumed to be true without qualification. We distinguish between incomplete information, and uncertain information.

3.2.1. Incomplete information.

In certain cases, an expert system has only incomplete information about the problem at hand. In cases of this type it is possible that the expert system assumes certain information to hold unless it receives evidence to the contrary. This type of knowledge, default knowledge, has been shown to play an important role in systems which embody common sense knowledge, and it can be expected that expert systems which rely on common sense reasoning will have to be able to reason with default knowledge as well.

3.2.2. Uncertain information.

Another type of imperfection has to do with uncertain information. Uncertainty has received a lot of attention in the context of expert systems (See for an overview, Parker, 1985). We distinguish between three types of uncertainty.

3.2.2.1. Uncertain terminology.

One form of imperfection of knowledge is due to uncertainty as to the exact meanings of the terms used in the domain in question. In the domain of marriage counselling for example, meanings of such basic terms as 'mental cruelty and 'neglect of the partner' are hard to make precise. A related problem is that different types of people often use the same term in different ways. Thus, in the medical domain patients and doctors often differ in their understanding of medical terms, such as e.g. palpitations (Beck et al., 1982, p1).

3.2.2.2. Uncertain data.

A second type of uncertainty is due to uncertainty in the data. In signal processing applications for example, the data are often noisy and hence their identification is problematic, thus giving rise to another source of uncertainty. Another source of uncertainty in signal processing applications is the fact that data will have to be reduced into a more compact format in order for the computer to be able to store them. This will lead to a loss of some information and hence uncertainty in the data.

3.2.2.3. Uncertain knowledge.

A third type of uncertainty is uncertainty in the knowledge itself. Often the connection between the antecedent and the consequent in an inference rule leaves room for some doubt. Most methods for dealing with uncertainty in expert systems are designed to deal specifically with this type of uncertainty.

Concluding Remarks

We have applied our classificatory scheme to a small number of existing expert systems. In particular, we applied it to MYCIN, VM, R1, and HEARSAY-II. The interested reader is referred to a longer version of this paper (Reichgelt & van Harmelen, 1985). We found that the scheme was applicable which we take as an indirect argument for its potential usefulness. After all, if the classification is going to be useful in the construction of new expert system, then it must applicable to already existing expert systems. We are therefore reasonably confident that the criteria which we have mentioned in this paper, are relevant to the knowledge engineer who is faced with the task of building an expert system.

The classification proposed here has to be followed by more explicit advice on what logics are most suited given the properties of the domain, and which control regimes are best given the properties of the task. The underlying intuition was that the choice of an appropriate logic depended on certain aspects of the domain, while the choice of control regime depended on the task. In this paper, we have tried to identify the relevant domain and task characteristics. Although we have made some remarks about what type of logic or control regime is required, this question needs to be tackled in a more systematic way, and we hope to do so in the near future.

Acknowledgements. The research reported in this paper was done in the Alvey-funded project "A Flexible Toolkit for Building Expert Systems". We would like to thank Maarten van Someren and Peter Jackson for their comments on an earlier version of the paper, as well as our industrial collaborators at GEC Research.

References.

Alvey, P. (1983). Problems of designing a medical expert system. Proceedings of Expert Systems 83, pp.20-42.

Beck, E., Francis, J. & Souhami, R. (1983). Tutorials in differential diagnosis (2nd edition). London: Pitman.

Bobrow, D. & Stefik, M. (1983). The LOOPS manual. Xerox.

Brachman, R. (1979). On the epistemological status of semantic networks. In Associative networks: Representation and use of knowledge by computers, ed. N. Findler, pp. 215-251. New York: Academic Press.

Breuker, J. & Wielinga, B. (1985). KADS: Structured Knowledge Acquisition for Expert Systems. VF-Memo 40, University of Amsterdam

Chandrasekaran, B. (1983). Towards a taxonomy of problem-solving types. AI Magazine, 4, 9-17.

Chandrasekaran, B. (1985). Generic tasks in expert system design and their role in explanation of problem solving. NAS/ONR Workshop on AI and distributed problem solving.

Clancey, W. (1984). Classification problem solving. AAAI-84, 49-55.

Fagan, L. (1980). Representing time-dependent relations in a medical setting. Ph.D. Diss. Computer Science Department, Stanford University.

Hart, P. (1982). Direction for AI in the eighties. Sigart newsletter, 79.

Hayes-Roth, F., Waterman, D. & Lenat, D. (eds.) (1983).. Building expert systems. Reading, Mass.: Addison- Wesley.

Miller, P. (1983). Medical plan analysis: The attending system. IJCAI-83, 239-41.

Parker, R. (1985). The treatment of uncertainty in expert systems. Technical Report 21, Internal project paper .

Reichgelt, H. & van Harmelen, F. (1985). Criteria for choosing a logic for expert systems. Technical Report EdU 5, Internal project paper.

Stefik, M., Aikins,J., Balzer,R., Benoit, J., Birnbaum, L., Hayes-Roth, F. , & Sacerdoti, E. (1982). The organization of expert systems: A tutorial. Artificial Intelligence, 18, 135-172. Also in F. Hayes-Roth, D. Waterman & D. Lenat (1983).

Williams, C. (1983). ART, the advanced reasoning tool, conceptual overview. Inference corporation.

GENERALISED ALPHA-BETA PRUNING AS A GUIDE TO EXPERT SYSTEM QUESTION SELECTION

C. S. Mellish,
Cognitive Studies Programme,
University of Sussex

Abstract. In many expert system applications, the task can be characterised as that of choosing one of a set of possible hypotheses to account for some given data by asking a set of questions of the user. In such an application, the expert system must be able to decide which questions are most relevant at a given time and when it is no longer productive to ask further questions. In this paper, we suggest that, given some assumptions about the form of the rulebase, techniques of alpha-beta pruning, originally developed for game-playing applications, can be usefully generalised to provide some guidance in this question selection problem.

The question selection problem

In expert systems applications such as PROSPECTOR (Duda et al 1979), the task of the expert program is to choose among a fixed set of hypotheses (in PROSPECTOR, classes of ore deposits) that might account for a set of data. To do this, the program must take account of volunteered information, and in addition may ask questions of the user. If such systems are to be useful in practice, it is most important that the user is not burdened with unnecessary questions. Thus one criterion for evaluating an expert system is the extent to which it asks the minimum number of questions before coming to a reasoned conclusion. There are two problems to be solved if a system is to perform well on this criterion. First of all, it is necessary to determine, at an arbitrary intermediate state of the reasoning, which questions might produce answers which affect the degree of belief in a given hypothesis. Secondly, it is necessary to determine at an arbitrary point whether asking more questions will produce any significant change in the degree of belief in a hypothesis.
Question selection involves deciding which basic information (to be obtained by questioning) is worth investigating to obtain an estimate for the likelihood of a given hypothesis. This is a similar problem to that of a chess program which has to decide which possible future board positions are worth investigating in order to evaluate the soundness of a possible next move. The chess program has the goal of evaluating as few board positions as possible, and this corresponds to the goal of asking as few questions as possible. Moreover, the chess program does not necessarily need a completely detailed analysis of all positions that may follow from two potential moves - it suffices to know that one move is better than the other. Similarly, in many expert systems it will suffice for the system to decide between two competing hypothesis without calculating the degree of belief in each one in great detail.

Chess programs use the techniques of minimaxing and alpha-beta pruning to restrict the number of board positions that they consider. We now investigate how these can be applied to the question selection problem in expert systems.

Alpha-beta pruning

The situation facing a chess program when about to choose a move can be represented as an AND/OR tree of possible future states of play. The OR nodes correspond to places where the (machine) player can choose a move. In general, the player need only consider one child of an OR node, since in the game it will be able to dictate which move is made there. On the other hand, the AND nodes correspond to those where the opponent has a turn. In general, the player needs to consider all the children of an AND node, since the opponent will dictate the move made, and the opponent's actions cannot be anticipated in advance.

At the bottom of the tree are particular board states that can be subjected to static evaluation. The value to the player of a given node in the tree is computed by maximising the scores of the child nodes (at an OR node) or minimising the scores of the child nodes (at an AND node). The top of the tree is the OR node corresponding to the current choice of next move. In fact, the player does not need to calculate the values of the daughters of this top node precisely; it suffices to know which one has the highest score. Alpha-beta pruning takes advantage of the fact that in general the minimaxing process does not have to take into account the whole tree. There are two basic configurations where optimisation can take place, illustrated in the following diagrams:

```
    ┌──AND──┐              ┌──OR──┐
    │       │              │      │
    5     ┌─OR─┐          100   ┌─AND─┐
 ·····     │    │          ····  │     │
          100   ...              5     ...
          ....                  ....
```

Assume that in each of these the trees are being traversed from left to right, and that the numbers represent nodes whose score has already been calculated. In the first case, the score of the AND node will be the minimum of 5 and whatever the score of the OR node is. Since the OR node is maximising, its score will certainly be more than 100. Therefore the score of the AND node is known to be 5 without the second child of the OR node having to be investigated. The second situation is similar; this time the second child of the AND node need not be investigated. In the literature, the second case is called alpha cutoff and the first is called beta cutoff. A good description of the history and properties of alpha-beta pruning is to be found in Knuth & Moore (1975).

We can represent the partial knowledge that we have of the score of a subtree by a closed interval that the eventual score will lie within. The maximisation and minimisation operations can be extended to deal with intervals instead of simple numbers. In this way, the evaluation of the first example tree can go as follows ("-inf" and "+inf" being the smallest and largest possible scores):

(1)

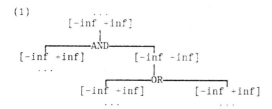

(2)

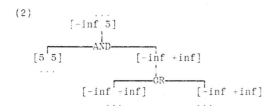

(3)

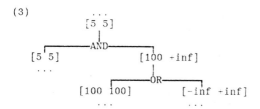

In (2), the first node has been fully evaluated, giving the interval [5 5]. This means that the value of the AND node is at most 5, and so its interval becomes [-inf 5] (each component of the interval is the minumum of the corresponding components for the child nodes). In (3), the second node has been evaluated to give the score 100. Although the interval at the OR node has still not converged to a point, minimisation at the AND node results in a completely determined value there.

The effect of alpha-beta pruning can thus be achieved by updating each score interval as soon as new information is available about the child nodes, and (working top-down) not further investigating any node whose interval has converged to a single value.

The inference net

How are the techniques of alpha-beta pruning to be generalised to attack the question selection problem? The inference net of a system like PROSPECTOR is in fact very like the AND/OR tree of a chess program, and there are obvious correlates to AND and OR in it. Indeed, any system of non-recursive IF-THEN rules involving logical AND and OR in their conditions can be displayed as an AND/OR graph without cycles and so is potentially amenable to these techniques. In this paper, we will talk about a rule system as if it is already presented in the form of an inference net, with top-level "goals" at the top of the net and propositions that can be questioned at the bottom.

Although simple minimisation and maximisation may be
sufficient evaluation functions for the AND/OR trees of chess programs,
many rule-based systems use complex numerical formulae for evaluating ANDs
and ORs. This means that parts of the tree will be "pruned" from
consideration on the basis of whether it is useful to narrow down a given
interval further, rather than on the basis of the interval having
converged to a precise value. In addition, it may be desirable to handle
other (possibly, semi-)logical connectives apart from AND and OR.

We will now specify a sufficient set of assumptions under
which generalised alpha-beta pruning can be applied to the question
selection problem. First of all, the system of rules must be non-recursive
and of the IF-THEN variety. Secondly, we must make assumptions about any
connectives and associated evaluation functions which are used in the
conditions of rules (these same assumptions must apply to any implicit
connective used to combine degrees of belief in a proposition obtained
from several rules). As in the maximisation/minimisation case, the
evaluation functions will operate on closed intervals rather than single
numbers. We will call these confidence intervals. Note that we are using
intervals here, not to represent uncertainty in the problem domain or
inference rules, but to represent incomplete computations of confidence
values - ranges within which they will fall. Thus, if this is desired, the
inference system will always, with sufficient effort, be able to reduce
all confidence intervals to point intervals. Uncertainty in the problem
domain is represented here by simple numbers, in the conventional way.

Each connective must have an evaluation function f which maps
sets of confidence intervals into single confidence intervals. f must be:

> monotonic - that is,
>   for all intervals i1 and i2 and all sets of intervals S
>   if i1 <= i2 then f(S U {i1}) <= f(S U {i2})
>
> (where "<=" denotes inclusion of intervals). This condition
> ensures that increasing information about any single
> proposition (that is, a contraction of its confidence
> interval) can only cause another proposition's interval to
> remain the same or contract.
>
> precise - that is, if S is a set of point intervals then   f(S)
> is a point interval
>
> This ensures that if a proposition has a non-point confidence
> interval, it is possible to narrow the interval further
> (either by asking a question if the proposition is at the
> bottom of the net, or by narrowing down the interval of
> another proposition).
>
> invertible - that is, the following two functions must be
> well-defined and computable for any set of intervals S which
> the connective may be applied to, any interval i in S and any
> numerical threshold thresh:

```
improve(S,i,f,thresh) =
        if there is no sub <<= S such that
                low(f(sub)) > thresh
            then FAIL
        otherwise if there is no i1 such that
                increases(i1,i,S,f,thresh)
            then SUCCEED
        otherwise if there is a least value X such that
                for all y > X,
                    increases([y high(i)],i,S,f,thresh)
            then <+ X>
        otherwise if there is a greatest value X such that
                for all y < X,
                    increases([low(i) y],i,S,f,thresh)
            then <- X>

worsten(S,i,f,thresh) =
        if there is no sub <<= S such that
                high(f(sub)) < thresh
            then FAIL
        otherwise if there is no i1 such that
                decreases(i1,i,S,f,thresh)
            then SUCCEED
        otherwise if there is a least value X such that
                for all y > X,
                    decreases([y high(i)],i,S,f,thresh)
            then <+ X>
        otherwise if there is a greatest value X such that
                for all y < X,
                    decreases([low(i) y],i,S,f,thresh)
            then <- X>
```

This condition ensures that obtaining a desired contraction of
an interval computed from a set of contributing intervals can
be reduced to contracting the contributing intervals. See the
Appendix for some notes on these definitions.

Here are some examples of connectives and associated functions
which satisfy the above conditions. We make no attempt to either justify
these connectives or provide their semantics, but they are all related to
actual connectives that have been used in expert systems. The point is
simply to indicate (informally) that the above assumptions are not very
restrictive in terms of the connectives chosen and that the techniques of
generalised alpha-beta pruning are therefore quite generally applicable.
With each connective, we provide the associated definition of "improve".
"worsten" is very similarly defined.

OR1. This first definition of OR uses maximisation as its evaluation
function (as in the chess application).

low(or1(S)) = max   low(i)
              i in S

high(or1(S)) = max   high(i)
               i in S

```
improve(S,i,or1,thresh) =
    FAIL if for all i1 in S, high(i1) <= thresh
    otherwise SUCCEED if low(i) > thresh or high(i) <= thresh
    otherwise <+ thresh>
```

OR2. This alternative definition of OR uses the standard probability function that assumes independence of the disjuncts. All numbers are assumed to lie in the range 0 to 1. It is defined here in such a way that it can only be applied to sets with two elements.

```
low(or2({i1,i2})) = low(i1) + low(i2) - (low(i1)*low(i2))
```

```
high(or2({i1,i2})) = high(i1) + high(i2) - (high(i1)*high(i2))
```

```
improve({i1,i2},i1,or2,thresh) =
    if high(or2({i1,i2})) <= thresh then FAIL
    otherwise if low(i) = high(i) or low(or2({i1,i2})) > thresh
        then SUCCEED
    otherwise <+ X>,
      where X is max(low(i1),(thresh-high(i2))/(1-high(i2)))
```

A similar formula can be written for "improve(...,i2,...,...)".

AND1. A version of AND that uses the standard probability function, taking the product of the probabilities of the conjuncts.

```
low(and1(S)) = product    low(i)
                  i in S
```

```
high(and1(S)) = product   high(i)
                   i in S
```

```
improve(S,i,and1,thresh) =
    if high(and1(S)) <= thresh then FAIL
    otherwise if low(i) = high(i) or low(and1(S)) > thresh
        then SUCCEED
    otherwise <+ X>,
        where X = max(low(i),thresh*high(i)/high(and2(S)))
```

COND. This connective can be used to express implications that have an associated weight w, this giving the "strength" of the implication. It is defined to only apply to sets with one element.

```
low(cond(w,{i})) = w * low(i)
```

```
high(cond(w,{i})) = w * high(i)
```

```
improve({i},i,cond(w),thresh) =
    if high(i) <= thresh/w then FAIL
    otherwise if low(i) > thresh/w then SUCCEED
    otherwise <+ (thresh/w)>
```

Determining relevant questions

If one is attempting to increase the degree of belief in a proposition above a given threshold, the "improve" procedures for the given connectives can be used as follows. "increase" takes a formula constructed of propositions and connectives (the definition of the proposition we are interested in) and returns the set of basic propositions which, when asked as questions, could contribute information that leads to the degree of belief in the whole formula increasing above the threshold (ie the "low" component of the interval does). In writing these formulae, we will often blur the distinction between a proposition, the definition of a proposition in terms of logical connectives and other propositions, and the confidence interval currently associated with a proposition.

```
     for any connective f,

     increase(f(S),thresh) =
         if improve(S,i,f,thresh) = FAIL for any i in S
             then FAIL
         otherwise,

         U        if improve(S,i,f,thresh) = SUCCEED then {}
       i in S     otherwise if improve(S,i,f,thresh) = <+ x> then
                     increase(i,x)
                  otherwise if improve(S,i,f,thresh) = <- x> then
                     decrease(i,x)

     for simple propositions i,

     increase(i,thresh) =
         if high(i) <= thresh then FAIL
         otherwise if low(i) > thresh then {}
         otherwise {i}
```

A definition for "decrease" can be produced similarly. In practice, it is useful to expand the above definition into cases, one for each connective. Thus, the cases for the examples we have considered above turn out as follows:

```
     increase(or1(S),thresh) =
         if for all i in S, increase(i,thresh) = FAIL then FAIL
         otherwise,

             U       increase(i,thresh)
           i in S

     increase(or2({i1,i2}),thresh) =
         if high(or2({i1,i2})) <= thresh then FAIL
         otherwise if low(or2({i1,i2})) > thresh then
             increase(i1,max(low(i1),
                         (thresh-high(i2))/(1-high(i2))))
             U increase(i2,max(low(i2),
                         (thresh-high(i1))/(1-high(i1))))
         otherwise {}
```

```
increase(and2(S),thresh) =
    if prod(high(S)) <= thresh then FAIL
    otherwise,

       U        increase(i,max(low(i),
     i in S                thresh*high(i)/high(and2(S))))

increase(cond(w)({i}),thresh) =
    if high(i) <= thresh/w then FAIL
    otherwise if low(i) > thresh/w then {}
    otherwise increase(i,thresh/w)
```

Evaluation of confidence intervals

For alpha-beta pruning to work correctly, it is essential that all confidence intervals are guaranteed to hold up-to-date values. Thus whenever a confidence interval associated with some proposition is altered (squeezed), all propositions which are defined in terms of that proposition need to have their confidence intervals re-evaluated. If some of these also change, the propositions defined in terms of them must be re-evaluated, and so on. In general, a change low down in the inference net may cause repercussions through large portions of the net higher up.

The propositions at the bottom of the inference net will obtain precise confidence values if they are asked as questions. In the meantime, they must be assigned sensible confidence intervals so that the calculations higher in the net are valid. They can either be given completely unrestricted confidence intervals (ie [-inf +inf] for suitable -inf and +inf) or restricted intervals based on a priori or volunteered information.

High level strategies

The confidence interval representation can help an inference system to adopt more sensible high-level strategies than exhaustive search. Such strategies can make the system's behaviour seem more directed and comprehensible. Indeed, a number of systems have attempted to build in such strategies explicitly (Clancey 1983). We here indicate how one might adopt and choose between high-level strategies on the basis of the confidence intervals of the main hypotheses.

Investigate Unknown Hypothesis H. This strategy might be applicable if hypothesis H had a completely unconstrained confidence interval ([0 1] if the confidences are probabilities). That is, nothing at all is currently known about H.

Exit With Solution H. This strategy might be applicable if the hypothesis H has a lower bound that is "significantly" above the upper bound of any other hypothesis:

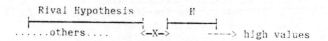

How small a value X would be a "significant" margin would presumably be application-dependent. Note that it is possible for the system to exit with complete confidence that H is the best hypothesis, even though the confidence intervals of H and other hypothesis may not have been reduced to points.

Confirm H. This strategy might be applicable if H looks like the best hypothesis but its lower bound has not yet become higher than the upper bound of a rival hypothesis:

Note that, in order to follow this strategy effectively, we are only interested in questions that could raise the lower bound of H above the upper bound of the rival.

Disconfirm H. In the same situation as shown above, an alternative strategy might be to try and reduce the upper bound of H so that it is lower than the upper bound of the rival. A similar strategy might be chosen for a situation like:

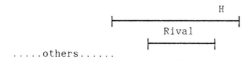

where decreasing the upper bound of H sufficiently (below the lower bound of the rival) would promote the rival immediately to the best hypothesis.

More complex strategies that might be adopted include differential diagnosis, where one would look for questions that would improve one hypothesis but have no effect on another.

Short example

Imagine a situation where the two highest ranking hypotheses, H1 and H2, have the confidence intervals [0 0.28] and [0.24 0.26] respectively. In this circumstance, we might adopt a strategy of "confirm H1". To confirm H1 as the winner, we have to move the low component of its interval above 0.26. Imagine that the inference net supporting H1 is as follows. Which questions would be suitable at this point?

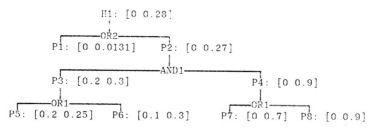

The set "increase(H1,0.26)" is to be computed. Since H1 is defined using an OR2, this set is:

increase(P1,0) U increase(P2,0.25)

((0.26 - 0.0131)/(1 - 0.0131) = 0.25 approx). The first of these is {P1}, since the lower bound of P1 can indeed potentially be raised above 0. Since P2 is defined using AND1, the second set is:

increase(P3,0.278) U increase(P4,0.833)

(0.25/0.9 = 0.278 and 0.25/0.3 = 0.833 approx). Both of the propositions P3 and P4 are defined using OR1, and so the union of these two sets is the union of the four sets:

increase(P5,0.278)
increase(P6,0.278)
increase(P7,0,833)
increase(P8.0.833)

The first and third of these are empty, since they make unreasonable demands on P5 and P7. The other two are non-empty, and so the final result is:

increase(H1,0.26) = {P1,P6,P8}

Conclusions

We have generalised techniques of alpha-beta pruning originally used for minimaxing in game playing to attack the question selection problem in rule based systems. These techniques will work with a class of logical or semi-logical connectives, and we have specified a sufficient set of conditions for a connective to be in this class. We have shown how generalised alpha-beta pruning can be implemented using confidence intervals and indicated how such intervals might help a system to choose a high-level strategy.

There are a number of theoretical limitations to the approach as described. We have described the techniques being applied with an acyclic inference net which is given in advance. It remains to be seen whether they can be applied to nets with cycles (corresponding to recursive rules) or to dynamically growing inference nets.

References

Clancey, W. (1983). The Advantages of Abstract Control Knowledge in Expert System Design. Proceedings of AAAI-83.

Duda, R., Gaschnig, J. and Hart, P. (1979). Model Design in the Prospector Consultant System for Mineral Exploration. In Expert Systems in the Micro Electronic Age, ed D. Michie. Edinburgh University Press.

Knuth, D. and Moore, R. (1975). An Analysis of Alpha-Beta Pruning. Artificial Intelligence Vol 6, No 4.

Appendix – notes on the definitions of 'improve' and 'worsten'

If i is an interval, low(i) is the lower bound and high(i) the upper bound on the interval.

For two sets of intervals S1, S2, S1 <<= S2 iff there is a 1-1 onto mapping g: S1 -> S2 and for all i in S1, i <= g(i).

"increases" is used to express the fact that a sub-interval i1 of an interval i, when substituted for i and given similar substitutions for the other elements of S, can cause the the evaluation of the set S (which contains i) to increase above a given threshold, that evaluation being performed by function f. "decreases" is the dual. They are defined as follows:

increases(i1,i,S,f,thresh) iff

        i1 < i and
            there exists sub <<= S - {i} such that
            low(f(sub U {i1})) > thresh but
            low(f(sub U {i})) is not > thresh

decreases(i1,i,S,f,thresh) iff

        i1 < i and
            there exists sub <<= S - {i} such that
            high(f(sub U {i1})) < thresh but
            high(f(sub U {i})) is not < thresh

Given our assumptions about connectives, it can be shown that:

For any S, i in S, f, thresh,

if increases(i1,i,S,f,thresh) then either
        a) increases([low(i1) high(i)],i,S,f,thresh) or
        b) increases([low(i) high(i1)],i,S,f,thresh)

and a similar result holds for "decreases". Further, there are a number of results of the following form:

If increases([low(i1) high(i)],i,S,f,thresh) then
        for all x >= low(i1) and <= high(i),
            increases([x high(i)],i,S,f,thresh)

EXPERT SYSTEMS TECHNIQUES:
AN APPLICATION IN STATISTICS

L. HaKong and F.R. Hickman
Department of Mathematical Sciences & Computing
Polytechnic of the South Bank
Borough Road, London SE1 0AA

ABSTRACT
   The problem of misuse of statistical packages and
hence statistical methods has long been recognised, but no
real solution has appeared, although related work in an
encouraging way can be seen. This problem can be tackled by
expert systems technology. However, one of the main
drawbacks which prevents a wider application of expert
systems techniques has been the difficulty in obtaining the
knowledge. This paper discusses the use of a formalised
method of knowledge acquisition, and reports on the initial
results, which are being implemented in a prototype called
SASS - Statistical Aid for the Social Scientist.

1   INTRODUCTION
1.1 Statistics and the Naive User
     There exists nowadays a fairly large choice of
reliable and well-documented statistical computation
packages which operate on mainframe computers, and the
number is also increasing for software on microcomputers
(Neffendorf 1983). Packages are developed so that they are
easy to use by non-statisticians or 'naive' users, and this
unfortunately has led to a misuse of the statistical methods
available. 'Naive' here refers to someone who is an expert
in his own field but does not have much knowledge of
statistics, other than the basic level or equivalent of an
introductory course.

As the number of statistical software increases, the number of users, more specifically 'naive' users also increases, and the problem of misuse of the methods increasingly becomes a pertinent one. This problem has been discussed at large in the statistical literature e.g.(Nelder 1977, Hooke 1980, Hunter 1981). No real solution has appeared yet, although work in the right direction can be seen e.g. (Gale & Pregibon 1982, Hand 1984).

Chambers (1981) summarizes the above discussion succintly:

"Statistical software in its present form, made widely available by cheap computing, will precipitate much uninformed, unguided and simply incorrect analysis. We are obliged to help."

1.2 Suggested Solution

1.2.1 The Expert System Technology. Feigenbaum(1982) defines an Expert System as follows:

"An Expert System is an intelligent computer program that uses knowledge and inference procedures to solve problems that are difficult enough to require significant human expertise for their solution.

The knowledge of an Expert System consists of facts and heuristics. The facts constitute a body of information that is widely shared, publically available, and generally agreed upon by experts in the field. The heuristics are mostly private, little discussed rules of good judgement that characterize expert-level decision-making in the field."

It follows that if the knowledge of how to use the methods properly - a form of statistical expertise - can be obtained and incorporated in a program, more 'intelligent' software can be made available to the user. This kind of expertise is highly unstructured and informal, and expert systems research specifically address such areas. Techniques for acquiring the knowledge and representing it in a form suitable for the computer have been devised, although they represent more a state of the art than an established technology.

1.2.2 Approaches to Statistical Expert System Building. There are basically two different approaches to helping the naive user, using expert system technology:

(i) Incorporate expertise in the use of a chosen method.
        This mainly implies that the assumptions underlying the statistical method chosen are not violated. An example of such an approach is REX (Gale & Pregibon 1982), a prototype built for doing regression analysis. Here, the user will need to have first made the decision that linear regression analysis is appropriate for this problem.

(ii) Incorporate expertise in guiding the user to select an appropriate statistical method.
        This approach ensures that the right method is chosen in the first place. An example of this approach is STATPATH (Portier & Lai 1983). The control strategy of the prototype is basically a binary tree search, where the end nodes of the tree represent the techniques. The system is quite restricted, and the work has not been followed up (personal communication 1985).

1.2.3 The Chosen Approach. In this research, the second approach was adopted for several reasons:

(i) The kind of user that one had in mind was one who would have sufficient understanding of the purpose of statistics, but insufficient familiarity of the various methods to know almost instinctively which one to select. The first approach would not be of much use if the user does not know which method to use in the first method.

(ii) The first approach requires the designer to be expert
in the use of a particular method, or working closely with
such an expert (Pregibon 1985). The second one can make use
of several experts who will each have a smaller commitment.
For this research, several expert statisticians can be
available for consultation but no particular one is directly
involved to any significant extent in the work.

2   EXPERT SYSTEM BUILDING

The traditional way to build an expert system is
to interview the expert with a view of representing what is
said in the form of a chosen representation scheme, usually
production rules.   A prototype is then built based on the
results of the interview, and this can be tested and
modified accordingly after reconsultation with the expert,
until a satisfactory level of performance is achieved. Such
an approach is being considered by Hand (1984), to build a
system for selecting a statistical tool.

However, this 'rapid prototyping' approach is
inherently very time-consuming and experience has shown that
a level of performance as desired is hardly ever achieved in
practice.   Furthermore, it forces one to represent the
knowledge in a predetermined format, which may not be the
right one.   Knowledge representation has been regarded as
being the determining factor in the performance of an expert
system (Young 1984). A different view, which has received
much interest in the literature, is that knowledge
acquisition is the crucial factor in expert system building
(Feigenbaum 1982).

The truth of the matter clearly lies between the
two i.e. it is believed that performance is a function of
both acquisition and representation of the knowledge.
Acquisition should not be initially guided by the
representation scheme (as is the case in the traditional
approach), but should reflect the expert's way of
problem-solving.   A representation scheme can then be

chosen, based on this initial knowledge. The refinement process can subsequently be carried out in the light of the scheme chosen. This approach can perhaps be termed 'slow prototyping' and is being adopted in this research. The view was largely influenced by the work of Breuker & Weilinga (1984) in the development of a methodology for knowledge acquisition.

3   DEVELOPING THE SYSTEM

In the traditional approach, the prototype itself is seen as a tool for further acquisition of knowledge. The initial set of rules (i.e. the initial knowledge base) does not seem to be crucial in validity, since the process of modifying it (the refinement cycles) is important in acquiring or refining the knowledge.

As hinted in the earlier section, it is believed that the knowledge for the first prototype is crucial as a properly chosen and represented, initial knowledge base can significantly reduce the number of refinement cycles. This consequently should reduce the interaction time with the expert, a situation highly desirable when considering cost of expert time.

The following stages describe the steps undertaken in acquiring knowledge for the domain of statistical method selection, and draws principally from the methodology as proposed by Breuker & Weilinga (1984).

3.1   Background Of The Domain

The 'domain' here denotes the entire subject of statistics. Several types of expertise were identified (HaKong 1985), two of which are more relevant to our problem of the naive user and have been incorporated in the approaches to system building (section 1.2.2). This stage is necessary to understand the importance of the task in a global way, as well as its validity. Information on the subject was obtained by interviewing the expert, and studying relevant articles and books e.g.(Hooke 1980, Hunter 1981, Chambers 1981).

The interview played a particularly important role in that it enabled one to formulate some preliminary design objectives, other than the problem-solving. These are primarily concerned with the necessity for good explanatory features and include:

(i) the ability to explain statistical terminology.

Statistics has its own terminology and this is very much a source of confusion for the naive user. Some form of clarification module must be incorporated.

(ii) the ability to answer 'why' questions

The system should be able to explain why a certain question was asked, or why a particular method was chosen. Here, sensible answers i.e. answers that clarify the situation, should be provided.

(iii) the ability to answer 'why not' questions

The naive user has some understanding of statistics and may sometimes wander why a different method (e.g. one that he is aware of or familiar with) has not been chosen. 'Why not' questions are equally as important and likely as 'why' questions, and again sensible answers must be given.

(iv) the ability to cope with unknown answers

The choice of a method requires the system to extract knowledge from the user, more specifically knowledge concerning the data and experiment. The user may feel unable to answer some questions. The system must be able to deal with the situation in a satisfactory way.

3.2 Choice Of The Ground Domain

Effective statistical work involves an extensive

interplay between the statistical knowledge and the ground domain knowledge i.e. the domain to which the statistical method is applied (Hand 1984). It was felt that the task of selecting a method would be more tractable if the work focuses on a specific ground domain. Social Sciences was chosen as the target ground domain, after an inspection through several curricula of degree-level courses that include a statistics module. Social scientists who had no deeper understanding of statistics before they did the course would appear to meet the requirements of the naive user.

3.3 Background Of The Sub-domain

The 'sub-domain' is a sub-task of the domain of statistical work. Here, it is the task of selecting a method for analysis of data. A literature search for the techniques mostly used by social scientists was carried out, principally from the textbooks by Blalock (1979), Everitt (1977) and Andrews et al (1976). The exercise showed that the statistical methods can basically be classified in three groups which are related to the number of variables of interest in the experiment, e.g. Andrews et al (1976). These groups can be termed the 'dimension' of interest to the user. An experiment which considers one variable only is termed a one-dimension experiment, and similarly for two variables experiments and more-than-two variables experiments.

3.4 Protocol Analysis

To verify and supplement the knowledge as obtained from the text-books, a series of examples of data-sets were provided to the expert for problem-solving. The expert was asked to 'think and comment aloud' as he solved the problems. All the sessions were tape-recorded for subsequent analysis.

3.5 Building An Interpretation Model

The process of building an interpretation model has been a very effective tool for acquiring knowledge for the system; its use is described in section 4. Weilinga & Breuker (1984) give the following definition:

"An interpretation model consists of a typology of basic elements, structuring relations and a representation of the inference structure for a class of domains. The elements are canonical, i.e. they are abstractions of the elements that constitute the knowledge in a specific domain."

In other words, an interpretation model makes explicit the different types of knowledge that may exist in a particular domain, and is therefore an epistemological framework. Using an interpretation model as a framework for understanding the data collected (from text-books, interviews and protocols) forces one to analyse the knowledge at an epistemological level. An interpretation model is built around the structure-support-strategy paradigm as suggested by Clancey (1983), when the importance of an epistemological analysis of knowledge for rule-based expert systems was underlined. (Brachman (1979) reached a similar conclusion for semantic-network systems.)

Some generalised interpretation models have been provided for particular classes of domains (Weilinga & Breuker 1984), but they seem too general to be useful in a specific domain. A more appropriate model was therefore developed for this research using the same basic elements as the general one for diagnostic tasks, since it has been claimed that the task of choosing the right statistical method is comparable to medical diagnosis (Hand 1984). The first interpretation model was developed from the knowledge acquired from the text-books by Blalock (1979) and Everitt (1977) mainly; it was then refined after consultation with the expert and an analysis of the protocols. The current version of the model is described in section 4.

3.6 Prototype Building

The derived interpretation model is an important tool for the prototype building as it keeps a record of the different types of knowledge that should be present in the system. The first prototype considers the methods for dimension-one experiments only. A suitable representation scheme and control strategy are chosen, which are outlined in section 5. The same control strategy will be applicable to higher-dimension experiments. The additional explanatory features are implemented simultaneously.

4 CURRENT VERSION OF THE INTERPRETATION MODEL

The basic elements of an interpretation model for diagnostic tasks as given by Weilinga & Breuker (1984) are: objects, knowledge sources types, strategic knowledge types, models (support knowledge), and structural knowledge types. Figure I gives the interpretation model developed for this task. Note that its derivation is very much a cyclic process. As the prototype is developed, the nature of the problem-solving will become clearer, and the model will subsequently be modified.

4.1 Objects

A typology of objects was obtained from the various sources of knowledge, mainly from Blalock (1979), Everitt (1977), and Andrews et al (1976). The objects can basically be categorized in two sets: the constraints to the statistical methods, and the methods themselves. A constraint here denotes any condition that restricts the choice of particular methods and includes the underlying assumptions to the statistical model of a method, as well as the objective of the experiment. The protocol analysis showed that the expert would check some of these constraints by established methods (e.g. the normality assumption), whereas others can only be verified by interaction with the user. Thus we see two kinds of constraints: data-directed

```
OBJECTS
   Constraints
      Data-directed Evidence
      Context-directed Evidence
   Hypotheses
      One-dimension Methods
      Two-dimension Methods
      Multi-dimension Methods
KNOWLEDGE SOURCES
   Identification of importance level of constraints
   Procedures for verification of data-directed constraints
STRATEGIC KNOWLEDGE
   Refinement Process
   Data-driven
SUPPORT KNOWLEDGE
   Statistical Theory
   Difference models
STRUCTURAL KNOWLEDGE
   Decision trees
   Lists of constraints and associated methods
```

Figure I

constraints which can be verified automatically, and
context-directed constraints which can only be verified by
interaction with the user. The statistical methods can be
termed 'hypotheses' as they denote possible candidates for
recommendation by the system. (This must not be confused by
the term 'hypothesis' as in the statistical terminology.)
These hypotheses can be classified in three groups, namely
one-dimension, two-dimension, and multi-dimension (cf.
Andrews et al (1976)).

4.2 Knowledge Sources
        From an expert point of view, some of these
constraints are more important than others, for a particular

dimension of experiment. This expertise can be captured as knowledge sources that derive the 'importance level' of a constraint given a particular problem.

Another set of knowledge sources are the procedures to verify automatically the validity of data-directed constraints.

4.3 Strategic Knowledge

Given an initial set of methods (initial hypotheses set), a refinement process can be carried out by checking the validity of a constraint. Any valid or applicable constraint will reduce the size of the initial set. The overall strategy is in a forward way (data-driven), since the refinement of the hypotheses occurs in the direction of contraint validation (which depends on data input by the user) to the hypotheses.

4.4 Support Knowledge

This type of knowledge is particularly important for generating good explanations (Clancey 1983). A crude explanation mechanism is immediately available by attaching to each statistical method the relevant constraints, and this could handle 'why' questions. However, this is unlikely to be satisfactory to some users. For example, when the user wants to test whether the mean of the population represented by his experimental data (his sample) is equal to a certain value, the system suggests the method 'z-test', if the number of cases in his sample is more than 100. When asked 'why' such method was chosen, the crude explanation mechanism would simply detect that it was because 'the sample size was more than 100'. This may be acceptable to some users and indeed sometimes the expert would give such answers. However, for users who wish a deeper level of understanding, a better explanation would be in terms of some statistical theory. In this example, the large sample means that the sampling distribution of the test statistic will be normally distributed, by the Central Limit Theorem. It is this 'normally distributed' property that allows the z-test to be chosen. Statistical theory is therefore a valuable source of support knowledge for giving good explanations.

When answering 'why not' questions, again a crude explanatory feature could be to simply list the corresponding sets of constraints for each method, and highlight the differences. The expert however would not give all detectable differences, and instead give the crucial one(s) only. This expertise can be captured in 'difference' networks, each representing the set of methods that are most likely to be compared. The nodes would represent the methods, and the links represent the crucial difference(s) between the two nodes. Each such 'difference' network would represent a set of methods with some common properties, the most important one being probably the fact that they would answer the same general objective of the user. For example, the methods 'mean', 'median', and 'mode' would belong to the same network of 'summary-measures', and are all candidates for a user wanting to summarize his data. Thus comparison across networks can be explained in terms of the objective of the user. For example, if he asks 'why not linear regression' when he wanted a summary measure, the system could point out that his objective was a 'summary measure' and not 'prediction'.

4.5 Structural Knowledge

One type of structure often given for implementing the task of selecting a technique in statistics is the decision tree (Andrews et al 1976). However, implementing the knowledge in the form of a decision tree would not provide the flexibility that one is seeking. To illustrate this, consider figure II, which represents part of such a decision tree. Notice that the five non-terminal and non-root nodes of the tree correspond to five constraints, which are: (a) ramdom-data objective, (b) time-ordered data, (c) difference-in-level objective, (d) dichotomy, and (e) small sample size.

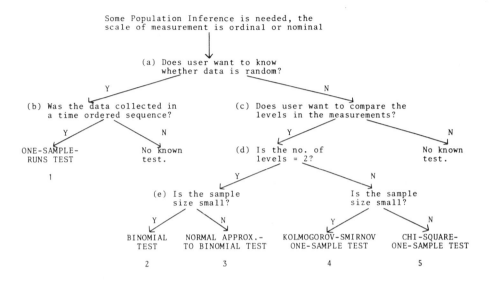

Figure II

In order to reach the end-nodes (which represent the methods), the tree structure requires that the 'constraints' be verified in the order as given. For example, 'random-data objective' must be verified before 'difference-in-level objective', or 'dichotomy' before 'small sample size'. A different order of verification of the constraints implies major reprogramming work.

The main shortcomings of the decision tree formalism are:

(a) its strictly procedural nature which does not seem to match the flexibility that experts seem to allow when performing the task. An expert does not appear to carry the verification process in the same order every time he solves the same task. Furthermore, different experts would solve

the problem in a different order which perhaps reflects
their particular area of work.
(b) the difficulty with which it would handle unknown
answers, as in Portier & Lai (1983).
(c) The combination of static and inference knowledge in the
tree, which makes it more difficult to alter the program.
Separating static from inference knowledge means that the
system can be expanded by simply expanding the static
knowledge.

The above were the main reasons for the need of an
alternative formalism, which is simply a 3-element list to
represent each constraint and related methods. Constraints
and methods were identified as objects in section 4.1, and
form the main part of the static knowledge. Each element of
a list represents the constraint name, a list of methods
that are applicable if the constraint is true, and a list of
methods that must be rejected if the constraint is false,
respectively. Thus the major part of the knowledge base
consists of a number of lists equal to the number of
constraints identified.

With the list-structure formalism, the order of
'importance' of the constraints is not implicit. Each list
contains information about a constraint, which is complete
i.e. it is not dependent on the other constraints. The
inference structure that makes use of this knowledge base is
described in section 5.5.

5 CURRENT STATE OF THE PROTOTYPE

The various types of knowledge as described in the
interpretation model are being implemented in a prototype
called SASS - Statistical Aid for the Social Scientist. The
language of implementation is NIAL (Nested Interactive Array
Language (Jenkins 1983)).

Figure III shows a structural diagram of the current system.

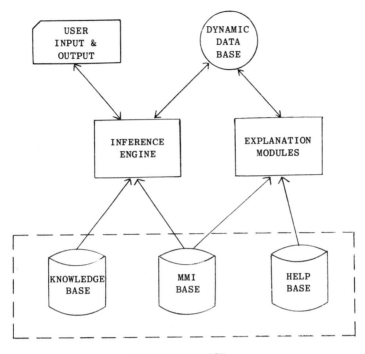

STATIC DATA BASE

Figure III

5.1 Static Knowledge Base

This refers to knowledge that does not change during the course of a session. It basically consists of 3 modules:

(a) Knowledge Base

This includes the set of lists of constraint-methods as described in section 4.5, a default list of constraints for each dimension of experiment, and a set of rules that alters the default list of constraints according to the situation in hand.

At present, SASS contains knowledge for one-dimension methods only. Work is under way to extend the knowledge base to include two-dimension methods.

(b) Help Base

This consists of knowledge to provide the user with good explanations, and includes a set of models based on statistical theory, a set of 'difference' models, and a glossary of statistical terms. They do not affect the basic inference structure and are accessed only by the explanatory modules, on request by the user. This help base is still undergoing development and is not yet fully integrated into the system.

(c) Man-Machine Interface

A natural language interface between the user and the system would be the ideal situation, but would be outside the scope of this research. To provide a seemingly 'natural' interface, canned text is stored, which are sets of questions and corresponding answers, each pair corresponding to a constraint.

5.2 Dynamic Data Base

The dynamic data base contains information relevant to the particular session i.e. it is the place where the user's data set, instantiated constraints (true or false), a list of hypotheses, are recorded. Its state at any time of the session represents the extent to which interaction between the user and the system has taken place. It is automatically erased at the end of a session, unless the user wishes to save it to continue the session at a later time. The dynamic data base is accessed by the inference structure to automatically check the validity of some constraints, and to ensure that the same questions are not asked to the user. The explanatory modules make use of this database to report to the user the particulars of his experimental data.

5.3   Inference Structure

5.3.1 Basic Control Structure. The control structure works basically in the following way: It first selects the right ordered list of constraints based on the dimension of the experiment. It then seeks to check the validity of each constraint, by either interacting with the user or applying statistical test to determine their validity. If a constraint is true, the initial set of hypotheses is reduced by rejecting the methods stored in the third item of its list (as found in the knowledge base). If a constraint is false, the methods in the second element of the list structure are rejected. If the validity of a constraint cannot be determined, the system will not reject any method, ensuring that an answer is always given to the user. A set of rules is applied to the ordered constraints list before any constraint validation takes place, which may result in a different ordered list.

5.3.2 An Example. We refer back to the five constraints ((a)-(e)) as identified in figure II. These may be relevant in other parts of the tree, but for the purpose of illustration we can assume that they are present only as seen in the sub-tree. These constraints are represented in the list structure as shown in figure IV, where each row represents a list. (The corresponding letters and numbers in figure II are used for purposes of demonstration).

```
( (a)  ( 1          )  ( 2, 3, 4, 5 ) )
( (b)  ( 1          )  (             ) )
( (c)  ( 2, 3, 4, 5 )  (             ) )
( (d)  ( 2, 3       )  ( 4, 5        ) )
( (e)  ( 3, 5       )  ( 2, 4        ) )
```

Figure IV

The initial hypotheses set contains methods 1-5. Note that

the union of second and third elements of a row does not necessarily give the initial set 1-5.

Suppose that a user wants to do a difference-in-level test, he has a large sample size, and his data is dichotomous. Figure V illustrates 2 ways (A and B) in which a method can be reached using the control structure described above:

	A	B	C
(a):	2,3,4,5	2,3,4,5	2,3,4,5
(b):	NA	NA	NA
(c):	2,3,4,5	2,3,4,5	2,3,4,5
(d):	2,3	(e): 3,5	2,3,4,5
(e):	3	(d): 3	(e): 3,5

NA: constraint does not discriminate between the remaining methods.

Figure V

In example A, the order in which the constraints are validated are as given in figure IV, and in example B, the order is altered by having constraint (e) before constraint (d). Example C shows the result if the validity of (d) was unknown i.e. if the data was not known to be dichotomous. In such a situation, the system would still give a choice of answers depending on the validity of the undetermined constraint.

6   CONCLUSION

In this paper, the need for an expert system to help the statistically naive user was briefly discussed. The various stages for acquiring the knowledge of the domain were described. A sub-domain of statistics was first chosen, namely the task of selecting a proper statistical method for analysing data in hand.   The major tool for acquiring the knowledge of the sub-domain was the development of an interpretation model. The initial results showed the various types of knowledge that are necessarily present in an ideal system. The results are being implemented in a system called SASS (Statistical Aid for the Social Scientist).

An immediate criticism of the approach may be the extent to which text-books have been used, principally in the use of simple examples for collecting the protocols. But while it is true that in real-life experiments the data collected have a more complex structure, it is also true that most complex data can be broken down in several simpler structures. Indeed it is good statistical practice to break down complex analysis into simpler forms which together may be enough to meet the objective of the experiment (Cox & Snell 1984). To do this breakdown would require ingenuity on the part of the user or the system depending upon the degree to which this ingenuity can be mechanised. This is the subject of current investigation.

The formalised approach to system building as adopted in this paper can only be encouraged. The experience obtained so far has helped the author to organise the work in an efficient way, hence obtain better insight in the task.

ACKNOWLEDGEMENTS
This work is supported by an ILEA research assistanceship. Many thanks to Peter Musgrove for several hours of expert advice in Statistics, and to Tom Addis, supervisor of Lise HaKong, for his continual support and valuable comments. Thanks also to Bob Phelps for his comments on an earlier draft.

REFERENCES

Andrews, F.M. et al. (1976). A Guide for Selecting
          Statistical Techniques for Analysing Social
          Science Data. Survey Research Center, Institute
          for Social Research, University of Michigan.

Blalock, H.M. (1979). Social Statistics, McGraw-Hill,
          3rd Edition.

Brachman, R.J. (1979). "On the Epistemological Status of
          Semantic Networks". In 'Associative Networks'
          N.V.Findler(Ed.), Academic Press, New York.

Breuker, J.A. & Weilinga, B.J. (1984). Initial Analysis for
          Knowledge Based Systems. Report 1.3, Esprit
          Project 12, University of Amsterdam.

Chambers, J.M. (1981). "Some Thoughts on Statistical
          Software". Proc. 13th Symposium on the Interface,
          Pittsburg, PA.

Clancey, W.J. (1983). "The Epistemology Of a Rule-based
          Expert System - A Framework for Explanation".
          Artificial Intelligence 20, 215-251.

Cox, D.R. and Snell, E.J. (1981). Applies Statistics.
          Chapman and Hall Ltd., London.

Everitt, B.S. (1977). The Analysis of Contingency Tables.
          Chapman and Hall Ltd., London.

Feigenbaum, E.A. (1982). "Knowledge Engineering for the
          1980s". Computing Science Department,
          Stanford University.

Gale, W.A. & Pregibon, D. (1982). "An Expert System for
          Regression Analysis". Proc. 14th Symposium on the
          Interface, New York.

HaKong, L. (1985). Expert System Techniques for Statistical
          Data Analysis. Progress Report, April, Polytechnic
          of The South Bank, London.

Hand, D.J. (1984). "Statistical Expert Systems: Design".
          The Statistician 33, 351-369.

Hooke, R. (1980). "Getting People to Use Statistics
          Properly". The American Statistician 34(1), Feb.

Hunter, W.G. (1981). "The Practice Of Statistics: The Real
          World is an Idea Whose Time Has Come.". The
          American Statistician 35(2), May.

Jenkins, M.A. (1983). The Q'NIAL Reference Manual. Release 1.0, Queen's University, Kingston, Canada.

Neffendorf, H. (1983). "Statistical Packages for Microcomputers: A Listing.". The American Statistician 37(1), Feb.

Nelder, J.A. (1977). "Intelligent Programs, The Next Stage in Statistical Computing". In 'Recent Developments In Statistics' J.R.Barra et al(Ed.), North Holland Publishing Company.

Portier, K.M. & Lai, P.Y. (1983). "A Statistical Expert System for Analysis Determination". Proc. American Statistical Association, Computing Section.

Pregibon, D. (1985). "A Do-It-Yourself Guide to Statistical Strategy". Workshop on AI and Statistics, April, AT&T Bell Laboratories, Princeton.

Weilinga, B.J. & Breuker, J.A. (1984). Interpretation of Verbal Data for Knowledge Acquisition. Report 1.4, Esprit Project 12, University of Amsterdam.

Young, R.M. (1984). "Human Interface Aspects of Expert Systems". In 'Expert Systems', J.Fox(Ed.), Pergamon Infotech.

A MODEL BASED EXPERT SYSTEM FOR HW TROUBLESHOOTING DRIVEN BY COMPILED CONTROL KNOWLEDGE

F. Giovannini
CSELT, via G. Reiss Romoli 274, 10148 Torino, ITALY.

F. Malabocchia
CSELT, via G. Reiss Romoli 274, 10148 Torino, ITALY.

Abstract. In this paper are outlined the experimental results about the development of diagnostic expert systems, within the ESPRIT project P96 "Expert System Builder". A mixed mode approach i.e. referring both to the deep and the shallow knowledge approaches has been chosen. A description of the four level structure of the system is outlined. Goals of the described research are the definition of a domain oriented knowledge representation formalism, the use of a unique model for all the diagnostic activities, the definition of an integrated set of AI tools working on it, and the definition of new diagnostic methodologies made possible by the availability of a declarative model.

1. INTRODUCTION

Troubleshooting digital electronics is a good domain for both basic and applied AI research. The application in itself is relevant and tractable [Dav 83] and quite a number of AI paradigms have to be considered. As a consequence troubleshooting electronic equipment is the application domain chosen in order to experiment and validate a hardware and software environment (AI and domain specific integrated tools) supporting the ES construction. This environment is under study within an ESPRIT project [Man 84]. This research is carried out according to a design-implementation loop referring both to the tools and the application. In the following we refer to the application only i.e. to the expert troubleshooting problem.
Expert troubleshooting systems can be divided into three classes:

1. ESs based on symptom-to-cause associations [Kin 82], i.e. ESs using compiled (shallow) knowledge; the majority of existing ESs belongs to this class.

2. Model based ESs [Dav 83], [Gen 84], i.e. deep knowledge based ESs, research in this field is still underway and no working ESs seem to exist till now.

3. Mixed mode ESs: research in the above fields have outlined a list of limitations in each of the two approaches; a way of overcoming these limitations is to exploit benefits of each approach in a single system.

The first class of ESs clearly depends on the specific equipment at hand. Conversely, model based systems are more complex, but device independent.

A promising idea seems to implement model based troubleshooting activities, managed via a high level strategy based on expert compiled knowledge.

The first hard problem in this research was the devising of a formalism in order to represent the knowledge about the model. In section 2.1 a domain oriented knowledge representation formalism is presented, with a simple example of description and a short list of advantages it provides. In section 2.2 are described the model access tools interpreting the formalism. The number and the variety of these tools is the best outcome of the use of such a model.

The second problem was to consider how to exploit the model expressiveness, in order to formulate the diagnostic tasks. The diagnostic tasks are described in section 2.3; one of them is new (e.g. network values reconstructor) while the other ones are analytical formalizations of activities to which a diagnostician is familiar. The improvement here is that while a human expert can use these heuristics only in easily recognizable circumstances, the use of a handy model allowed the understanding of the implicit motivations of each task and then its analytical formulation.

The third problem was how to obtain the best results from this model based diagnosis adding expert control metaknowledge, the results are shown in section 2.4

2. SYSTEM STRUCTURE

In this section we describe the structure of the system (see fig. 1) which implements the mixed mode approach to diagnosis: different levels help to clarify the structure of the reasoning process, its control and its access to the model.

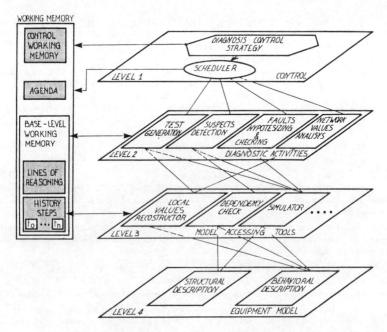

Fig. 1 - The 4-Levels of a troubleshooting expert system.

Entities of the system are:

- The model (structural and behavioral).

- Model interpreters (the model is shared among different interpreters, one of them is the simulator which interprets the model to obtain the outputs of the circuit).

- Diagnostic tasks (which use interpreters as an interface to access the model).

- Control heuristics organize and manage diagnostic activities. Besides scheduling tasks, such heuristics are crucial to recognize unsolvable problems, e.g. fault equivalence.

Figure 1 can be easily summarized considering the model description as the system database, the model interpreters as the the DBMS, and the two higher levels as the diagnostic expert system, with domain tasks at level 2 and their metalevel control knowledge at level 1.

2.1 Model description

Model description can be subdivided into structural and behavioral. In the first case we used a SUBTLE like formalism [Gen 82], implemented using an object oriented paradigm [Bra 82]. Behavioral description instead expresses the components functionality, and uses B-FORM, a specially developed Lisp-like formalism.

Structural description. The HW we consider is a multilevel HW without unbroken loops of combinational modules. Main properties of the structural description are:

a. At each level we have networks built up with boxes (modules), and connections.

b. Modules are considered to be typed objects.

c. Each sequential type definition must be completed with a timing definition, specifying both timing triggering conditions and output delays.

Multilevel description is obtained by allowing each box to be a network by itself.
Following this approach we can represent the structure of digital HW, to complete our task we have now to devise a behavioral description.

Behavior-formalism (B-FORM). The behavioral information pertaining to a module can be expressed in a Lisp derived formalism. A B-FORM function contains both Lisp-like functions and especially defined functions. Lisp-like used functions are: cond, or, and, not, and the main ones working on numbers. We use the "term" Lisp-like to mean that the corresponding Lisp functions were taken as a model for our functions, and then specialized following our constraints. On the other hand, ad hoc functions were needed to express domain peculiarities such as the I/O HW actions, and the state variables handling.

Example of description:

```
(deffunct multiplexer4
  (cond ((= (in 1) 0) (out 1 0))
        ((= (in 1) 1) (out 1 (in 1)))
        ((= (in 1) 2) (out 1 (in 2)))
        ((= (in 1) 3) (out 1 (in 3))))))
```

Advantages of this model representation formalism are:

- It is a high level language allowing the description of complex devices.

- It is a language that can be executed by a very small interpreter built upon Lisp.

- It is a descriptive language which allows, with a limited effort to infer all the relations among inputs and outputs, otherwise hidden.

2.2 Model interpreters

Model interpreters consist of a set of programs working on a shared description. Some of them correspond to tools available in CAD systems, the new ones turned out to be feasible adopting the handy model representation formalism.

Simulator. Different experiences demonstrated the need of a simulator, that would be not mainly (or not only) a powerful number cruncher [Lie 83], but a simulator that would be able to:

1. process data shared among other programs and then not directly suited to it (the same HW description must be used by all programs needing it).

2. allow partial simulations.

3. allow intermixed level simulations.

4. allow alternative simulations changing something at some intermediate instant.

5. allow a change in the behavior of a subcircuit.

6. keep a track during its computation in order to reconstruct each step.

7. process symbolically a subcircuit behavior.

With these goals in mind, the simulator has become not just a program standing by itself and fed by inputs to compute outputs, but an interpreter of the behavioral and structural description able to process declarative data depending on their meaning.

Partial simulation: in our program the simulator has to be called on a single module at any depth inside a network. This feature allows to direct focus of attention over one module and, at the same time, to have a partial simulation of the upper level network.

Intermixed level simulation: when the simulator processes a module, it is applied to the network inside the module. This network con tains some modules, whose behavior can be represented either by their B-FORM function or (recursively) by the simulation of their own contained network, and so on till we have description levels. We have an intermixed level simulation when we replace in a simulation (with a "subnet" option), a module with its contained network which in turn becomes part of the upper network for the following simulations.

Alternative simulations: sometimes in diagnosis it is useful to avail of the capability of backtracking a simulation aiming at testing hypotheses generated about a fault behavior. For this reason one important feature for a simulator used in a diagnostic task is the ability to restore any previous state and then to be restarted over different data. Different data can be:

a. values forced into a point in the circuit.

b. values forced into a state variable.

c. a different behavior function for a module.

Local values reconstructor. The problem tackled by this task can be stated as: "given a module behavior function in B-FORM, and an incomplete list of known values on its inputs, outputs, and state variables, find the missing values that can complete the known situation".

  For a state variable we are interested in a value at time t and in a value at time t+1, in fact we can have for example its initial value unknown, and its final value known, and so on. That means that our variables can be: inputs, outputs, initial state values, final state values. Note that simulation is a very particular case of this task and happens when we know exactly all inputs and all state variables and want to discover what will be the next values on outputs and on state variables.

  What we have achieved in this work is to solve the problem with a subset of the possible functions we can generate in B-FORM. This subset contains also functions not invertible for mathematical analysis owing to a lack of injectivity. That means that there can be more than one solution.

  Example: the following figure is drawn from a dribble-file reporting two significant cases of the application of the local values reconstructor to the PLA contained in the AM2910 circuit. The first case is when information supplied is not sufficient to generate a single solution, and then two numerical solutions are generated. In the second case the supplied information is contradictory and this is the result. The third case is more interesting because the available information is not enough and a symbolic constraint is returned. Its meaning can seem obscure but it simply states that (out 1) and (in 4) have the same value.

```
(inver-cond b-pla nil '(((out 4) 1) ((out 5) 0)))
(((AND (= (IN 1.) 6.) (= (IN 3.) 0.))
  (((OUT 1.) 1.) ((OUT 2.) 1.) ((OUT 3.) 1.) ((OUT 6.) 0.)))
 ((AND (= (IN 1.) 6.) (= (IN 3.) 1.))
  (((OUT 1.) 2.) ((OUT 2.) 1.) ((OUT 3.) 1.) ((OUT 6.) 0.))))
```

```
(inver-cond b-pla
          '(((in 2) 1))
          '(((out 2) 0) ((out 4) 1) ((out 5) 0) ((out 6) 0)))
"contradiction"

(inver-cond b-mux
          '(((in 1) 3) ((in 2) 0) ((in 3) 1) ((in 5) 2))
          nil)
(((((IN 4.) ((IN 4.)) (OUT 1.) ((OUT 1.)))) NIL)
```

<u>Control finder</u>. Sometimes it is important to discover, for a module whether it has highly effective inputs as regard to the behavior. In a HW language they are called control wires, conditional inputs, and so on. They, for the fact that the output is "highly effected" by them (i.e. the module function has a higher injectivity degree respect to other inputs), are given with high relevance in an expert diagnosis.

In an expert system for diagnosis, we can choose to represent that information, for example, attaching a label to those inputs which are considered highly effective by an expert. This of course is feasible, but the same goal can be achieved using a B-FORM behavior description. If we define that a highly effective input is a value tested in each condition, and/or highly used in actions, then we have a way to discover all the inputs that can turn out to be useful for an expert diagnosis.

It is worth noting that this method has a strong analytical power in finding such inputs because, given the behavior definition, we can find not only the special purpose inputs, devoted by the designer to control functions, but also all "hidden" inputs having such property.

This task, perfomed within modules, can be performed on modules networks also. The idea is of looking for modules having functional and topological properties typical of control modules. (e.g. are the sources of other module's control inputs).

<u>Dependency checker</u>. Similar to the previous method is the dependency checker, which is in charge of discovering the functional dependencies of outputs on inputs. The question to be answered is: "at a given time which inputs did affect the observed output and which did not?" This task is carried out by syntactically studying the B-FORM function in the context of the simulation data.

This tool is a simple example of qualitative reasoning. In fact the relations among the pins of a module at a given time are properties of the module itself at that time and can be recognized as a strengthening of the general relations expressed by the module behavior.

Example: the following lines are drawn from a dribble-file reporting the application of the dependency-checker to three of the AM2910 modules. This tool gets a B-FORM function, the number of an output and a specific instant. The answer is a list of input ports from which depend the considered output at the given instant. The instant is important because, at two different moments, the given output may depend on different input pins.

```
(dependency-check 'b-inc 1 0)
(1 2)

(dependency-check 'b-pla 5 0)
(1)

(dependency-check 'b-pla 3 0)
(3 1)

(dependency-check 'b-mux 1 0)
(5 2)
```

Temporal dependency checker. This tool derives, by the timing specifications and delays of each module, the instants in which a value in a certain point of the circuit is affected by the values in a preceding point
of the circuit. The problem faced with in this case is the same as in the
previous one, but temporal dependency checker allows to study functional
dependencies for sequential modules. Both are used by the reasoned trace
task described in section 2.3.

The difference from the previous case is that an output at a
time t, can depend in the first case only on the inputs at time t. For
sequential modules we also have to take into account all past inputs which
may have affected the current output value.

Behavior composition. In some cases it is useful to cluster together a
group of modules and to look at them as if they were a single one. Behavior composition gets the descriptions of some connected modules and
returns the description of the higher level one. This tool is under development.

Loop detector. The loop detector analyses the structural description of a
circuit and returns the list of all contained loops. A loop can be defined
as a path, starting at an output of a box and ending at an input of the
same box. Every loop is represented by giving the sequence of boxes and
connections involved in the loop itself. It is even possible to find loops
inside other loops; that is, loops between boxes included in an outside
loop.

Example: the loop detector is here applied to a sample circuit. The program is written in MRS [Gen 84a], and then the outputs are
MRS assertions. MRS makes use of an ad hoc interface with the model representation formalism.

Relevant topological description of the sample circuit:

```
(conn (in 1 board) (in 1 m1))
(conn (out 1 m2) (in 1 m3))
(conn (out 1 m3) (in 1 m4))
(conn (out 1 m5) (out 1 board))
(conn (out 1 m1) (in 1 m2))
(conn (out 2 m2) (in 2 m1))
(conn (out 1 m4) (in 1 m5))
(conn (out 2 m5) (in 2 m4))
```

Loop detector generated facts:

```
p307: (loop (m4 m5) ((in 1 m5) (out 1 m4) (in 2 m4) (out 2 m5)))
p293: (loop (m1 m2) ((in 1 m2) (out 1 m1) (in 2 m1) (out 2 m2)))
```

2.3 Diagnostic tasks

At the moment we consider four main diagnostic tasks, that
are: reasoned trace, exhaustive diagnosis, network values analyzer and
test generation. In the following we will sketch the ideas underlying each
task giving an example of how they work. The examples in this case will be
imaginary simple ones, because real examples would require too much space
to be explained. In fact these tasks work on the overall description of
the circuit and some of them are very complex.

Reasoned trace. This task is in charge of tracing back, throughout the circuit stucture, the incorrect output values, having the goal of recognizing the subset of modules that can have affected the observed results. Such a task makes use of the circuit's structure and behavior. The motivation of this task is that if a module has an incorrect output, then for the single fault assumption, either the module itself is faulty, or it has (had if sequential) at least one incorrect input from those affecting the output. Goal of this trace is to discard all data paths which were not able to affect (structurally or functionally) the incorrect output.

      Example: suppose that (figure 2) the control input S is expected to select B, then:

1. either MUX is faulty.

2. or a faulty value came from S.

3. or S did not supply a faulty value, -> S is selecting B.

In all the three previous cases A is not the responsible of the incorrect behavior, then its path is not traced backward.

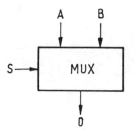

Figure 2

Exhaustive diagnosis. This task consists of hypothesizing a fault, and comparing its simulation with the observed outputs, aiming at discarding the hypothesis if it could not have generated the observed behavior. This task needs a careful expert control to select only easily verifiable hypotheses, that are likely to be false. It is generally used to discard wire stuck-at's, but in particular cases it can lead to acquit entire circuit regions, that is when we can show the inconsistency of faulty values on data paths from there.

      Example:

Let us suppose the situation outlined in figure 3:

- the value observed on output O2 was 1 instead of 0;

- both the other outputs, O1 and O3, showed a correct 1;

- all suspectable components are dashed.

Let us consider the wire W as suspected. If the expected value on it was 1, then we can hypothesize a stuck-at 0 on it. The simulation of this fault supplies the values 0 1 1 for the primary outputs; as these values are different from the previous observed ones we can deduce:

1. W is not stuck-at 0.

2. All modules driving W cannot be responsible of the previously observed misbehavior. Thus they are no longer suspected (single fault hypothesis).

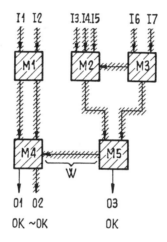

Figure 3

Network values analyzer. This task is devoted to increment the current diagnostic knowledge, about the equipment under diagnosis. It uses the local values reconstructor with the goal of inferring what values could have given rise to the observed misbehavior.

When applying the local values reconstructor to a module, we assume that the module is fault-free, but at some points in the network we arrive at an inconsistency (at least one exists). Such a fact implies that at least one of the assumptions is false and then that one of the considered modules is the faulty one (single fault).

This task, initially proposed for electronic circuits [Sus 75] propagation techniques, is applied here to circuit containing sequential logic and complex transfer functions. The main result in this work is the generation and solution of constrained equations obtained from the B-FORM description.

Example: suppose we have a configuration like in figure 4 with the notation convention of having expected values between square parentheses, and reconstructed values without parentheses.

Suppose we observed a 1 on the primary output instead of a 3. Applying the local values analyzer program we can reconstruct that the multiplier inputs were (1 1). The value 1 on the output of the shifter is

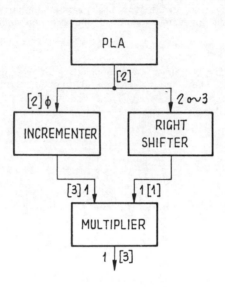

Figure 4

exactly the expected value, then with the single fault assumption we can conclude that the shifter can not be the responsi ble of the observed mis- behavior.

For the incrementer the expected value is 3, while the recon- structed one is 1. We can not conclude anything then we go backward: the reconstructed value on the incrementer input is 1, while the ones on the shifter input can be either 2 or 3. As 0 is not consistent with 2 and 3, we have a contradiction. Till now the hypotheses we made for applying the local values reconstructor are:

1. multiplier must be ok, and

2. incrementer must be ok.

A contradiction implies that at least one of them is faulty and then (single fault) the other modules (the PLA) are no longer suspected.

Example of qualitative reasoning. Owing to a lack of injec- tivity of single modules, we can find that a large number of inputs could have produced a given output for a module. In this case could be a burden trying to propagate backward this large set of data. The idea in this case is to infer a common property of the solution components i.e. they can be represented as a a*n+b series with n ranging in a given interval. In this case we propagate backward this weaker property instead of the actual solution. Propagating a weaker property can weaken the inferences we could do, but sometimes a faster incomplete solution can be more desirable than a complete slow one.

In the following there is the example of the identification of one of the possible properties that this program is able to recognize:

```
(np+a '(3 9 15 1 13 7))
(+ (* 6 I) (1 3))

(included '(3 9 15 1 13 7))
(1 15)
```

The first command np+a gets a list of numbers and represents them as two series which are: 6*n+1 e 6*n+3, while "included" simply recognizes the validity of such series.

Test generation This task can be performed in two alternative ways. In one, a test library is provided by the expert, along with a set of rules that manage their application in order to dynamically generate the best test sequence.

In the other, a test generation task instead is in charge of dynamically generating the next test pattern when it is needed. This second part has not been implemented yet, but the main tools are already available i.e. local values reconstructor, which in this case will be used to propagate backward to the primary inputs the pattern generated for a module inside the network. The idea is to generate plausible fault hypotheses, along with a pattern that could be able to exploit the functionality of the model.

Example (figure 5): suppose that the other diagnostic tasks could not go further, then we can generate a test aiming at discarding the hypothesis that B could have propagated the misbehavior (or was the only faulty path). We search (with the dependency checker and the local values reconstructor) for a pattern with such inputs "don't care". A misbehavior on the output unmarks B.

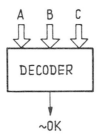

Figure 5

2.4 Control heuristics

At this level a choice of the next task to apply is carried out. Expert knowledge about the efficiency and effectiveness of each task is considered in order to decide what to do next. Each of the diagnostic tasks has a list of applicability conditions derived partly by the expert, and partly by statistics of experiments.

For example the reasoned trace is very useful at the very beginning of diagnosis, while as diagnosis goes on its effectiveness decreases. For the network values analyzer instead the effective ness increases as the diagnosis goes on. Exhaustive diagnosis has to be

carefully managed and its effectiveness depends on the topological configuration assumed by suspected modules, not tied to a particular
diagnostic stage. Test generation is used when the other tasks are not
applicable.

However control heuristics are more complex because take into
accout also the computational complexity of each task along with the tools
it uses to access the model.

Besides control heuristics are in charge of formulating the
diagnostic plan depending on the circuit under test, while heuristics
about the diagnostic task control allow the dynamical updating of such a
plan. At this level are considered also heuristics to stop the diagnostic
tasks when equivalent faults are recognized and then diagnosis cannot go
further.

3. CONCLUSION

The results presently achieved are:

- The formulation of a special purpose formalism, that can express all
  facts relevant for diagnosis, without loosing in access and computation
  efficiency.

- Tools for accessing model are all sharing the same model representation, some of them are well known tools for diagnosis, other ones are
  new, and their formulation has been made possible, because of the formalism expressiveness.

- A practical way of mixing model based and expert based diagnosis has
  been outlined. The advantage in this case is a consistent gaining in
  efficiency.

- An internal organization of the system, which may turn out to be
  general has been shown.

In addition, limited examples of the use of qualitative
reasoning have been tackled. The system presented here has been written
partly in MRS [4] and partly in ZETALISP on Symbolics 3600 and experimented at first on a combinational circuit drawn from a speech synthe-
sizer. Then the devised techniques have been experimented on an integrated
circuit for microprogram control sequencing: AM 2910 [ADM 83]. The circuit
has been chosen as representative for its components, which typically make
HW diagnosis a complex task, e.g. sequential modules, PLAs etc. We have
implemented reasoning activities which use both deep and shallow
knowledge, with the purpose of:

- organizing the flow of diagnosis with expert strategies;

- providing the model description and its manipulation facilities with
  powerful and specialized procedural attachments.

Presently the effort is to apply it on a board with 130 commercial ICs.

4. REFERENCES

[ADM 83] Advanced Micro Device, Bipolar Microprocessor Logic and Interface, Am 2900 Family, 1983 Data Book.

[Bra 82] R. J. Brachman, H. L. Levesque, "Competence in Knowledge representation",Proc.AAAI-82, Pittsburg, Pennsylvania, August 1982.

[Dav 83] R. Davis, "Reasoning from first principles in electronic troubleshooting", Int. J. Man-Machine Studies (1983) 19, 403-423.

[Gen 84] M. R. Genesereth: "The use of design descriptions in automated diagnosis" Stanford Heuristic Programming Project Memo HPP-81-20, January 1984.

[Gen 84a] M. R. Genesereth, R. Greiner, M. R. Grinberg, D. E. Smith, "The MRS dictionary", Stanford Heuristic Programming Project, Report No. HPP-80-24, January 1984.

[Gen 82] M. R. Genesereth, M. Grinberg, J. Lark, "SUBTLE manual", Stanford Heuristic Programming Project, Memo HPP-81-11 (Working Paper), May 1982.

[Lie 83] H. Lieberman, "An object oriented simulator for the Apiary", Proc. AAAI-83, Washington, Maryland, August 1983.

[Kin 82] J. J. King, "Artificial intelligence techniques for device troubleshooting", CSL-82-9 (CRC-TR-82-004), Computer Science laboratory, Hewlett-Packard Company, Palo Alto, August 1982.

[Man 84] F. Manucci et al."Project P96, Expert System Builder, Proc.ESPRIT Conference, ESPRIT technical week 1984.

[Sho 84] Y. Shoham, D. V. McDermott, "Knowledge inversion", Proc. AAAI-84, Austin, Texas, August 1984.

[Sus 75] G. V. Sussman, R. M. Stallmann "Heuristic Techniques in Computer-Aided Circuit Analysis", IEEE trans. on circuits and systems, vol. cas-22, no. 11, November 1975.

ESCORT: THE APPLICATION OF CAUSAL KNOWLEDGE TO REAL-TIME PROCESS CONTROL

Andy Paterson, Paul Sachs and Michael Turner

PA Computers and Telecommunications
Rochester House, 33 Greycoat Street
London SW1P 2QF

Abstract

The ESCORT demonstration system has shown the feasibilty and usefulness of a real-time expert system to ease the cognitive overload experienced by operators of process plant. The work described here deals with two omissions from the original demonstration system and gives ESCORT the ability to reason about the dynamics of the plant and the interactions between different parts of the plant. The approach used is based on causal reasoning. The creation and maintenance of an hypothesis structure that allows reasoning in real-time using current and historic data is presented.

1. Introduction

ESCORT (Expert System for Complex Operations in Real Time) is an expert system that deals with the problem of cognitive overload experienced by operators of process plant. The system analyses the plant data to identify control and instrumentation failures and provides the operator with advice on crisis handling and avoidance.

ESCORT has been developed as a demonstration system to show the feasibility of developing a real time expert system. It has been described at length elsewhere [Sachs et al., 1985; Sargeant, 1985] and is summarised below.

Since the completion of the ESCORT Demonstration System (EDS) in February 1985 we have been investigating ways of enhancing the system to provide more flexiblity in the problem solving approaches used and, in particular, to deal with non-local events and reasoning with time.

This paper describes the work done on these and other aspects of the system since the completion of the EDS.

2. The process control domain

Processes in oil refineries, chemical plants, power stations etc. are nowadays largely controlled by computers or digitally based systems. These computer systems serve the following functions:

- to control the process
- to shut down the plant if it gets out of control
- to provide information to the operators to allow them to manage the plant.

If a process variable (eg. level, pressure, temperature) moves outside set limits despite the control system's attempts to control it then an alarm is sounded and the operator must take some action to remedy the situation. If he doesn't then some or all of the plant may automatically shut down.

2.1. Cognitive overload

In the past the values of process variables were displayed to the operator on standard size (eg. six inch by three inch) meters. The amount of data available to the operator was therefore limited by the number of meters that could be fitted on the panel in the control room. As a result only the more important variables were displayed in the control room. A computerised system, however, has no such limitations. Anything measured can be displayed to the operators. This results in a vast increase in the amount of data that the operators must cope with. For example, the operators of British Gas' Morecambe Field development will have access to around 35,000 items of data. The rate at which the process data changes can also be very great (500 lights went on and off in the first minute of the Three Mile Island incident (Baur, 1983)). Trying to make decisions on the basis of large amounts of data that can change rapidly leads to cognitive overload with the possible consequence that the operator misperceives the real state of the process plant and hence takes incorrect "corrective" action, often causing some or all of the plant to shut down.

2.2. The process plant used for ESCORT

The ESCORT demonstration system operates using data from a simulation of part of an existing North Sea oil platform. Part of the plant is shown in figure 1. The diagram shows two of the five vessels simulated, their connecting pipes, control valves and indicators. The purpose of the plant is to separate out natural gas liquids (NGL) from the mixture of gas, NGL and glycol input through the pipe on the left. The NGL is output from the bottom of VX2. The pipes on the right lead to heating and cooling systems.

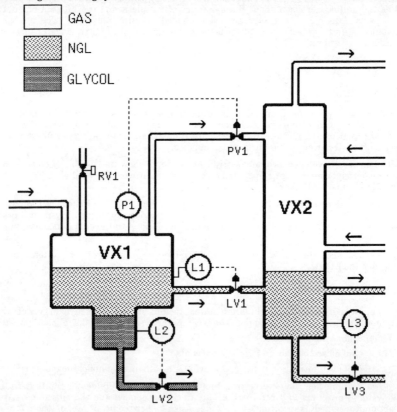

Figure 1.

The plant control system is configured as a number of control loops in which the position of the output valve is controlled by the process variable which it affects. For example, in VX1 there is an NGL level sensor (normally called a level transmitter). Its output goes to a controller which compares the level with what it ought to be (its set point). If the level is too high then the controller sends a signal to the valve to open further. If the level is too low then the valve is closed a little. There are also alarms that activate if the process variable becomes too high or too low. The combination of transmitter, controller, valve and alarms is known as a control loop.

Most of the problems in process plants are caused either by operator errors (eg. adjusting a controller set point incorrectly) or by failure of the control and instrumentation systems (eg. a control valve sticking). Failure of part of the plant itself (eg. a pipe rupturing) is considerably rarer. The faults that can occur in the simulation include control valves sticking open or closed, transmitters failing high or low, and level and pressure switches failing. In addition, the person operating the simulation may make errors in controlling the process.

3.   Limitations of the ESCORT demonstration system

The EDS successfully indicated the feasibility of using a real time expert system to reduce the cognitive load on process operators. Oil and gas industry personnel who have seen the system have generally been very positive about the usefulness of such a system (Pitcher, 1985). The advice provided by the EDS is sufficient for simple process plants in which there is little interaction between the different parts of the plant. The EDS does however have some limitations that must be overcome if ESCORT is ever to be implemented for a complex process plant. The two most important of these are described below.

3.1. Dealing with non-local events

A fault in a particular control loop can cause alarms to occur in both that control loop and other control loops (in which there may be no fault). The first of these we have termed local events - where the event (in this case an alarm) and the fault that caused it are in the same control loop. The second we have termed non-local events - where the event and the fault are in different loops. Non-local events are a major cause of cognitive overload since they can be far more numerous than local events and obscure the location of the real problem. The EDS can correctly diagnose local events. However, it cannot deal with non-local events since its search for a cause is constrained to the control loop in which the event occurred.

3.2. Reasoning with time

The EDS takes a "snapshot" of the plant data every second. This snapshot contains all the data on the process control data buses - the same information as is available on the operator's console. Any advice is based solely on the data contained in one snapshot - previous snapshots and conclusions cannot be taken into account. Thus, although the EDS operates in real time it does not "know" about time (real time in this context means "fast enough to give the operator advice when he needs it"). However, having a knowledge of the past is essential in certain circumstances. For example, where the original fault has been fixed but non-local effects still persist the system must know what happened in the past in order to draw the correct conclusions. It is the ability to refer to past data and diagnoses in order to reason about the dynamics of the plant and to understand what is currently happening in the plant that we have referred to as reasoning with time.

3.3. An illustration

This section contains a simplified example of a situation in which non-local events occur and reasoning with time is necessary. Some points should be noted about the following example. Firstly, the original problem is an operator error and all control systems function correctly. Secondly the rate at which gas is input to VX1 is constant. Figure 2 shows in a graphical form what happens to the pressures and levels involved (the numbers on the graph refer to the stages given below). The sequence of events is as follows.

1.   The operator accidentally opens pressure relief valve RV1 for 10 seconds.

2.   The pressure in VX1 (P1) drops from 36 bars to 22 bars causing a low pressure alarm to occur in VX1. The low pressure alarm is considered to be a local event since the EDS associates relief valves such as RV1 with the loop controlling the same pressure.

3.   NGL is normally driven from VX1 into VX2 by the pressure difference between the two vessels. However, the pressure in VX1 is now lower than that in VX2. The flow therefore ceases (there are one-way valves to stop reverse flow) causing the NGL level in VX1 (L1) to rise rapidly.

4. An NGL high level alarm occurs in VX1. This is the first non-local event.

5. The pressure in VX1 is recovering towards its set point (it has been rising gradually since RV1 was closed). The initial alarm now ceases.

6. There is now sufficient pressure in VX1 to force NGL into VX2. As a result L1 starts falling. The NGL level in VX2 (L3) starts rising. LV3 opens 100% but cannot cope with the increased input from VX1.

7. A high level alarm occurs in VX2. This is the second non-local event.

8. As NGL empties out of VX1 level L3 continues to rise, eventually causing the process to shut down completely.

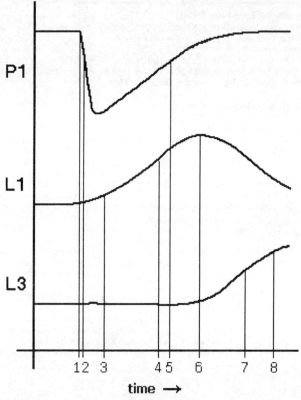

Figure 2.

To summarise, one fault causes three alarms, one local and two non-local. The second non-local event causes the process to shut down. By the time this second non-local event occurs the original cause and local event have disappeared. ESCORT's task is to relate all these alarms to the one cause. If only the snapshot of stage 8 is available then there is no information available to indicate what caused the problem.

4.   Overview of approach taken

The solution developed uses a deeper knowledge of the process plant than that possessed by the EDS. The EDS treats control loops as isolated systems and cannot reason about how one affects another. We have therefore incorporated rules that deal with causal reasoning about the process rather than just heuristic "rules of thumb" about individual control loops. This allows the system to reason from one control loop to another. The system's current view of what is going on in the plant is represented in an hypothesis network. Each hypothesis represents some assertion that may be true, false or unknown (uncertainty is discussed in section 7.2).

An hypothesis network (an example is shown in figure 6) is similar in appearance to an inference network. There are, however, three significant factors that set this approach apart from the usual inference network approach.

1. To allow reasoning with time, the information about a particular assertion is divided into three types (definition, truth values and links with other assertions) which are stored separately.

2. The hypothesis network is not pre-defined - it grows and contracts as necessary. The system has explicit knowledge of how to construct this hypothesis network.

3. The primary function of the links between hypotheses is to represent explanations of cause rather than logical inference.

The three main data types used for holding information on assertions are described in section 4.2. Section 5 explains how these are used to construct a network.

4.1. Plant representation

In order to reason about a process plant a representation of it is required. There are two parts to this: a definition of the components used to make up a plant and a representation of how these components are connected to each other.

Each type of component of the process plant is described by a class in a Class Inheritance Lattice (CIL) (Stefik et al., 1983). Figure 3 shows a small excerpt of the CIL used by ESCORT. A class inheritance lattice is primarily a way of defining data types. Its two main features are that a child class is considered to be a specialisation of the parent and that the child inherits the definition of the parent but can add to or change it. For example, a control valve is a specialisation of (or kind of) valve and therefore inherits the definition of valve which includes variables such as position (open or closed). Note that the CIL only defines how objects are described - it does not define the objects themselves.

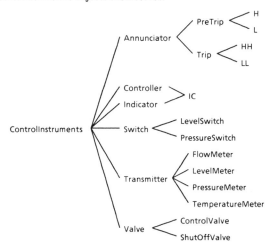

Figure 3.

The actual representation of the plant itself is contained in another lattice whose elements are instances of classes. Figure 4 gives, as an example, two representations of the instance lattice for part of the vessel VX1. The one on the left gives the class of each instance. The one on the right gives the name of each instance. The names shown are those used in the simulation which are different from the simplified names shown in figure 1. The correspondance is as follows: VX01 = VX1, P0101 = P1, L0101 = L1, RV01 = RV1.

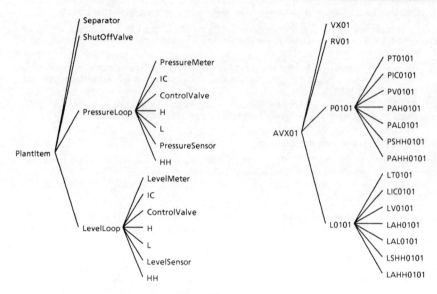

Figure 4.

4.2 Hypothesis representation

The usual way of representing an assertion is with one data type or record. However, when reasoning with time is involved two of the requirements for an assertion representation are that:

- the system should be able to keep an arbitrarily long history of the assertion's truth values

- having two hypotheses refer to the same assertion but at different times (eg. "Is the valve stuck now?" and "Was the valve stuck five minutes ago?") should not result in the duplication of the assertion's definition.

A representation has been developed which uses three data types - hypotheses, super-hypotheses and time-slots.

4.2.1. Hypotheses

An hypothesis represents the question "Is a particular assertion true at a particular instant?". Hypotheses are the main reasoning blocks of the system. An hypothesis does not contain a definition of the assertion or its truth value. Instead it contains pointers to these items. This allows the system to have several hypotheses which all refer to one assertion definition (super-hypothesis) but refer to different times without there being any duplication.

4.2.2. Super-hypotheses

A super-hypothesis contains a description of an assertion (eg. low pressure) together with a location (eg. VX1). It also contains a pointer to a list of time-slots which hold the assertion's truth values. Thus, a super-hypothesis together with its list of time-slots contains everything that is known about an assertion and does not refer to any particular moment in time.

4.2.3. Time-slots

A time-slot contains a time interval together with a truth value. Each super-hypothesis has associated with it a list of time-slots that indicate when in the past the assertion was true or false. Whenever the truth value of an assertion is changed a new time-slot is created and pushed onto the front of the list. This allows the system to maintain an arbitrarily long history of the truth value of an assertion.

Figure 5 shows an example of how these three data types are used together.

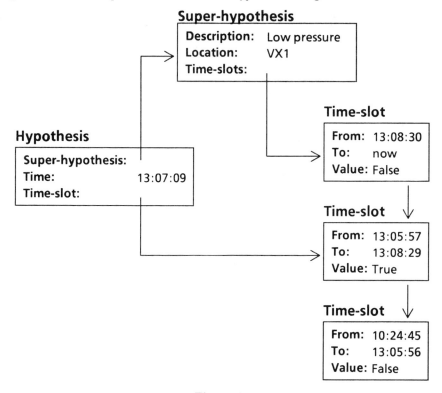

Figure 5.

5. Creating the hypothesis network

5.1. Creating hypotheses, super-hypotheses and time-slots

Hypotheses are created only as a result of events. An event is some "interesting" occurrence in the plant (most usually an alarm going off). For instance, referring back to step 2 of the example, when the low pressure alarm occurs an hypothesis is created to represent this. If a super-hypothesis for this hypothesis exists then the hypothesis is linked to it. If not then a new super-hypothesis is created together with a new time-slot.

5.2. Knowledge about generating the network

When considering an assertion there are three questions that ESCORT needs to consider.

1. How to establish if the assertion is true or not?
2. If it is true do we need to establish a cause?
3. If so, what are the possible causes?

The algorithm used to generate the network reflects this. Its main stages are as follows.

1. Test if the assertion is true or not.
2. Test if it is a terminal assertion.
3. If the assertion is false or terminal then stop, otherwise generate possible causes (more assertions).

The knowledge to answer these questions resides with the class of the object to which the assertion refers. For example, the assertion "control valve LV1 is stuck open" refers to LV1 which is an instance of ControlValve. The class ControlValve contains three rulesets; one to work out if assertions about control valves are true, one to determine whether they need further investigation and another to give possible causes.

5.3. An example of creating an hypothesis network

Figure 6 shows a simplified version of the hypothesis network at step 4 of the example given in section 3.3. Those hypotheses with a bold surround represent events. The letter in the box to the right of an hypothesis shows its initial truth value. All hypotheses refer to the present (step 4) unless otherwise specified.

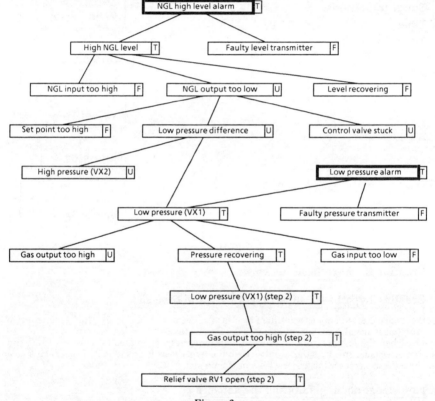

Figure 6.

Taking the hypothesis "NGL output too low" as an example, this has been created as a possible explanation or cause for "high NGL level". When considering this hypothesis the system first tries to establish if it's true. It is not possible to determine this directly since there is no measurement of flow in the pipe between VX1 and VX2. Its truth value is therefore initially "unknown". The system then establishes if the hypothesis is terminal or not. In general terminal hypotheses represent faults (eg. a stuck valve). It is sufficient to establish what the fault is - it is not within the scope of ESCORT to establish why a fault occurred. Non-terminal hypotheses generally represent symptoms rather than faults (eg. high level). Here a cause for the condition must be found. The third stage of investigating low NGL output is to postulate possible causes. The ruleset responsible for this looks at the plant representation and works out what could possibly cause low NGL output. In this case there are three possible causes, all of which are then investigated in the same manner as low NGL output.

6. Deleting the network

In the current system super-hypotheses and time-slots are never deleted. In a real ESCORT system that would have to operate continuously these would have to be garbage collected when no longer used.

6.1. Deleting hypotheses

Once an hypothesis has been created it is rechecked periodically to see if its truth value is still correct. The frequency of rechecking depends upon the type of hypothesis - some things tend to change much faster or slower than others. If the new truth value is false then we consider whether to dispose of the hypothesis completely. The method of deleting false hypotheses is as follows:

1. if the hypothesis has no parent (ie. is not a cause for anything) then delete it
2. try to delete each of its children.

For instance, at stage 5 in the example the low pressure alarm ceases. The hypothesis that represents this therefore becomes false. It has no parent and is deleted. It has two children. The faulty transmitter hypothesis is deleted since it no longer has a parent. The low pressure hypothesis still has one other parent so is not deleted. This hypothesis can only be deleted once "NGL high level alarm" becomes false and is deleted.

This approach results in hypotheses only being deleted when it is certain they will not be needed again.

7. Further work

The work described here has greatly enhanced ESCORT's capabilities. There are, however, some weaknesses in the current approach and some areas that we have as yet not investigated. The first two points discussed in the following sections will have to be tackled before ESCORT is implemented for a complex process plant. The third point is not essential but suggests an interesting extra capability for ESCORT.

7.1. Uncertainty

The main purpose of the work described here was to establish a software architecture that would allow reasoning about non-local events and time. Detailed consideration of uncertainty was deliberately postponed until a view of the architecture had become clearer. The current system uses a three valued logic. An ESCORT system for a complex process plant will, however, require a more detailed representation of uncertainty. The main types of uncertainty encountered when reasoning about a process plant are:

1. The a priori liklihood of a simple occurence (eg. given no evidence, how likely is it that a valve has stuck).
2. The degree of belief in a conclusion (eg. having taken into account all the evidence, is the valve stuck?).
3. Confidence in analogue transmitter readings. There are several ways in which the reading may be wrong:
    - noise
    - miscalibration (eg. always reading 5% high)
    - the transmitter can stick at a previous reading
    - the transmitter can fail to 0% or 100%, sometimes intermittently.

We have not yet worked on developing an approach which deals with uncertainty satisfactorily.

7.2. Truth propagation

An hypothesis network has two functions:

- to allow generation of explanations
- to allow propagation of truth values.

In the current system if an hypothesis has a truth value of unknown then it inherits the truth value of its children (true if any child is true, false if all children are false, unknown otherwise). This does not allow conjunctions to be represented but the changes required to allow this are small. More seriously, there is an assumption that if A explains B then A implies B, which is not necessarily true. For example, low output might be explained by a set point adjusted too high but a set point too high only implies high level if the control system is working correctly. The solution to this is to make the rules for truth propagation explicit rather than implicit in the rules for generating explanations of cause.

7.3. Reasoning about the future

The approach described here has shown how hypotheses can refer to the present or the past. It would be a simple task to extend the representation to allow hypotheses to refer to the future. In order to generate the future state of the plant rules would be required that predicted the behaviour of the plant. The feasibility of writing such rules has not been investigated. Reasoning about the future is potentially very useful. In the example a high level in VX2 could be predicted as soon as RV1 was opened and preparatory action taken before there was any sign of a problem in VX2.

8. Concluding remarks

The ESCORT demonstration system showed the feasibility of an expert system operating in real time. It also demonstrated the usefulness of an expert system to ease the cognitive overload experienced by process plant operators, even though its conclusions were limited to local faults.

The software approach presented here has given ESCORT the ability to:

- maintain hypotheses about the past and use them when reasoning
- reason about how one control loop interacts with another
- correctly diagnose and explain the causes for non-local events.

All of these are achieved with the system operating in real time. As a result ESCORT's effectiveness in dealing with cognitive overload is greatly increased.

9. Acknowledgement

The authors would like to thank Artificial Intelligence Ltd. for the use of their facilities in producing camera-ready copy.

10. References

Baur, P. (1983) "Strategies for eliminating human error in the control room", Power. May 1983.

Pitcher, G. (1985) "Expert systems mean less operator load", Control Systems. May 1985.

Sachs, P.A., Paterson, A.M. and Turner, M.H.M. (1985) "ESCORT - An Expert System for Complex Operations in Real Time", to appear in Expert Systems.

Sargeant, R.A.E. (1985) "Experience of building a real time expert system", Proc. Apollo Forum "An Introduction to Artificial Intelligence".

Stefik, M., Bobrow, D.G., Mittal, S. and Conway, L. (1983) "Knowledge Programming in LOOPS: Report on an experimental course", The AI Magazine. Fall 1983. pp. 3-13.

A REVIEW OF KNOWLEDGE-BASED PLANNING TECHNIQUES

Austin Tate

Knowledge-based Planning Group
Artificial Intelligence Applications Institute
University of Edinburgh

ABSTRACT

Planning systems have been an active research topic within Artificial Intelligence for over two decades. There have been a number of techniques developed during that period which still form an essential part of many of today's planners. This paper introduces the techniques, attempts to classify some of the important research themes in AI planning and describes their historical development.

There has been a recent surge of interest in planning systems at both the research and applications levels. This paper should act as a brief introduction to the large volume of literature on the subject. An extensive bibliography is provided and cross-referenced throughout the text.

1. Introduction

General purpose planning systems which can automatically produce plans of action for execution by robots have been a long standing theme of AI research. A large number of techniques have been introduced in progressively more ambitious systems over a long period. There have been several attempts to combine the planning techniques available at a certain time into prototypes able to cope with realistic application domains.

Planning research has often built on earlier work. There have usually been full written accounts of the techniques employed and these have been in a form where the central ideas could be abstracted out from the application

---

This article is derived from an earlier invited paper for the U.K. Alvey IKBS Expert Systems Research Theme Workshop at Abingdon, Oxfordshire, U.K. in April 1984.

Where names of planning systems and other AI software are described in the paper, the bibliography is annotated with the name of the system in square brackets.

domain and re-implemented or incorporated in other systems. A "tradition" of using a simple block stacking domain for examples has aided comparison and improved understanding (though today's more sophisticated planners barely show their true worth on these simple problems). Several researchers have used a set of problems to facilitate efficiency comparisons between the various systems, so introducing a (mildly) competitive spirit into the production of realistic prototype planners.

Planning research involves many of the areas of principal concern to AI:

- Search and choice making

- Knowledge Representation

- Learning

In this respect planning is a useful forcing ground for general techniques developed in other sub-fields of AI as well as being a generator of techniques itself. Planning also introduces its own problems:

- Representing and reasoning about time, causality and intentions

- Uncertainty in the execution of plans and dealing with the "real world"

- Sensation and perception of the "real world" and beliefs about it

- Multiple agents who may cooperate or interfere

- Physical or other constraints on suitable solutions

Planning also has some features in common with many other Expert Systems applications (as well as the general areas of search control and knowledge representation):

- Need to justify solutions

- Knowledge elicitation

Planners have been applied to a variety of application domains (as well as the simple explanatory domains such as block stacking). A selection is shown in Table 1.

Table 1: Applications tackled by Knowledge-based Planning Systems

Domain	Planner	
Robot Control	STRIPS	[22]
Simple Program Generation	HACKER	[71]
Mechanical Engineers apprentice supervision	NOAH	[59]
House Building and Elect. Turbine Overhaul	NONLIN	[74]
Experiment Planning in Molecular Genetics	MOLGEN	[69]
Electronic Circuit Design	NASL	[45]
Journey Planning	OPM	[30]
Job Shop Scheduling for Turbine Production	ISIS-II	[25]
Aircraft Carrier Mission Planning	SIPE, AIRPLAN	[88][43]
Naval Logistics	NONLIN	[77]
Voyager Spacecraft Mission Sequencing	DEVISER	[78]
Planning conversations	KAMP	[2]

Plans have also been used as a basic data structure in systems used to explore other areas of AI such as:

- Story understanding [62][83]

- Speech and text generation [48]

- Office systems modelling [21]

Diagram 1 shows many of the major planning systems developed in AI and how they relate to one another. No attempt has been made to add planners developed in the last year or two to the diagram since they often draw on techniques from many of the systems shown. A bibliography is attached to this paper to act as an entry point to the literature. However, it is con- venient to briefly survey the field on the basis of areas of interest rather than chronologically, since many themes recur.

2. Search Space Control

A planner is organised so that it defines a search space and then seeks a point in that search space which is defined as a solution. Planners differ as to how they define their search space. Some (most of the pre-1975 planners) define points in the search space as "states" of the application's world at various times. This "state search space" can be traversed by applying any applicable operator to some chosen state leading to a different point in the search space. A problem solution can be defined as the sequence of operators that can traverse the search space from some initial state to some state defined as meeting the goal criteria.

Other (most of the post-1975) planners define points in the search space as partially elaborated plans. One point in this space is transformed into another using any applicable planning operation such as the expansion of an action to a greater level of detail, the inclusion of an additional order- ing contraint between actions to resolve some interaction, etc.. Given some initial (skeleton) plan defining a point in this "partial plan search

space", a set of decisions have to be taken which lead to a fully detailed
plan that meets the goal criteria and various constraints.

Many search control methods are aimed at reducing the initial search space
defined by the planner. Other techniques are then geared towards choosing
a path through the search space that leads as quickly as possible to a
solution.

State Space Search
Early approaches to planning sought to apply legal "moves" to some
initial state to search for a state that satisfied the given goals.
There was a great deal of overlap with game playing work.   Heuristic
evaluation functions were employed to rate the various intermediate
states produced to estimate their "closeness" to a goal state (e.g.,
in the Graph Traverser [12]).

State space search of some description is often used to control the
selection of alternatives in other search strategies, but is not often
used for search in the actual problem space in general planners today.

Means-end Analysis
To reduce the number of intermediate states considered, only those
operators or activities that can satisfy some outstanding goal may be
considered. These in turn can introduce new (hopefully simpler) sub-
goals. This was introduced in GPS [51] and used in many later systems.

Search Reduction through Least Commitment/No Alternatives Considered
Some systems, especially ones which introduced important new techniques, did not search through the possible alternatives at all (e.g.,
NOAH (Sacerdoti [59])). Selections were made on the basis of the
information available locally and then a commitment to that solution
path was made. Of course, this often means that some problems could
not be solved. However, since these systems were often demonstrated
on particular applications for which a technique was most appropriate,
the search was often successful at arriving at a solution directly.

Very often, techniques demonstrated in isolation in such a way were
incorporated in later planners that could search alternatives and use
the method alongside others depending on its relevance.

Depth-first Backtracking
A simple method of considering alternative solution paths (especially
when there are only a few to choose from due to the use of means-end
analysis, etc.) is to save the state of the solution at each point at
which there are alternative ways forward and to keep a record of the
alternative choices. The first is chosen and search continues.   If
there is any failure, the last choice point saved state is restored
and the next alternative taken (if there are none, "backtracking" continues up one more level). Simple stack based implementation techniques can be used for this process (e.g., in the PROLOG language).

Beam Search
A search method which considers all possible solutions within a pre-

constrained area so that they can be compared. Such a method is normally used when tight search space constraints are known and hence the solution space considered by the beam search is expected to be small. It is also normally employed along with other heuristic search methods so that a choice can be of the "best" solution found amongst the solutions to some sub-problem which have been proposed by a beam search (e.g., in ISIS-II [25]).

One-then-Best Backtracking

Since there is often good local information available to indicate the preferred solution path, it is often appropriate to try the best choice indicated by local heuristic information before considering the many alternatives that may be available should the local choice prove faulty. Taken to the extreme, depth-first search gives something of the flavour of such a search strategy. However, gradual wandering from a valid solution path could entail backtracking through many levels when a failure is detected.

An alternative is to focus on the choice currently being made and try to select one of the local choices which seems most promising. This continues while all is going well (perhaps with some cut-off points to take a long, hard look at how well things are going). However, if a failure occurs, the WHOLE set of alternatives which have been generated (and ranked by a heuristic evaluator) are re-considered to select the re-focussing point for the search (e.g., in NONLIN [74]).

Dependency-Directed Search

It is well known that any backtracking system based on saved states and resumption points (whether depth-first or heuristically controlled) can waste much valuable search effort. There may be several unrelated parts to a solution. If it so happens that backtracking on one part has to go back beyond points at which work was done on an unrelated part, all effort on the unrelated part will be lost. Examples of work that has explored this important area includes Stallman and Sussman [67], NONLIN+Decision Graph [7], and MOLGEN [69] to some extent.

Some systems do not keep saved states of the solution at choice points. Instead they record the dependencies between decisions, the assumptions on which they are based and the alternatives from which a selection can be made. They then use methods of undoing any failure by propagating the undoing of all dependent parts of the solution. This leaves unrelated parts intact irrespective of whether they were worked on after some undone part of the solution.

Opportunistic Search

Some systems do not take a fixed (goal-driven or data-driven) directional approach to solving a problem. Instead a current "focus" for the search is identified on the basis of the most constrained operation that can be performed. This may be suggested by comparison of the current goals with the initial world model state, by consideration of the number of likely outcomes of making a selection, by the degree to which goals are instantiated, etc.. Any problem solving component may summarise its requirements for the solution as constraints on

possible solutions or restrictions of the values of variables
representing objects being manipulated. They can then suspend their
operation until further information becomes available on which a more
definite choice can be made. (e.g., MOLGEN [69])

Many such systems operate with a "blackboard" through which the various components can communicate via constraint information (e.g.,
HEARSAY-II [17] and OPM [30]). The scheduling of the various tasks
associated with arriving at a solution may also be dealt with through
(an area of) the blackboard.

Meta-level Planning

There are a number of planning systems which have an operator-like
representation of the different types of operations that a planner can
perform. A separate search is made to decide which of these is best
applied at any point before decisions are taken about the details of
the particular application plan being produced (e.g., MOLGEN [69] and
Wilensky [84]). This technique is often used in opportunistic
planners.

Distributed Planning

Some systems have gone further in distributing the sources of problem
solving expertise or knowledge. They allow fully distributed planning
with the sub-problems being passed between specialised planning
experts. The use of the experts or the types of things they can do
may be controlled through a centralised blackboard and executive (with
a system rather like priority scheduling of parallel processes) or may
be controlled in a more distributed fashion via pairwise negotiation.
Examples of relevant work include Smith's [65] Contract Net, Corkill
[5], Kornfeld [37], Konolige and Nilsson [36], Georgeff [26], Corkill
and Lesser [6], etc..

Work is underway to interleave the time spent planning, sensing the
state of the world to gather information and execution (e.g., Doran
and Trayner [13], Drummond [15], etc.).

Pruning of the Search Space

Besides the basic methods of reducing the search space by selection of
relevant operators in means-end analysis, many other methods of reducing the search space size have been employed in planners. Some are
identified here:-

- by considering "higher priority" goals first in hierarchical
  planners (e.g., ABSTRIPS [57] and LAWALY [64]). See below.

- by detecting and correcting for interactions in an intelligent
  fashion (e.g., Waldinger [80] with Goal Regression and in INTER-
  PLAN [72], NOAH [59] and NONLIN [74]). See section 4 below.

- by using applicability conditions and other information restricting ways that goals can be satisfied (e.g., "Typed Preconditions"
  in NONLIN [73], DEVISER [78], etc.).

- by rejection of states or plans that are known to be impossible

or   in violation of some rule about the state or plan (e.g., WAR-
PLAN [81] "IMPOSS" statements and Allen and Koomen's [1]   "Domain
Constraints").

-      by checks on resource usage levels, time constraints on   actions,
etc. (e.g., NONLIN [77], DEVISER [78] and SIPE [88]).

3. Hierarchy/Abstraction Levels

The order in which several simultaneous goals are tackled can have a marked
effect   on   the   efficiency   of   the   search process for a solution.   In some
early planners, it can make the difference between finding a   solution   and
looping round on the same goals repeatedly or getting solutions with redundant steps.   Some approaches to ordering the various goals involve separating   the goals into levels of importance or priority (the more abstract and
general goals being worked on first and the more concrete or detailed   levels being filled in later).

Strict Search by Levels
The early hierarchical systems (e.g., ABSTRIPS [57], LAWALY [64], NOAH
[59])   formed   a   solution   at the most abstract level and then made a
commitment to this solution.   The lower levels were then planned using
the pre-set skeleton plan formed at the upper levels.   No backtracking
to the higher levels was possible.

Non-strict by Levels
Later systems (e.g., NONLIN [74]) treat the abstraction   levels   as   a
guide   to   a   skeleton   solution,   but are able to re-plan or consider
alternatives at any level if a solution cannot be found, or   if   problems   with   part of a solution indicate that a higher level choice was
faulty.

Opportunistic by Levels
Other hierarchical systems use the abstraction levels as one guide   to
the   ordering   of   goals,   but   have other mechanisms that can be considered alongside this.   Some systems are able   to   determine   when   a
particular   choice   (at whatever level) is sufficiently constrained to
be a preferable goal to work on at any time (e.g., MOLGEN [70]).

4. Goal Ordering and Interaction Detection and Correction

Planners can be split into two basic types with respect   to   the   way   that
they   tackle   several   simultaneous   goals. The "linear" planners make the
"linearity assumption" - that solving one goal and then following it by the
solution   to   a   further   goal is often successful because the solutions to
different goals are often   decoupled.   The "non-linear" planners take   a
"least-commitment" approach   by representing a plan as a partially ordered
network (a graph) of actions and goals and only introducing ordering   links
between actions or goals when the solutions demand this.

In both types of systems, the solutions to one goal may interact   with   the
solutions   to   the others.   Planners can be categorised by their ability to
detect and in some cases correct for the interactions.

Linear - Interactions Ignored
    If the separate sub-goals are solved sequentially and then a simple
    check made to see if the conjunction of goals then holds (e.g., in
    STRIPS [22]), this can lead to mutual goal or subgoal interference
    which at best can lead to redundant actions in the plan and at worst
    may get the planner into an endless cycle of re-introducing and trying
    to satisfy the same goal over and over again.

Linear - Interactions Detected
    In early systems that recognised the importance of detecting "bugs"
    with the "linearity assumption" (e.g., HACKER [71]), corrections were
    attempted by backtracking to points where alternative goal orderings
    could be tried (as part of the overall search space). This could
    solve some types of problems.

Linear - Interactions Detected - Corrected by Action Regression
    One method of correcting for detected interactions is to allow the
    interfering action (just being introduced to satisfy some goal) to be
    placed at different (earlier) points in the partial linear plan until
    a position is found where there is no interaction (e.g., WARPLAN
    [81]). Unfortunately this can lead to the inclusion of redundant
    actions since the action may not be necessary (or may not be the best
    choice) when moved earlier in the plan.

Linear - Interactions Detected - Corrected by Goal Regression
    The problem of regressing the actual action chosen to satisfy a goal
    back through the plan to correct for an interaction can be solved by
    regressing the goal itself when an interaction with some particular
    solution fails (e.g., Waldinger [80]). This has the advantage that
    redundant actions are not included if the goal is already solved at
    some earlier point in the plan.

Linear - Interactions Detected - Corrected by Analysis
    A technique called "Goal Structure" was introduced in INTERPLAN [72]
    to record the link between an effect of one action that was a precon-
    dition (subgoal) of a later one. This representation is additional to
    the ordering links between the actions themselves (as some actions
    have effects that are used much later in the plan). Sussman [71]
    referred to this as the "teleology" of the plan.

    Interactions are detected as an interference between some new action
    or goal being introduced and one or more Goal Structure ranges (origi-
    nally called "Holding Periods" in INTERPLAN). A table called a "tick-
    list" was built to represent the relationships between actions and the
    goals they achieved for later points in the plan. A minimum set of
    goal reorderings (called the "Approach") could be suggested that
    corrected for the interactions found. This considered fewer re-
    orderings of the given goals and subgoals than the regression methods.

Non-linear - Interactions Detected - Limited Correction
    The first non-linear planner, NOAH [59], incorporated code called
    "critics" which were used to search for interactions between parts of
    the plan. It used a Table of Multiple Effects (TOME) to aid in dis-
    covering the interactions. The TOME was modelled on the concept of

Goal Structure as it appeared in INTERPLAN. Once detected, NOAH could correct for interactions in a limited way suited to the applications it was employed on. This was primarily due to the limitation in NOAH that no alternatives could be considered - the best choice was committed to at each stage.

Non-linear - Interactions Detected - Corrected by Analysis
The detection of interactions by analysis of the underlying "Goal Structure" was added to a non-linear planner, called NONLIN, modelled on NOAH. The combination in NONLIN [74] was more effective than its earlier use in the linear INTERPLAN system. In NONLIN, the minimum set of orderings necessary to resolve any interaction could be suggested by the introduction of ordering links into a partially ordered plan only when this became essential. The NONLIN system could consider alternatives if failures on any chosen search branch occurred.

Similar analyses of a representation of the effect and condition structure of a plan to detect and correct for interactions have been included in PLANX-10 [4], SIPE's "Plan Rationale" [88] and Dean's TNMS [10].

Non-linear - Interactions Detected and Corrected - Time Limits Handled
When individual goals or actions in a plan have time constraints on when they can be satisfied or performed, the detection and correction of interactions must be sensitive to the temporal displacement introduced (e.g., in DEVISER [78]). This normally further limits the number of legal solutions that can be proposed. There may also be a need to link the plan to externally induced events (beyond the control of the planner and possibly occurring at pre-specified times). The DEVISER system added such capabilities to a NONLIN-like planner.

Non-linear - Interactions Detected and Corrected - Resources Handled
The use of objects being manipulated as scarce resources on which usage conflicts occur and need to be avoided was incorporated in the MOLGEN [69] and SIPE [88] planners.

5. Planning with Conditionals and Iterators

Most of the search space control techniques, goal ordering and interaction correction mechanisms developed in AI planners to date have been orientated towards the generation of plans which are fully or partially ordered sequences of primitive actions. However, there has been some effort on the generation of plans which contain conditionals ("if ... then ... else ...") and iterators ("repeat ... until ...").

Black Box Approach to Conditionals and Iterators
A conditional or iterator which can be modelled as a single entity and for which the differences between the multiple paths or the individual loops are not important can be handled by many of the planning systems and techniques already described. NOAH [59] explicitly dealt with such packaged conditionals and iterators. SIPE [88] was able to deal with iteration which repeated a planned action sequence on each member of a set of parameters (which could be objects or points on an

aircraft flight trajectory).

Conditionals: Branch and Case Analysis
Conditionals were handled in WARPLAN-C (Warren [82]) by branching the
plan at the conditional and performing separate planning on the two
branches using the assumption that the statement in the conditional
was true in one branch and false in the other. This lead to a case
analysis of the separate branches to produce a plan that was tree-
structured.

Conditionals: Branch and Re-Join
There has been relatively little work in the mainstream AI planning
literature which has attempted a full treatment of conditionals which
can branch and rejoin later in the plan and for which the black box
approach was not sufficient. However, work on automatic programming
and theorem proving has considered this area. See, for example, Luckham and Buchanan [42] and Dershowitz [11]. The latter reference has
an extensive bibliography of papers on automatic programming and shows
how AI planning research overlaps with this work.

Formal Models of Plans and Actions
Plan representations and formalisms which are more powerful than the
orderings on actions basis of many AI planners are now being explored.
For example, Petri-nets (Drummond [15]), formal models of processes,
actions and states (see section 7 of this paper), etc.. Some of these
allow for the representation of and reasoning about iterative and conditional statements in plans.

6. Time and Resource Handling

It is becoming increasingly important in planning systems to perform on
realistic applications where resources of various types are limited. Also,
planners are being used in domains where time considerations and matters
beyond the control of the planning system itself must be accounted for.
Several systems have explored this area.

Compute Time and Resource Usage
In a project planning domain, NONLIN [73] maintained information about
the durations of the various activities and used this to compute earliest and latest start times for each action. A critical path of
actions could be found. A "cost" measure could also be kept with each
activity. This information was used in an extension to the NONLIN
planner that could selectively remove costly activities or lengthy
activities from a plan and replace them with others that either
reduced the cost or the duration depending on the limitation that was
exceeded [7]

More recent work on NONLIN (Tate and Whiter [77]) has added the capability of representing multiple limited resources and making selection
from appropriate activities on the basis of reducing some overall computed "preference" between them.

Objects as Resources
SIPE [88] is able to reason about competing demands for the use of

scarce objects (such as a ladder or a key). An analysis of the objects used and returned by actions or objects "consumed" by them can be used to linearize the plan to prevent usage conflicts.

Event and Time Specifications for Actions
DEVISER [78] allows a "time window" to be specified for any goal or action. External events can be described as having some effect at a particular time. The planner propagates the temporal links between these time windows, progressively narrowing them as they become constrained by other actions. It can detect when some plan step prevents a goal from being achieved or an activity from being executed at the required time. In such a case, backtracking will consider alternative solutions.

AIRPLAN (Masui, McDermott and Sobel [43]) was able to reason about time intervals and how actions suggested in them could interfere, etc..

O-Plan (Open Planner Architecture) (Bell and Tate [3]) the successor to NONLIN, uniformly represents time constraints (and resource usage) by a numeric (minimum, maximum) pair which bound the actual values for activity duration, activity start and finish times, and delays between activities. The actual values may be uncertain for various reasons such as the plan being at a high abstraction level, not having chosen values for objects referred to in the plan, uncertainty in modelling the domain, etc.. Constraints can be stated on the time (and resource) resource values which may lead to the planner finding that some plans are invalid.

Flexible Time Handling
Very much more flexible handling of the propagation of temporal constraints between the steps of a plan is being considered in the widespread research effort on temporal logic (e.g., McDermott [46], Allen and Koomen [1], etc.).

Soft Constraints
ISIS-II [25] allows a wide variety of constraints on the problem to be specified. Some of these can be in the form of preferences or "soft" constraints which are used to guide the search for acceptable solutions.

7.   Domain Representation

Many AI systems have introduced formalisms or constructs for capturing the information about the application domain and for making that knowledge available to a planning system. Once again, later systems have often built on the best aspects of earlier efforts.

Differences
The early means-end analysis systems selected appropriate operators to apply to a problem by considering the "differences" between the goal state and the initial state. The General Problem Solver (GPS [51]) associated the operators for the problem with the "differences" they could reduce.

Add/Delete/Precondition Lists
Using ideas from problem solving in a "situational calculus" (McCarthy and Hayes [44], Green's QA3 [28]) and the notion of differences from GPS, STRIPS [22] took the assumption that the initial world model was only changed by a set of additions to and deletions from the statements modelling the world state (everything else remaining unchanged). This is called the "STRIPS assumption". STRIPS then defined an operator as having an add-list, a delete-list and a preconditions-list (to state the applicability or sub-goaling conditions). Operators could be selected on the basis of goals which occur on their add-lists (statements added to the world model).

Abstraction Levels on Goals
The hierarchical systems introduced the ability to specify the abstraction or criticality levels of the various statements that could be made about a world state (e.g., ABSTRIPS [57], LAWALY [64]).

Partial-orders on plan parts in hierarchical planners
The first non-linear planner, NOAH [59], allowed plan steps to be kept in parallel until some cause was found to linearise them. NOAH had procedurally specified "SOUP" (Semantics Of User's Problem) code to introduce appropriate methods of achieving goals or orderings to correct for interactions into the network of actions.

Declarative Partial-order representation
Later planners introduced declarative representations for operators in extensions of the STRIPS operator type of formalism (e.g., NONLIN's Task Formalism [74] and SIPE Notation [88]). As well as add, delete and precondition lists, an "expansion" of the operator to a lower level of detail could be specified as a partial order on suitable sub-actions and sub-goals.

Intent of plan steps
Some systems distinguish between ordering relationships on actions and the purpose of each action or goal with respect to the other parts of the plan at which they are required. Such information was first made available through the STRIPS "triangle tables" [23] to aid in re-use of parts of plans in new situations. In HACKER [71], the information is kept as protection intervals (Sussman used the term "teleology") and was used to detect "protection violations" which led HACKER to consider alternative ways to perform a task being tried. In INTERPLAN [72] and NONLIN [74][76] such information (called "Goal Structure") was used to be more precise about interaction detection and aided in suggesting the corrections (for this, "typed conditions" could be stated in an operator description). PLANX-10 [4] has internal structures similar to Goal Structure. SIPE's "Plan Rationale" [88] is a more limited version that reflects only the main outcomes of given actions.

Typed Preconditions
There is often a distinction between applicability conditions for an operator and sub-goals to be introduced to enable the operator to achieve its purpose. AI languages used for planning have recognised this distinction by providing two types of goal statement (e.g., in

POPLER [94]). NONLIN [74] and DEVISER [78] allow this same distinction between goals simply to be checked if they already hold and goals that can cause further introduction of operators and sub-goals.

NONLIN introduced other condition types, as well as those mentioned above, to reflect internally managed goals and actions within the control of a particular operator's "manager" ("supervised") and those beyond the manager's control ("unsupervised"). These different types of condition are useful in differentiating between the various methods by which goals can be satisfied and enabling the system to recover from planning failures in more appropriate ways.

Resources
      The definition of shared objects as resources and the declaration of the use of such resources in operators was provided in SIPE. The declaration of multiple consumable resources, their limitations and preferences as to which should be minimised in solutions has been added to NONLIN. DEVISER can also handle consumable resources (such as fuel).

Time Windows and Events (e.g., DEVISER [78])
      DEVISER has provided a method for specifying a time window on goals and activities. External events and their time of occurrence can also be given. Delayed events caused some time after a planned action can be specified.

Property Inheritance
      Some planning systems make use of extensive knowledge representation schemes that can express the type of objects and the properties that instances of the types can inherit (e.g., SIPE [88], PLANX-10 [4] and CALLISTO [61]). This can significantly increase the size of problems that can be tackled.

Action Logics and Formal Models
      Formal models of actions, processes and states have been a recurring theme of AI work and this has impacted on AI planning work. Some of the work has its roots in Process models and Finite State Automata. The majority of the AI planning techniques reviewed in this paper are most suited to planning for discrete activities. Some of the work on formal models and action logics admit reasoning about continuous processes. Such topics require a survey in their own right and are only briefly touched upon here. Example references include Moore [49], McDermott [45], Lansky [38], etc.. Recent research in AI planning is taking more account of such work.

8. Support Languages and Data Base Systems

Some early planning systems were implemented in specially tailored languages designed to allow search and pattern directed inference (e.g., PLANNER [100], POPLER [94], CONNIVER [112] and their derivatives). The depth-first search strategy of the logic programming language PROLOG [93] was used in WARPLAN [81], probably the first planner to be implemented in that language. In other cases a base AI Programming language was augmented by suitable language extensions (e.g., QA4 [108], QLISP [109], etc.).

However, most systems have been implemented in a combination of an AI language with a knowledge representation language such as UNITS [111] in LISP (for MOLGEN [69]), HBASE [89] in POP-2/POPLOG [110] (for INTERPLAN [72] and NONLIN [74]), etc.. Separate research and development on knowledge representation languages (e.g., KRL [91], PEARL [95], LOOPS [90], KEE [103], SRL [98], Knowledge Craft [92], ART [102], etc.), parallel reduction machines and large content addressable memories (e.g., NETL [97], FACT [106], etc.) is an important source of support for new planning work.

9. Planning Bibliography

[1]   Allen, J.F. and Koomen, J.A. (1983) "Planning Using a Temporal World Model", IJCAI-83, pp 741-747 Karlsruhe, West Germany. [TIMELOGIC]

[2]   Appelt, D.E. (1985) "Planning English Referring Expressions", Artificial Intelligence, 26, pp 1-33. [KAMP]

[3]   Bell, C.E. and Tate, A. (1985) "Using Temporal Constraints to Restrict Search in a Planner", Proceedings of the Third Workshop of the Alvey IKBS Programme Planning Special Interest Group, Sunningdale, Oxfordshire, UK, April 1985. Available through the Institute of Electrical Engineers, London, UK [O-PLAN]

[4]   Bresina, J.L. (1981) "An Interactive Planner that Creates a Structured Annotated Trace of its Operation", Rutgers University, Computer Science Research Laboratory, Report CBM-TR-123. [PLANX-10]

[5]   Corkill, D.D. (1979) "Hierarchical Planning in a Distributed Environment", IJCAI-79, pp 168-175, Tokyo, Japan.

[6]   Corkill, D.D. and Lesser, V.R. (1983) "The Use of Meta-level Control for Coordination in a Distributed Problem Solving Network", IJCAI-83, pp 748-756, Karlsruhe, West Germany.

[6b] Currie, K. and Tate, A. (1985) "O-Plan - An Overview of the Open Planner Architecture" BCS Expert Systems Conference, Warwick, UK. December 1985.

[7]   Daniel, L. (1983). "Planning and Operations Research", in "Artificial Intelligence: Tools, Techniques and Applications", Harper and Row, New York. [NONLIN]

[8]   Davis, R. and Smith, R. (1983) "Negotiation as a Metaphor for Distributed Problem Solving", Artificial Intelligence, 20, pp 63-109.

[9]   Davis, P.R. and Chien, R.T. (1977) "Using and Re-using Partial Plans", IJCAI-77, Cambridge, Mass., USA.

[10] Dean, T. (1985) "Temporal Reasoning Involving Counterfactuals and Disjunctions", IJCAI-85, Los Angeles, Calif. [TNMS]

[11] Dershowitz, N. "Synthetic programming", Artificial Intelligence, 25, pp 323-373.

[12] Doran, J.E. and Michie, D. (1966) "Experiments with the Graph Traverser Program" Proceedings of the Royal Society, A, pp 235-259. [GRAPH TRAVERSER]

[13] Doran, J.E. and Trayner, C. (1985) "Distributed Planning and Execution - Teamwork 1", Computer Science Technical Report, University of Essex, UK [TEAMWORK]

[14] Doyle, J. (1979) "A Truth Maintenance System", Artificial

Intelligence, 12, pp 231-272.

[15] Drummond, M.E. (1985) "Refining and Extending the Procedural Net", IJCAI-85, Los Angeles, Calif.

[16] Duffay, P. and Latombe, J-C (1983) "An Approach to Automatic Robot Programming Based on Inductive Learning", IMAG, Grenbole, France. [TROPIC]

[17] Erman, L.D., Hayes-Roth, F., Lesser, V.R. and Reddy, D.R. (1980) "The HEARSAY-II Speech-understanding System: Integrating Knowledge to Resolve Uncertainty", ACM Computing Surveys, 12, No.2.

[18] Fahlman, S.E. (1974) "A Planning System for Robot Construction Tasks" Artificial Intelligence, 5, pp 1-49.

[19] Faletti, J. (1982) "PANDORA - A Program for Doing Commonsense Reasoning Planning in Complex Situations", AAAI-82, Pittsburgh, Pa., USA, Aug, 1982. [PANDORA]

[20] Fikes, R.E. (1970) "REF-ARF: A System for Solving Problems stated as Procedures", Artificial Intelligence", 1, pp 27-120.

[21] Fikes, R.E. (1982) "A Commitment-based Framework for Describing Informal Cooperative Work", Cognitive Science, 6, pp 331-347.

[22] Fikes, R.E. and Nilsson, N.J. (1971) "STRIPS: a New Approach to the Application of Theorem Proving to Problem Solving", Artificial Intelligence, 2, pp 189-208. [STRIPS]

[23] Fikes, R.E., Hart, P.E. and Nilsson, N.J. (1972a) "Learning and Executing Generalised Robot Plans", Artificial Intelligence, 3. [STRIPS/PLANEX]

[24] Fikes, R.E., Hart, P.E. and Nilsson, N.J. (1972b) "Some New Directions in Robot Problem Solving", in "Machine Intelligence 7", Meltzer, B. and Michie, D., eds., Edinburgh University Press. [STRIPS]

[25] Fox, M.S., Allen, B. and Strohm, G. (1981) "Job Shop Scheduling: an Investigation in Constraint-based Reasoning", IJCAI-81, Vancouver, British Columbia, Canada, August 1981. [ISIS-II]

[26] Georgeff, M. (1982) "Communication and Interaction in Multi-agent Planning Systems", AAAI-3.

[27] Georgeff, M. and Lansky, A. (1985) "A Procedural Logic", IJCAI-85, Los Angeles, Calif., Aug 1985.

[28] Green, C.C. (1969) "Theorem Proving by Resolution as a basis for Question Answering" in Machine Intelligence 4, eds. Meltzer, B. and Michie, D., Edinburgh University Press.

[29] Hayes, P.J. (1975) "A Representation for Robot Plans", Advance papers

of IJCAI-75, Tbilisi, USSR.

[30]   Hayes-Roth, B. and Hayes-Roth, F. (1979) "A Cognitive Model of Planning", Cognitive Science, pp 275-310. [OPM]

[31]   Hayes-Roth, B. (1983a) "The Blackboard Architecture: A General Framework for Problem Solving?", Heuristic Programming Project Report No. HPP-83-30. Stanford University. May 1983.

[32]   Hayes-Roth, B. (1983b) "A Blackboard Model of Control", Heuristic Programming Project Report No. HPP-83-38. Stanford University. June 1983. [OPM]

[33]   Hendrix, G. (1973) "Modelling Simultaneous Actions and Continuous Processes", Artificial Intelligence, 4, pp 145-180.

[34]   Kahn, K. and Gorry, G.A. (1977) "Mechanizing Temporal Knowledge" Artificial Intelligence, 9, pp 87-108.

[35]   Konolige, K. (1983) "A Deductive Model of Belief", IJCAI-83, pp 377-381, Karlsruhe, West Germany, Aug 1983.

[36]   Konolige, K. and Nilsson, N.J. (1980) "Multi-agent Planning Systems", AAAI-1, pp 138-142, Stanford, Ca., USA.

[37]   Kornfeld, W.A. (1979) "ETHER: a Parallel Problem Solving System" IJCAI-79 pp 490-492, Tokyo, Japan.

[38]   Lansky, A. (1985) "Behavioral Planning for Multi-Agent Plans", SRI AI Center Report.

[39]   Latombe, J-C. (1976) "Artificial Intelligence in Computer-aided Design - The TROPIC System", Stanford Research Institute AI Center Technical Note 125, Menlo Park, Ca., USA.

[40]   Lenat, D.B. (1975) "BEINGS: Knowledge as Interacting Experts", IJCAI-75, pp 126-133, Tbilisi, USSR. [PUP]

[41]   London, P. (1977) "A Dependency-based Modelling Mechanism for Problem Solving", Dept of Computer Science, University of Maryland, Memo. TR-589.

[42]   Luckham, D.C. and Buchanan, J.R. (1974) "Automatic Generation of Programs Containing Conditional Statements", AISB Summer Conference, University of Sussex, UK, pp 102-126, July 1974.

[43]   Masui,S., McDermott, J. and Sobel, A. (1983) "Decision-Making in Time Critical Situations", IJCAI-83, pp 233-235, Karlsruhe, West Germany, Aug, 1983. [AIRPLAN]

[44]   McCarthy, J. and Hayes, P.J. (1969) "Some Philosophical Problems from the Standpoint of Artificial Intelligence", in Machine Intelligence 4, ed. Meltzer, B. and Michie, D., Edinburgh University Press.

[45] McDermott, D.V. (1978) "Planning and Acting", Cognitive Science, 2.

[46] McDermott, D.V. (1982) "A Temporal Logic for Reasoning about Processes and Plans", Cognitive Science, 6, pp 101-155.

[47] McDermott, D.V. and Doyle, J. (1979) "An Introduction to Non-monotonic Logic", IJCAI-79 pp 562-567, Tokyo, Japan.

[48] Mellish, C.S. (1984) "Towards Top-down Generation of Multi-paragraph Text", Proceedings of the Sixth European Conference on Artificial Intelligence, pp 229, Pisa, Italy, September 1984.

[49] Moore, R. (1980) "Reasoning about Knowledge and Action", SRI AI Center Report No. 191.

[50] Mostow, D.J. (1983) "A Problem Solver for Making Advice Operational", Proc. AAAI 3, pp 179-283.

[51] Newell, A. and Simon, H.A. (1963) "GPS: a Program that Simulates Human Thought", in Feigenbaum, E.A. and Feldman, J. eds Computers and Thought (McGraw-Hill, New York, 1963). [GPS]

[52] Reiger, C. and London, P. (1977) "Subgoal Protection and Unravelling During Plan Synthesis", IJCAI-77, Cambridge, Mass., USA.

[53] Rich, C. (1981) "A Formal Representation for Plans in the Programmer's Apprentice", IJCAI-81 pp 1044-1052, Vancouver, British Columbia, Canada.

[54] Rich, C., Shrobe, H.E. and Waters, R.C. (1979) "Overview of the Programmer's Apprentice", IJCAI-79, pp 827-828, Tokyo, Japan.

[55] Rosenschein, S.J. (1980) "Synchronisation of Multi-agent Plans", AAAI-2.

[56] Rosenschein, S.J. (1981) "Plan Synthesis: A Logical Perspective", IJCAI-81, Vancouver, British Columbia, Canada.

[57] Sacerdoti, E.D. (1973) "Planning in a Hierarchy of Abstraction Spaces", Advance papers of IJCAI-73, Palo Alto, Ca., USA. [ABSTRIPS]

[58] Sacerdoti, E.D. (1975) "The Non-linear Nature of Plans", Advance papers of IJCAI-75, Tbilisi, USSR. [NOAH]

[59] Sacerdoti, E.D. (1977) "A Structure for Plans and Behaviour", Elsevier-North Holland. [NOAH]

[60] Sacerdoti, E.D. (1979) "Problem Solving Tactics", IJCAI-79, Tokyo, Japan.

[61] Sathi, A., Fox, M.S. and Greenberg, M. (1985) "Representation of Activity Knowledge for Project Management", IEEE Special Issue of Transactions on Pattern Analysis and Machine Intelligence, July, 1985. [CALLISTO]

[62] Schank, R.C. and Abelson, R.P. (1977) "Scripts, Plans, Goals and Understanding", Lawrence Erlbaum Press, Hillsdale, New Jersey, USA.

[63] Siklossy, L. and Roach, J. (1973) "Proving the Imposssible is Impossible is Possible: Disproofs based on Hereditary Partitions", IJCAI-73, Palo Alto, Calif. [DISPROVER/LAWALY]

[64] Siklossy, L. and Dreussi, J. (1975) "An Efficient Robot Planner that Generates its own Procedures", IJCAI-73 Palo Alto, Ca., USA. [LAWALY]

[65] Smith, R.G. (1977) "The Contract Net: a Formalism for the Control of Distributed Problem Solving", IJCAI-77 pp 472 Cambridge, Mass, USA.

[66] Smith, R.G. (1979) "A Framework for Distributed Problem Solving", IJCAI-79, Tokyo, Japan.

[67] Stallman, R.M. and Sussman, G.J. (1977) "Forward Reasoning and Dependency Directed Backtracking", Artificial Intelligence, 9, pp 135-196.

[68] Steele, G.L. and Sussman, G.J. (1978) "Constraints", MIT AI Lab Memo 502.

[69] Stefik, M.J. (1981a) "Planning with Constraints", Artificial Intelligence, 16, pp 111-140. [MOLGEN]

[70] Stefik, M.J. (1981b) "Planning and Meta-planning", Artificial Intelligence, 16, pp 141-169. [MOLGEN]

[71] Sussman, G.A. (1973) "A Computational Model of Skill Acquisition", M.I.T. AI Lab. Memo no. AI-TR-297. [HACKER]

[72] Tate, A. (1975) "Interacting Goals and Their Use", IJCAI-75, pp 215-218, Tbilisi, USSR. [INTERPLAN]

[73] Tate, A. (1976) "Project Planning Using a Hierarchical Non-linear Planner", Dept. of Artificial Intelligence Report 25, Edinburgh University. [NONLIN]

[74] Tate, A. (1977) "Generating Project Networks", IJCAI-77, Boston, Ma., USA. [NONLIN]

[75] Tate, A. (1984a) "Planning and Condition Monitoring in a FMS", International Conference on Flexible Automation Systems", Institute of Electrical Engineers, London, UK July 1984. [NONLIN]

[76] Tate, A. (1984b) "Goal Stucture: Capturing the Intent of Plans", European Conference on Artificial Intelligence, Pisa, Italy, September 1984. [NONLIN]

[77] Tate, A. and Whiter, A.M. (1984) "Planning with Multiple Resource Constraints and an Application to a Naval Planning Problem", First Conference on the Applications of Artificial Intelligence, Denver, Colorado, USA. December 1984. [NONLIN]

[78] Vere, S. (1983) "Planning in Time: Windows and Durations for Activities and Goals", IEEE Trans. on Pattern Analysis and Machine Intelligence, PAMI-5, No. 3, pp. 246-267, May 1983. [DEVISER]

[79] Vilain, M.B. (1980) "A System for Reasoning about Time", AAAI-2.

[80] Waldinger, R. (1975) "Achieving Several Goals Simultaneously", SRI AI Center Technical Note 107, SRI, Menlo Park, Ca., USA.

[81] Warren, D.H.D. (1974) "WARPLAN: a System for Generating Plans", Dept. of Computational Logic Memo 76. Artificial Intelligence, Edinburgh University. [WARPLAN]

[82] Warren, D.H.D. (1976) "Generating Conditional Plans and programs", Proceedings of the AISB Summer Conference, pp 344-354, University of Edinburgh, UK, July 1976. [WARPLAN-C]

[83] Wilensky, R. (1978) "Understanding Goal-based Stories", Dept. of Computer Science, Yale University, Research Report No. 140.

[84] Wilensky, R. (1981a) "Meta-planning: Representing and Using Knowledge about Planning in Problem Solving and Natural Language Understanding", Cognitive Science, 5, pp 197-233.

[85] Wilensky, R. (1981b) "A Model for Planning in Complex Situations", Electronics Research Lab. Memo. No. UCB/ERL M81/49, University of California, Berkeley, Ca., USA.

[86] Wilensky, R. (1983) "Planning and Understanding", Addison-Wesley, Reading, Mass.

[87] Wilkins, D.E. and Robinson, A.E. (1981) "An Interactive Planning System", SRI Technical Note 245. [SIPE]

[88] Wilkins, D.E. (1983) "Representation in a Domain-Independent Planner", IJCAI-83, pp 733-740, Karlsruhe, West Germany. [SIPE]

10. Bibliography on Support Languages, Databases and Background

[89] Barrow, H.G. (1975) "HBASE: a Fast Clean Efficient Data Dase System", D.A.I. POP-2 library documentation. Edinburgh University. [HBASE]

[90] Bobrow, D.G. and Stefik, M.J. (1983) "The LOOPS Reference Manual", Xerox Palo Alto Research Center, Ca. USA. [LOOPS]

[91] Bobrow, D.G. and Winograd, T. (1976) "An Overview of KRL - a Knowledge Representation Language", Xerox PARC Repport CSL-76-4, Xerox Palo Alto Research Center, Ca. USA. [KRL]

[92] Carnegie Group Inc. "Knowledge Craft", Commerce Court at Station Square, Pittsburgh, PA 15219, USA. [Knowledge Craft, SRL+]

[93] Clocksin, W. and Mellish, C. (1981) "Programming in PROLOG", Springer-Verlag. [PROLOG]

[94] Davies, D.J.M. (1973) "POPLER 1.5 Reference Manual", D.A.I. Theoretical Psychology Unit Report no.1, Edinburgh University. [POPLER]

[95] Deering, M., Faletti, J. and Wilensky, R. (1981) "PEARL: An Efficient Language for Artificial Intelligence Programming", IJCAI-81, Vancouver, British Columbia, Canada, Aug, 1981. [PEARL]

[96] Elcock, E.W., Foster, J.M., Gray, P.M.D., McGregor, J.J. and Murray, A.M. (1971) "ABSET, a Programming Language based on Sets: Motivation and Examples", in Meltzer, B. and Michie, D. Machine Intelligence 6, (Edinburgh University Press). [ABSET]

[97] Fahlman, S.E. (1979) "NETL: a System for Representing Real World Knowledge", MIT Press, Cambridge, Mass. USA. [NETL]

[98] Fox, M. (1983) "SRL User's Manual", Technical Report, Robotics Institute, Carnegie-Mellon University, Pittsburgh, Pa., USA. [SRL]

[99] Hendrix, G. (1975) "Expanding the Utility of Semantic Networks through Partitioning", IJCAI-75, Tbilisi, USSR.

[100] Hewitt, C. (1972) "Description and Theoretical Analysis (using schemata) of PLANNER", MIT AI Lab. Memo no.MAC-TR-256. [PLANNER]

[101] Hillis (1981) "The Connection Machine" MIT AI Lab Memo 640.

[102] Inference Corporation (1985), "ART Manual", 5300 West Century Blvd, 5th Floor, Los Angeles, CA 90045. [ART]

[103] IntelliCorp (1985), "KEE System Manual", 707 Laurel Street, Menlo Park, CA 94025-3445. [KEE]

[104] Jiang, Y.J. and Lavington, S.H. (1985) "The Qualified Binary Relationship Model of Information", University of Manchester, Department of Computer Science, Internal Report IFS/2/85.

[105] McDermott, D.V. and Sussman, G.J. (1972) "The CONNIVER Reference Manual", M.I.T. AI Lab. Memo no.259. [CONNIVER]

[106] McGregor, D.R. and Malone, J.R. (1981). "The FACT Database: A System using Generic Associative Networks", Research Report No. 2/80, Department of Computer Science, Univ. of Strathclyde, UK. [FACT]

[107] Nii, H. P. and Aiello, N. (1979) "AGE (Attempt to Generalize): A Knowledge-based Program for Building Knowledge-based Programs", IJCAI-79, Tokyo, Japan. [AGE]

[108] Rulifson, J.F., Derkson, J.A. and Waldinger, R.J. (1972) "QA4: A Procedural Calculus for Intuitive Reasoning", Technical Note 73, SRI International Menlo Park, Ca., USA. [QA4]

[109] Sacerdoti, E.D., Fikes, R.E., Reboh, R., Sagalowicz, D. and Waldinger, R.J. (1976) "QLISP: a Language for the Interactive Development of Complex Systems", SRI Technical Note, SRI International, AI

Center, [QLISP] Stanford, Ca. USA.

[110] Sloman, A. (1983) "POPLOG - a Multi-purpose, Multi-language Program Development Environment" Cognitive Studies Programme, University of Sussex, UK. [POPLOG]

[111] Stefik, M.J. (1979) "An Examination of a Frame-structured Representation System", IJCAI-79, pp 845-852 Tokyo, Japan. [UNITS]

[112] Sussman, G.A. and McDermott, D.V. (1972) "Why Conniving is Better than Planning", MIT AI Lab. Memo 255A. [CONNIVER]

11. Recommended Reading

A good and reasonably up-to-date account of AI planning techniques and systems is given in Charniak and McDermott's Introduction to Artificial Intelligence textbook [114]. In particular, chapter 9 and sections of chapters 5 and 7 are relevant.

Somewhat earlier material is provided in Elaine Rich's Artificial Intelligence textbook [116]. Nilsson's book on the Principles of Artificial Intelligence [115] provides a uniform treatment of planning techniques available up to the time it was published. There are several useful summaries of early AI planning work in the Handbook of Artificial Intelligence [113] volume I section II.D and volume III sections XI.B, XI.C and XV.

[113] Barr, A. and Feigenbaum, E.A. (1981) "The Handbook of Artificial Intelligence" William Kaufmann, Los Angeles, Calif.

[114] Charniak, E. and McDermott, D.V. (1985) "Introduction to Artificial Intelligence", Addison-Wesley.

[115] Nilsson, N.J. (1980) "Principles of Artificial Intelligence", Tioga Press, Palo Alto, Calif.

[116] Rich, E. (1983) "Artificial Intelligence", McGraw-Hill, New York.

Acknowledgements

Thanks go to my colleagues in the Artificial Intelligence Applications Institute and the Department of Artificial Intelligence at Edinburgh University for their comments on drafts of this paper. Mark Drummond was especially helpful in updating an earlier draft to the present paper.

The support of my colleagues at Systems Designers Scientific for the work of the AIAI Knowledge-based Planning Group is gratefully acknowledged.

Figure 1: A Taxonomy of AI Planning Systems

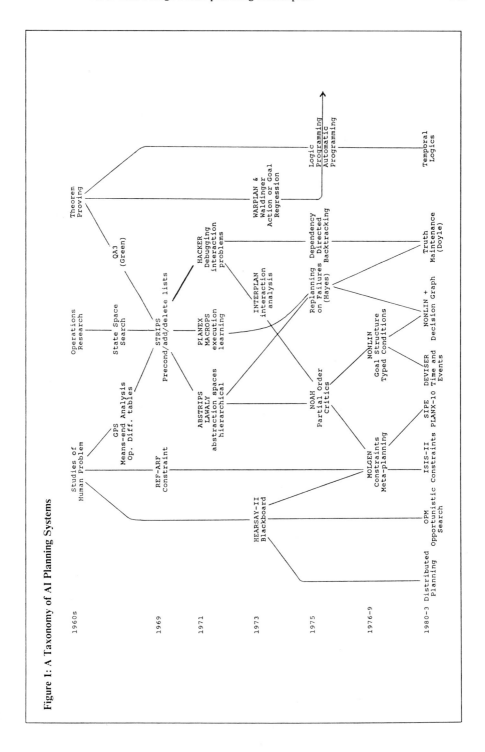

ALLOCATING ABILITIES TO ACTORS

C. Trayner

Computer Science Department, Essex University, Colchester,
Essex CO7 OBE

Abstract Multi-agent planning systems and their relation to
expert systems are described. The problem of distributing
abilities amongst a non-identical set of agents is discussed.
A method is proposed and the results of tests on it are
described.

1 INTRODUCTION

The relationship between Expert Systems and other branches of
AI has often been subject to phases of appearing to diverge and
subsequently converging. Currently the relevance of planning techniques to
expert systems seems to be emerging (Zhang 1985). Moreover multiple-
processor techniques are beginning to migrate from general computing into
the AI sphere. Although in the short or medium term they provide no real
defense against combinatorial explosion they can offer other advantages.
The design of such multi-actor systems is currently poorly understood,
though it seems clear that in realistic domains it will not be a trivial
task: one should probably think in terms of expert systems to assist.
There is thus a growing commonality of interest between expert systems and
multiple-agent planning systems.

Many of the purposes for which AI planning systems are being
developed stand to benefit from the availability of multi-agent systems.
These are AI systems in which multiple agents are distributed in some
fashion, either co-operating or competing in some activity. We consider
here only co-operating teams. The actors communicate to share the work in
some fashion (e.g. Smith (1979), Corkill (1979)). In moving from a single-
actor to a multi-actor situation many additional complications are brought
in, such as the underlying communications (Trayner 1985), contractual
behaviour (Smith 1978) and strategies of co-operation (Cammarata et al

1983). The distribution of abilities amongst actors has received some attention (Corkill & Lesser 1983) though less thoroughly so: this is the subject of the present paper.

2 BACKGROUND

There are several reasons for preferring a distributed set of planners and executors to a single actor controlling all. These include
- Cost(many small mass-production actors rather than one large small-production one).
- Reliability (a single failure will not bring down the whole system).
- Flexibility (of the system to be re-configured).
- Feasibility (for domains with very large numbers of actions, which may be impractical for one agent to contain).

Many of the characteristics of such actors (like the technique of evolving a plan using any abilities available) are likely to be uniform across the whole team. Others (such as the abilities available, the domain knowledge) need not be. The question of allocating the abilities to the actors deserves attention. Three methods (from a spectrum) are:
- At one extreme, all actors could have all abilities. Although this would have certain advantages (see the speculation under further work, below) it would leave the actors' sizes uncontrolled.
- The abilities could be distributed across the actors in some fashion such that each actor had a subset of the full gamut of abilities.
- At the other extreme, most of the actors could have no or virtually no abilities themselves. They would refer for all knowledge of how to perform tasks ('technique knowledge') to one or a few actors ('sages') which would specialise in providing techniques. This would however tend to increase the inter-actor communication load enormously.

Our TEAMWORK research is concentrating on the middle course and the present paper considers such allocation.

3 REQUIREMENTS

Given a set of actors and a set of abilities, the basic requirement is to distribute the latter amongst the former in such a way that
- the team can perform any task which it could were all actors to have all technique knowledge;

- the techniques are, broadly speaking, evenly distributed (so that no actor's need for storage becomes too large);
- the inter-actor communication requirement does not get too large.

Such division of labour is of course well known in human practice, where one encounters such specialities as thatchers and lamplighters, but the problem is to choose the groupings in an efficient way. (Human practice is no guide, suiting a set of actors with different characteristics and moreover additional motives.) Doran (1984) has speculated that the grouping can usefully be chosen by considering the extent to which techniques refer to each other. If one finds a subset of techniques which co-refer to a great extent then one tries to group them together, and expects to find groupings which can be described as specialisms. We now consider ways of doing this and the results thereof.

4 PROPOSED TECHNIQUE

Stated more precisely, the hypothesis is that a set of abilities in a real-world domain will tend to be clustered by way of their references to each other; furthermore that if one allocates such clusters each to an actor then the communication requirement will be reduced with no loss of team ability. By communication requirement is meant the amount of inter-actor communications needed during planning and execution.

By 'references to each other' is meant the calling by one ability of another to perform some subsidiary function. (For instance screwing an object to a wall involves drilling holes, holding the object against the wall and screwing in the screws: in this sense it refers to drilling, holding and screwing abilities.)

In referring to 'allocating a cluster to an actor', by actor is meant one such or a set of identical actors. If one finds that the abilities of a rat catcher form a convenient cluster, for instance, there is no objection to having several rat catchers if the quantity of trade justifies it.

By 'team ability' is meant qualitative ability: whether the team can achieve the goal or not. Quantitative ability —how efficiently it does it— depends not only on the clustering here considered but also on (int. al.) the degree of cloning referred to above.

5 TESTS

5.1 The domain

The tests involved a real-world domain, albeit a small one, since real-world problems are of interest. (Imaginary-world domains could have clustering characteristics varying from no clustering (all abilities referring to all others exactly once) to extreme clustering (abilities grouped into totally isolated subsets); analysis thereof would only tell one about the assumptions involved in defining such worlds and nothing about designing teams of actors for real-world activities.) A domain was required with a reasonable range of abilities, a goodly proportion involving expansions of actions into component acts (and thus referring to other abilities). Furthermore the domain would preferably be one where human conventions exist for grouping the abilities, allowing comparison of the generated grouping with human practice. The domain chosen concerns the installation of water-heating components, involving work with pipes, cable, boilers and hot tanks.

5.2 Domain observation

TEAMWORK 1, a simple multi-actor planning and executing system (Doran et al (1984), Trayner (1984)), was used to represent the domain and perform the task within it. References by abilities to other abilities were logged during task performance. This amounted to observation of the simulated domain: finding the characteristics of typical tasks encountered. This provided the frequency of reference data for the cluster analysis which in turn informed the grouping of actors.

5.3 Domain analysis

Many cluster analysis techniques have been developed and refined over the last twenty years. Those used were a form of agglomerative clustering, specifically complete-linkage and single-linkage cluster analysis (Sneath & Sokal (1973), Dunn & Everitt (1982)). Objects (here the abilities available to members of the team) are regarded as being distributed in some space and as being related pair-wise by some proximity measure. Here the proximity is the number of calls by either ability to the other. (Calls in either direction are taken to contribute to the proximity, since being in the same cluster is symmetric.) Agglomerative clustering involves starting with the acts distributed as widely as possible -one actor to each ability- and repeatedly joining the closest pairs of acts. Thus one moves from a system with one actor per ability towards one with a single actor having all acts. (Fig. 1.)

Fig 1. Hierarchical clustering: as further clustering takes place, moving from left to right, the process agglomerates succesively (1) and (2), (4) and (5), (3) and (4,5) and finally (1,2) and (3,4,5).

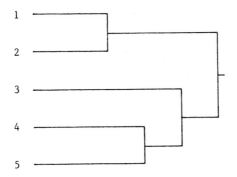

Agglomerative techniques group objects hierarchically, conforming to human canons of preference in organisational and computer-system design. Single-linkage and complete-linkage clustering both satisfy the requirements of being invariant under scaling of the proximity values. They are also relatively insensitive to permutation of their order and minor changes in their values (Cunningham & Ogilvie 1972). (Although these results refer to a stress measure they give some confidence that clustering will be similarly unaffected.) Both techniques have at least theoretical drawbacks, but single-linkage clustering is susceptible to chaining (fig. 2), an effect which can tend to agglomerate two clusters falsely on the basis of a few common links. Complete clustering on the other hand tends to produce tight, distinct clusters (Sneath & Sokal 1973).

Fig 2. Chaining: the objects shown joined by lines agglomerate early thus drawing together what are really two separate clusters. The lines show the first six linkages.

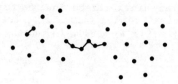

Many other agglomerative clustering techniques exist: the present pair was chosen not because they are universally superior but because they represent to some extent the field with its facilities and its problems.

Performing the cluster analysis on the frequency-of-reference data collected above agglomerates the techniques into successively fewer and larger clusters: the clusters should be clear and convincing for the first part of the hypothesis to hold. If at stage **s** of the analysis there are **n** clusters $G_{s,1}$, $G_{s,2}$, ... $G_{s,n}$, then the second part of the hypothesis presented can be restated as saying that there is benefit in assigning a cluster $G_{s,i}$ to each of **n** actors. Thus the cluster analysis generates recommendations for alloting techniques to actors. (Note that this does not give complete freedom over the choice of team size since the values of **n** are determined by the exigencies of the clustering in the particular domain and with the particular clustering technique used. Since in reality there will be other constraints on the choice of team size, cluster analysis may not be able to suggest an optimal team size. This is in effect a quantisation problem. Such clustering may also interact problematically with any wish to associate the actor planning some part of the task with that carrying it out: other constraints will probably affect the assignation of abilities to executors.)

TEAMWORK 1 was again used to simulate the behaviour of the fuller systems of interest here. (The frequency of communication is the present concern, not its temporal pattern or the planning abilities of the planner.) Two tests were run for each level **s** above: firstly with **n** actors having the abilities assigned according to the recommendations of the cluster analysis, secondly with the abilities assigned randomly to the **n** actors. (In the second test the random assignment was such that each actor had at least one technique (otherwise it would not be an **n**-actor setup); moreover several tests were made and their results averaged.) The communication requirements of the two cases were compared.

6 RESULTS

The task was the assembly of the heating installation shown in fig. 3. This involves five components, four pipe joints and one electrical joint. The 11 actions are listed in table 1.

The complete-linkage cluster analysis generated two stages between the extremes of 11-actor and 1-actor systems; the single-linkage generated three. These stages and their clusterings are shown in table 2. The complete-linkage clusterings certainly seem clear and convincing, not being a slow accretion of extra techniques in random order where no natural groupings exist. The single-linkage clusters are perhaps less so. For the non-degenerate cases (all except **s**=1 and its highest value), tables 3 and 4 compare the communication requirements of the analysis-recommended and (averaged) random tests. The random cases are markedly more verbose, around 65%-85% so.

Fig 3: The heating system to be built, constituting the task

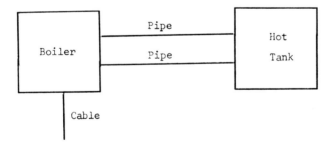

Table 1: Abilities distributed within the team

1: fix appliance to wall   7: flux pipe
2: fix pipe to wall   8: insert pipe into appliance
3: fix cable to wall   9: solder pipe into appliance
4: join pipe to appliance   10: strip cable sheath
5: join cable to appliance   11: strip cable inner insulation
6: screw cable to terminals

Table 2: Successive groupings recommended by the analysis

Analysis Stage s	------------ Groupings recommended by ---------------	
	complete-linkage analysis	single-linkage analysis
1	1,2,3,4,5,6,7,8,9,10,11	1,2,3,4,5,6,7,8,9,10,11
2	1,2,3,4+7+8+9,5,6,10,11	1,2,3,4+7+8+9,5,6,10,11
3	1+2+4+7+8+9,3,5,6,10,11	1+4+7+8+9,2,3,5,6,10,11
4	1+2+3+4+5+6+7+8+9+10+11	1+2+4+7+8+9,3,5,6,10,11
5		1+2+3+4+5+6+7+8+9+10+11

Table 3: Stages of complete-linkage analysis with resulting communication requirements

Analysis Stage s	Number of actors n	--- Communications Requirement ---	
		Random assignment	Complete-linkage clustering
1	11		
2	8	21.6	13
3	6	24	13
4	1		

7 FURTHER WORK

These tests seem to indicate that Doran's (1984) speculation is correct. It would be highly desirable to extend the tests, principally in two respects.

Firstly they should be extended to larger real-world domains. A suggested target for the next stage would be the assembly of something like a dozen components, requiring abilities drawn from something like fifty techniques, not all of them in use for all tasks. This would probably require the writing of a special-purpose simulator: the tests described here, using a LISP planning and executing system on a PDP-10, stretched the available resources almost to the limit.

Secondly, other clustering techniques should be assessed and the quality of the resulting recommendations compared. Other agglomerative techniques exist and much discussion has taken place on their relative merits (such as Jardine & Sibson (1968), Cunningham & Ogilvie (1972)). Much of this is related to fields remote from planning, however, and its relevance here is debatable: all that can be said at the moment is that some of the other methods deserve investigation. Non-hierarchical techniques (Jardine & Sibson 1968) should also be considered.

Additionally, it would be interesting to question the initial assumption that this distributed-ability arrangement is always best. It is a common human experience that the distribution of specialities brings in its train scheduling problems. ("I know I'm late finishing the wiring – the plumber keeps getting in my way.") One might speculate that, in a

Table 4: Stages of single-cluster analysis with resulting communication requirements

| Analysis Stage s | Number of actors n | --- Communications Requirement --- | |
		Random assignment	Single-linkage clustering
1	11		
2	8	21.6	13
3	7	24.2	13
4	6	24	13
5	1		

situation where storage space for technique knowledge is not a limiting factor, it might be preferable to revert to the arrangement of all actors having all abilities. The work could be allocated not according to ability but according to geographical area.

8 CONCLUSION

Cluster analysis can usefully inform the distribution of abilities across actors in a co-operative team environment. Further work needs to be done in assessing the relative merits of different cluster analysis techniques.

9 ACKNOWLEDGEMENTS

This work has been conducted with the aid of SERC grant GR/C/44938. I would also like to thank Jim Doran and Sam Steel for many fruitful discussions on these topics.

10 REFERENCES

Cammarata, S, McArthur, D. and Steeb, R. (1983) Strategies for Cooperation in Distributed Problem Solving. IJCAI-83 pp. 767-770.

Corkill, D.D. (1979) Hierarchical Planning in a Distributed Environment. IJCAI-79 pp. 168-175.

Corkill, D.D. & Lesser, V.R. (1983) The use of Meta-level control for coordination in a distributed problem solving environment. IJCAI-83 pp. 748-756.

Cunningham, K.M. and Ogilvie, J.C. (1972) Evaluation of hierarchical grouping techniques: a preliminary study. Computer Journal 15 pp. 209-213.

Doran, J. 1984 (1984) First thoughts on designing teams of actors. ALVEY Planning SIG IKBS Planning Systems R&D in the UK Fleet, Hampshire.

Doran, J., Steel, S., Trayner, C. and Wilks, Y. (1984) Meta-planning and Communication in TEAMWORK. ECAI-8: Proceedings of the sixth European conference on Artificial Intelligence. p.281 Elsevier, Amsterdam.

Dunn, G. and Everitt, B.S. (1982) An introduction to mathematical taxonomy. CUP, Cambridge.

Jardine, N. and Sibson, R. (1968) The construction of hierarchic and non-hierarchic classifications. Computer Journal 11 177-184

Smith, R.G. (1978) A Framework for Problem Solving in a Distributed Processing Environment. (PhD thesis) Stanford University STAN-CS-78-700.

Smith, R.G. (1979) A Framework for Distributed Problem Solving. Procedings of IJCAI-79 pp.836-841.

Sneath, P.H.A. and Sokal, R.R. (1973) Numerical Taxonomy W.H.Freeman, San Francisco

Trayner, C. (1984) The TEAMWORK 1 Program ALVEY Planning SIG IKBS Planning Systems R&D in the UK Fleet, Hampshire.

Trayner, C. (1985) TEAMWORK 2: Non-Planning Aspects. Internal paper, Essex University

Zhang, X. (1985) MTPS: An Expert System for Medical Treatment Planning. Internal paper, Essex University

CHOICE MAKING IN PLANNING SYSTEMS

D. Croft,
Department of Artificial Intelligence,
University of Edinburgh.

Abstract

The question of control in AI programs is a vast, and largely unexplored area of study. In this paper, one aspect of control - choice making - is considered for a planner. A program, MODPLAN, is presented, which is able to model a planner (Tate's NONLIN) in terms of the choices it makes during the planning process. The types of choice made by NONLIN are discussed, and two categories of choice type are isolated. Making choices is treated as a generate and test problem. Choice making heuristics are examined, and the possibility of learning them is considered. Finally, the potential of MODPLAN as a general planning program modeller is discussed.

Topic: Description of a planner whose operation is centred around the making of choices.

Keywords: Planning, control, choice making, learned heuristics, NONLIN.

1. Introduction

During planning, a planner is called on to make many choices. For instance, there may be several operators applicable for refining an action, or there may be several methods available for resolving a goal conflict. When and how these choices are to be made is generally coded into the control structure of the planner. This is undoubtedly a disadvantage if the user wishes to change the control structure. However, more importantly from the point of view of the current discussion, the explicit and uniform representation of the choices made during planning opens up the possibility of guiding the planner so that the <u>best</u> choices are made in any given problem solving situation. In this paper, three methods for guiding the making of choices are considered:

(1)   Interactively - the user is given relevant information about the current state of the plan and a list of possible choices, and then allowed to select a choice for himself.

(2)   Automatically - Under the control of explicitly stated user defined choice making heuristics.

(3)   Automatically - Under the control of <u>learned</u> choice making heuristics.

The first two of the above choice making methods have been implemented in a program called MODPLAN, written in PROLOG ([CLOCKSIN, 1981]). Interactive choice making is not discussed in detail in this paper; methods for automating choice making are described in section 4.

MODPLAN's operation is centred around the choices made during planning; MODPLAN models planners in terms of these choices. The first step in this modelling process is, therefore, to discover the <u>types</u> of the choices being made by the planner being modelled and the <u>information</u> used in making them. The order in which choices of different types are made then defines the control structure of the planner; the effects that the choices have on the plan are described by a <u>Plan Modification Formal-ism</u>.

2. Making Choices; How NONLIN is Modelled

The planner currently modelled by MODPLAN is Tate's NONLIN ([TATE, 1977]). Ten choice types were identified as being important for NONLIN, including choosing which node in the plan network to expand, choosing which operator to use to perform an expansion, and choosing a method to correct an interaction between conflicting goals. In addition, a dummy "stop" choice type was used, to mark the point at which planning had been completed.

MODPLAN's operation is controlled at the highest level by a recursive function. At each level in the recursion, a choice of a given type is made. Making a choice consists in selecting a decision from a list of possible decisions generated at this level in the recursion. Having selected the decision, the system will execute the meta-level action (ie., implement changes to the plan, if there are any to be made) associated with it. Such actions are specified in terms of the "Plan Modification Formalism" (PMF) mentioned in the Introduction. The type of a choice at a given level in the recursion is decided by a simple scheduling function; this function also detects plan completion. MODPLAN's choice making process is summarised in diagram 1.

The choices thus made are stored in a tree. Nodes in the tree correspond to choice-points in the planning process, and are represented as PROLOG structures. Arcs correspond to a chronological ordering on the choices made, and are represented as pointers in the choice-point structures.

The choice-point structures contain several pieces of information, including a unique number (for identification purposes), the type of the choice made, and a list of decisions. The list of decisions per-

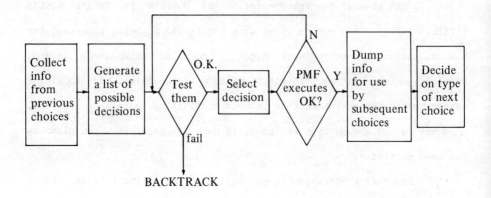

diagram 1 MODPLAN's choice making process.

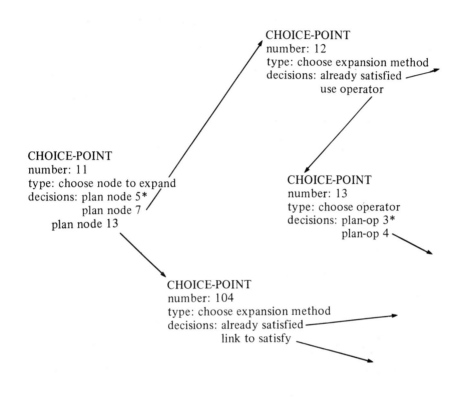

diagram 2 A few nodes in MODPLAN's choice-point
         tree.

forms two functions. First, it specifies all possible ways in which the

plan could be changed at this point. Second, for those decisions that

have already been tried, and have succeeded, it points to the subsequent

choice-points in the tree. A small piece of such a tree is illustrated

(notionally) in diagram 2. Decisions to which links are attached have

already been tried; those marked with a "*" have been tried but have led to failure.

The planner has at its disposal the Plan Modification Formalism already mentioned, which is used to specify changes to be made to the plan. It is a simple programming language, with about a dozen primitive plan altering operators, plus another thirteen high-level plan altering functions. Six conditionals are defined, allowing the language to test for certain conditions relating to the state of the plan.

A piece of PMF is a PROLOG structure, with arguments giving the name of the PMF, a pattern for passing arguments to it, a body defining the lower-level PMF that, if executed, would achieve the purpose of this piece of PMF (the body is null for primitive PMF), and a list of applicability conditions.

Primitive PMF is defined by PROLOG functions that act on the plan directly. Examples are the PMF that adds a new node to the plan network and the PMF that removes contributors to conditions in the Goal Structure. High-level PMF is defined in terms of the lower-level PMF that would have to be executed in order to achieve it. This lower-level PMF may be primitive, or it may contain further pieces of higher-level PMF. This allows PMF definitions to be nested. Examples of high-level PMF are the PMF that implements the expansion of a node specified by an operator, and the PMF that reorders network nodes during interaction correction.

As an illustration, one piece of high-level PMF that is used when selecting an expansion method is shown in diagram 3 (capitalised words indicate variables). The diagram shows the PROLOG version of this piece of PMF, as used by MODPLAN internally. In English, we can understand it as meaning that if the expansion method chosen for node number 'Nodenum' allows the node to be satisfied by already existing effects in the plan, then change the type of this node to 'phantom', so long as the

```
pmf(expmethod,
    node(Nodenum,Type,Pattval),
    alreadysatisfied,
    [pmf(changetype,changetype(Nodenum,phantom),_,[],[])],
    [type(Type,goal)]).
```

diagram 3 Implementing an expansion method -
a MODPLAN PMF definition

applicability condition "current node type is 'goal' " holds.

The high-level PMF operators are all associated with particular choice types; for some choice types, no change in the plan is involved. The PMF definitions for these choice types have null bodies. The remaining high-level PMF definitions are given in table 1.

The choice types used by MODPLAN can be split into two categories, depending on how they obtain their decision lists:

(1) Choices whose decision lists are derived from the information in the plan. In a NONLIN-type planner, choices between alternative plan nodes to expand or unsupervised conditions to satisfy are examples of this category. These choices do not directly affect the plan.

(2) Choices whose decision lists are derived from high-level PMF definitions. Very often, there is more than one way of changing the plan to achieve some meta-goal, such as "correct this interaction". For choice types in this category, alternative techniques are embodied in the high-level PMF definitions.

Once a list of decisions has been generated (and passed by a failure-detection mechanism), a choice can be made. Choice making can be

PMF name	Effects on plan
Expmethod	Used in conjunction with choices where an expansion method is chosen for a plan node; may change the type of the node being expanded.
Operator	This applies a predefined domain operator; in so doing, it can affect the network of plan nodes, the goal structure and the table of effects.
Contributor	One means of satisfying a goal is to take advantage of beneficial interactions; this may involve adding new links to the plan network.
Instantiate	Will cause instantiations to be made for the variables in a previously selected condition; changes may occur to the goal structure.
Correctint	Causes an interaction to be corrected, which may involve the addition of extra links to the plan network and changes to the goal structure.

table 1 Plan altering high-level PMF

under user control, or it can be done automatically by MODPLAN. The user can single-step from choice to choice, or he can request the planner to make any number of choices automatically. When making a choice in automatic mode, the system will apply a user defined heuristic to give each of the decisions in the decision list a grading. The decision with the highest grading will then be selected. The heuristics are discussed in a later section.

As hinted above, a failure detection mechanism is brought into action between the creation or changing of a decision list and the making of a choice. It performs a set of tests over the entire list of decisions. If the decision list passes these tests, then MODPLAN moves on to the task of decision selection. Otherwise, the choice as a whole is failed, and MODPLAN backtracks to the previous choice. Decisions leading to failing choices are given a status "fail" to prevent them from being reselected.

The choices made by MODPLAN are not independent; the way in which one choice is made can directly affect several others, and indirectly affect many others. An information passing protocol was developed to enable choices to pass on relevant information to dependent choices. At each of the choice making levels in the planner's recursion, two things are done. First, before even the list of decisions has been generated, information from previous choices must be picked up from the information passing structure. Second, once the choice has been made, any information generated must be packaged and dumped into the information passing structure for the use of subsequent choices. Much of the information thus passed is redundant, since it could have been extracted from the plan. However, it would be wasteful to have to extract exactly the same information from the plan at several successive choice-points; better to preserve it and pass it on.

MODPLAN's control structure is determined by the way in which one choice type follows on from another. At a given choice-point, the type of the next choice to be made must be determined. The function for doing this takes as input the current plan, the current choice-point tree, and any information passed on from previous 'choices. It outputs the type of the next choice to be made. The next choice type will be dependent mainly on the types of recently made previous choices. Other factors may be influential, including the number of outstanding expandable nodes and the number of outstanding uncorrected interactions. The control structure thus defined is fixed, cyclic in nature, and derived from NONLIN. It operates roughly as follows:

(1)   Choose a node in the plan network to expand; if none, goto (6).

(2)   Select a method to expand this node.

(3)   Choose instantiations for variables within the expansion.

(4)   Check for interactions. If any are found, select one to be corrected, and select a method to correct it. Repeat until all interactions have been corrected.

(5)   Goto (1).

(6)   If there are any unsupervised conditions, select one to be satisfied, and select a method for satisfying it. Repeat until all unsupervised conditions are satisfied.

(7)   Stop.

Each step represents choices to be made. If failure occurs, the system backtracks to the previous choice. The user only has a say in the way in which choices can be made; the ordering of choices is embedded in MODPLAN's program code.

3. Refocusing

Since MODPLAN records the choices made during planning in a tree, there is obvious potential for moving about in this tree, so that planning can be restarted at any point, and so that alternative plans can be generated. This is known as refocusing - we are refocusing the attention of the planner.

MODPLAN cannot store plan states, apart from the current one.

When the user has selected the choice that he wants to refocus on, the system will examine the choice-point tree to find the point at which the current branch meets the branch on which the selected choice-point lies. The system will then backtrack to this meeting point, and from there, plan forwards until it arrives at the selected choice-point. The planning is guided by the existing record of choices in the tree. The user can now recommence interactive planning from his selected "target" choice-point.

Since the choice-point tree will generally be quite large, it is not practical to present the user with the entire tree and expect him to pick his target. Instead, he is given a facility whereby candidate lists of potential target choice-points are incrementally shrunk by applying incomplete user-specified information. The information may relate to some property that the target has as a tree node, eg., its position in the tree, or it may relate to the way in which decisions recorded at it affect the plan.

4. Automating Choice Making

Two methods for the automating of choice making will be considered here - using predefined heuristics, and using learned heuristics. The first has been implemented, albeit in a rather crude way, in MODPLAN. The second has not.

When making choices, one of the problems that confronts both humans and machines is finding the information that is relevant. For a planner, the information available can be overwhelming, since even to represent a small plan requires a lot of information.

No techniques are described here for deciding on the relevance of information, although it might be noted in passing that the choice type could be used to suggest, in broad terms, which information to include and which to exclude. It is also possible that, given the information a human uses in choice making, the system could learn which information to retain, and how to extract it.

In MODPLAN, user defined heuristics are regarded as operational expressions of planning policies. The user may invent any number of policies - eg. "minimise plan network linearity" or "find shortest path through solution space". The operationalisation of these policies consists in writing heuristics, for several or all of the choice types, that are believed to achieve the meta-goal embodied in the policy. The term operationalisation is due to Mostow ([MOSTOW, 1979]), and he describes a number of techniques for operationalising advice initially expressed in a non-effective form. Only the most trivial of these techniques is used in MODPLAN, namely goal specific operationalisation.

In MODPLAN, the user has at his disposal about ten different primitive information extraction functions. He can build up more sophisticated functions in the form of function nets. Nodes in the net correspond to primitive functions, and arcs to arguments passed. Information sources (ie. the plan and the current decision list) and information destinations (ie. operationalisations for currently active policies) are also represented as nodes in the net. An interpreter uses the net to control information extraction; the relevant information thus extracted is passed onto the operationalisations.

The language that MODPLAN provides for describing heuristics is not very powerful. It has two primitive functions for grading decisions; these functions obtain their inputs from the information extraction function net and the decision currently under consideration, and their outputs are fed into an arithmetic expression. Evaluation of this expression gives a grading for the decision under consideration.

If we wanted MODPLAN to <u>learn</u> its choice making heuristics, we would have to define for the learning program a set of examples and the attributes and classifications of these examples. As examples, then, the system would be given decisions that had been tried. Output from the information extraction function net would provide the attributes. The classification of a decision would depend on how well it had succeeded or how badly it had failed. A simple heuristic could be written to give, say, five possible classifications on the axis very good to very bad. Decisions would be taken from selected choice-points in the choice-point tree. The system would apply a different learning process to each choice type, since the rules governing choice making for one type of choice would almost certainly be different from those for other choice types. The selection of choice-points for use as examples would be at the discretion of the user, but he would be given special facilities to feed the learning system with all choices on a particular branch in the choice-point tree. This means that it would be possible, for instance, to supply the learning program only with choices lying on the shortest path to a solution.

Since the classifications used by the system would have more than two possible values, the rules that the system builds up would be disjunctive. Furthermore, the example classifying heuristic would not always be right; conflicting examples could arise. These considerations are likely to affect the learning algorithms selected to tackle the heuristic learning problem.

5. Some Results

To find out how changing choice making heuristics could affect MODPLAN's performance, a number of experiments were performed. MODPLAN has several plan performance assessment functions built into it, that enable the user to find out to what extent the planner has been failing and backtracking, and at which choice types the problems have been arising.

MODPLAN was called upon to solve a classic three-blocks problem. Initially, it was tested out with heuristics that used no information at all, apart from the order of decisions in decision lists. That is, it just tried out each decision in turn, until one of them worked. These heuristics tended to make the paths through the solution space rather long, and the planner tried a lot of dead-end paths before finding a correct solution. By using the performance assessment functions, the choice types most likely responsible for the problems were identified. Heuristics using more information were then written, and substituted for the original unintelligent heuristics. The performance improved; and by repeating this cycle of running the planner and then re-writing heuristics several times, the system's performance was improved to the stage where it found the solution without search.

Of course, these heuristics had become tailored somewhat to this particular problem. When applied to a problem involving five blocks, they did not fare so well. Modifying them so that the five-blocks problem was solved reasonably efficiently caused a deterioration in the performance on the original three-blocks problem.

Thus, to find heuristics which, for a given domain, will work fairly well for all problems within that domain, could involve a substantial amount of trial and error experimentation.

6. Modelling Other Planners

The concepts used in building MODPLAN were aimed at an ability to model any planner in terms of the choices that it makes. Flexibility-wise, MODPLAN falls some way short of such an aim - to accommodate a planner other than NONLIN would entail significant alterations to the program code, although MODPLAN's basic framework could be retained in many cases. The following list outlines the most important factors that would have to be taken into account if a new planner was to be modelled:

(1)   Language. MODPLAN is written in PROLOG, and any serious attempt to change the program would require a good working knowledge of PROLOG.

(2)   Plan representation and modification. MODPLAN represents a plan as a PROLOG structure. A new plan representation would demand modifications to this structure, and to the primitive PMF that operates on it.

(3)   Choice types. If the types of choice made by MODPLAN are to be changed, then corresponding changes would have to be made to the high-level PMF definitions. Furthermore, the functions describing the control structure and the protocol for passing information between choices would be different.

(4)   Meta-planning. MODPLAN's control structure currently uses an agenda-based task scheduling system, resorting to backtracking if failure occurs. Programs such as MOLGEN ([STEFIK, 1981])

and PANDORA ([WILENSKY, 1981],[FALETTI, 1982]), whioh uoc
multi-level control structures, could not conveniently be
modelled by MODPLAN - some fairly fundamental changes in program structure would be involved.

(5)   <u>Dealing</u> <u>with</u> <u>failure</u>. If a choice leads to failure, MODPLAN
will backtrack to the previous choice. More sophisticated
means of dealing with failure, such as dependency-directed
backtracking ([HAYES, 1975], [DANIEL, 1982]), would require
additions to the choice-point tree and changes in the way in
which the tree is updated at the point backtracked to. Means
of discovering dependency relationships would also have to be
incorporated.

7. Conclusions

MODPLAN is able to model a planner, NONLIN, in terms of the
choices that it makes. Facilities for guiding choice making are available. Routines have been provided to allow a user to assess how well the
planner is performing under a particular set of choice making heuristics.
Experiments with a simple blocks world problem showed that performance
improvement could be obtained by incremental modification of choice making heuristics. Making explicit the choices made by a planner enables us
to consider the possibility of a system that <u>learns</u> choice making heuristics. The potential of MODPLAN as a general planning program modeller
was examined, and some fairly serious difficulties were uncovered.

The work outlined in this paper is discussed in more detail in
my thesis, see [CROFT, 1984].

References

[CLOCKSIN, 1981] Clocksin, W.F. and Mellish, C.S. (1981). Programming in prolog. Springer-Verlag.

[CROFT, 1984] Croft, D. (1984). Choices made by a planner: Identifying them and improving the way in which they are made. M.Phil thesis, University of Edinburgh.

[DANIEL, 1982] Daniel, L. and Tate, A. (1982). A retrospective on the "Planning: a joint AI/OR approach" project. University of Edinburgh DAI Working Paper 125.

[FALETTI, 1982] Faletti, J. (1982). PANDORA - A program for doing commonsense planning in complex situations. In AAAI, 185 - 188.

[HAYES, 1975] Hayes, P.J. (1975). A representation for robot plans. In IJCAI 4, 181 - 188.

[MOSTOW, 1979] Mostow, J. and Hayes-Roth, F. (1979). Operationalising heuristics: some AI methods for assisting AI programming. In IJCAI 6, 601 - 609.

[STEFIK, 1981] Stefik, M. (1981). Planning and meta-planning. In Artificial intelligence 16, 141 - 170.

[TATE, 1977] Tate, A. (1977). Generating project networks. In IJCAI 5 888 - 893.

[WILENSKY, 1981] Wilensky, R. (1981). Meta-planning: Representing and using knowledge about planning in problem solving and natural language understanding. In Cognitive science 5, 197 - 233.

THE ECO BROWSER

David Robertson*
Robert Muetzelfeldt**
Dave Plummer*
Mike Uschold*
Alan Bundy*

* Department of Artificial Intelligence,
University of Edinburgh.
** Department of Forestry and Natural Resources,
University of Edinburgh.

Keywords : browser

ABSTRACT

The ECO Browser is the prototype of a Prolog browser for a large knowledge base of loosely structured observational information. Its purpose is to provide a way for users quickly to access the information they require without necessarily having predetermined ideas about the things that are of interest to them. The browsing mechanism is based on simple principles. We adopt an approach which relies on a gradual narrowing of the area of interest, until the desired information is found. Recent small scale tests suggest that this method is natural and easy to use, although a short introductory session is often required. Several extensions to the current system are suggested, including the incorporation of intelligent guidance methods.

1. Introduction

ECO [Uschold *et al* 84] is an intelligent front end which helps ecologists construct models of dynamic ecological systems. Its users must have access to a body of ecological information from which they can extract the information they need to build a specific ecological model. Offering facility presents three major problems:

* A large variety of ecological information must be represented.

* Users must be allowed to search through it in a flexible, efficient manner.

* Users cannot be expected to know exactly what type of information they
want before using the browser.

This paper describes a method of tackling these problems in an ecological context
but these techniques may be useful in other areas where the knowledge is loosely
structured.

2. Browser Requirements in an Ecological Domain

As ecology covers a broad range of interests, the type of information
required will differ widely between individual users. Therefore, the system used to
browse around the knowledge base must be based on a mechanism which is largely
independent of the ecological context in which it is used. It must operate in a way
which seems natural to inexperienced users and must give them control over the
selection of information without overburdening them with complex commands.
Users may not know exactly what information they need until they have seen part of
the knowledge base. The browsing system should lead novice users if necessary,
but should allow experienced users to find the information they need quickly. As
the task is exploratory in nature, the system should permit users to backtrack to
previous states in the browsing session if they have not found what they are
looking for in the first instance.

2.1. Knowledge representation

Ecological information is often obtained in the form of observational
records which may be of varying complexity and may refer to differing aspects of a
similar situation. For instance, three ecologists may each make an observation
about deer.

1. The weight of male deer in Scotland is, on average, 50 kilos.

2. The body weight of a male deer was 45 kilos.

3. The weight of a deer is about 100 pounds.

Each real world observation corresponds to a *record* in the knowledge base. The
bits which make up each record are informally referred to as *items* (eg. deer,
Scotland). All the examples above refer to deer but the differences in detail
between records means that they may not all be useful to specific users. For
example, someone who was interested in deer in Scotland would only want record 1
but someone who was interested in deer weight in general could be interested in

any of the three records. Loosely structured records do not lend themselves directly to efficient browsing but relationships between the items which constitute each record may be used to provide a graph of related items. Such a graph is used by the ECO browser to help users isolate the records which most closely match their requirements. (A separate program which we do not describe is used to convert the set of loosely structured records into this graph.)

2.2. Using the browser on large knowledge bases

The current version of the ECO browser represents both the records and relationship graph as Prolog facts. This presents problems of storage space and real time searching speed which has limited the size of our test knowledge base to about 120 records, each with about six constituent items. To overcome this, the prototype system must be re-implemented to provide the following:

* Fast access to the records which refer to a selected node on the graph.

* A large data storage capacity is essential, and may require secondary storage management.

* It will be necessary to tag all the records which have been selected at a particular time and to quickly find which records carry a specific tag, in order to allow previous selection states to be restored. If a large number of records are available, then a large number of tags will need to be applied for each selection. Also, when returning to a previous selection state it will be necessary to check all records for the appropriate tag.

It is possible that these requirements would be satisfied by using existing knowledge representation tools, such as Loops [Bobrow & Stefik 81], ART [Clayton 84], or NETL [Fahlman 79]. The former two are frame-based and have hash coded patterns and relationships for efficiency. The latter uses a parallel network approach designed for anticipated parallel hardware. Special purpose hardware for high speed information retrieval is already being developed [MacGregor 84] which may also support the ECO browsing strategy. This paper is concerned with the way search should be controlled and displayed to users and does not concentrate on knowledge representation. However, efficiency problems must be overcome if the system is to prove useful for practical applications. Also, the browser, in its current form, is unsuitable for search graphs which are very deep and/or have high branching rates. A discussion of this problem appears in section 3.3.

3. The Browsing Mechanism

The ECO browser supports two main types of activity:

1. *Search for items of interest.* This assumes no prior knowledge of what may be contained in the knowledge base. Users are faced with a menu of general items (eg. habitat, nutrients, organism). They may then search for further items which are related to these (eg. organisms subdivide into the categories of plants and animals; animals then subdivide into reptiles, fish, mammals, etc.).

2. *Select records.* At any point during the search, users may select records which pertain only to items in which they express interest.

This section describes these actions and the method for displaying information to users. A variety of additional commands and special features are described in section 4.

3.1. Searching for items of interest

At the start of a session, users are positioned at the most general node in the graph – the root node. From there, they are encouraged to search for more specific items of interest by being shown the nodes connected directly below that node. This process can be repeated until one of two things happen:

* They find an item which interests them and select the records to which it applies (see below).

* They reach a leaf node of the graph, below which there are no more specific items.

Users can continue to search and select by jumping back up the graph and travelling down different pathways toward various selection points. This process continues until a user has selected as finely as s/he needs.

3.2. Selecting records

One selects records relevant to a particular item by selecting that item. Selecting an item causes the records which contain that item – either explicitly, by containing the item itself, or implicitly, by containing one of its descendants – to be tagged as belonging to the set of records which are available to the user at that time. All other records are discarded as irrelevant.

This process can be illustrated using the examples of records in section 2.1. If the item "weight" is selected then all three records would be retained, since they all refer to some type of weight. However, if the item "male" was then selected, only records 1 and 2 would be tagged as being available. If further selection of the item "body weight" occurred then only record 2 would remain because this is the only record which contains types of "weight", "male" and "body weight".

A side effect of selecting records is that items which were previously available for the user to select are made unavailable. This occurs because by reducing the number of records in this way, the diversity of information in the remaining records tends to decrease. Using the current example, if record 3 were the only record left then selection of "male" would not be possible. It is undesirable to have this as an irreversible process, so additional features have been added to allow the undoing of selections.

3.3. Displaying information to users

At all times, users should be aware of their position in the graph; the number of records which are available and the items which they have selected. This information must be conveyed succinctly and, in our case, within the limitations of a standard VDU display (the potential of graphics facilities will be discussed later). The display which is currently in use adresses the following requirements:

* Users should have an indication of their position relative to other nodes in the graph. In particular, displaying a path upwards through the graph via more general nodes provides a context for the current position, while an indication of possible paths downward through the graph is given by displaying the children of the current node.

* A record of past selections should be shown, to remind users of the items in which they have shown interest.

* The display format should be the same throughout the session so that users become familiar with the layout as soon as possible.

* Items which are specific types of the current item should be easily accessed without having to provide their names.

* Users should know how many records remain available as they progressively refine their ideas about what interests them.

Taking the example from section 2.1, the display would appear as in 3-1 if a user had selected "weight", "male" and "body weight" in that order. It is possible that the amount of information shown on this display could overwhelm users – particularly if the graph were deep and with a high branching rate. It would be useful to limit the display in two ways.

* If a user is positioned at a great depth in the graph, only a limited number of nodes should be shown as context – perhaps those nearest to the current position on a path back to the most general node.

* If the user is positioned at a node which has a large number of children, there should be some way of restricting the number of children displayed. This suggests a need for some form of user guidance, which will be discussed in section 8.3.

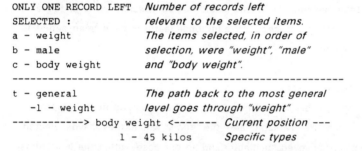

```
ONLY ONE RECORD LEFT    Number of records left
SELECTED :              relevant to the selected items.
a - weight              The items selected, in order of
b - male                selection, were "weight", "male"
c - body weight         and "body weight".
-------------------------------------------------------------
t - general             The path back to the most general
   -1 - weight          level goes through "weight"
------------> body weight <------- Current position ---
            1 - 45 kilos     Specific types
```

Figure 3-1:   Sample of a standard display

4. Additional Features

Simple searching and selecting operations were found to be insufficient for easy operation of the system and a number of extra features were added. These options allow more sophisticated use of the mechanisms described above.

4.1. Undoing selections

Users may change their mind about selections they have made and want to undo the effects of their actions back to a specified point. The Browser provides a command which returns the records which were available when some previous item was selected. This is possible because the system maintains a tree of selection states, with each node representing a list of records relating to a particular selected item. For example, if someone selected "weight" followed by "male" and "body weight" and then undid the selections back to "weight", finally selecting "50 kilos", the selection tree would have the structure shown in figure 4-1.

Numbers in brackets are available records at each node.

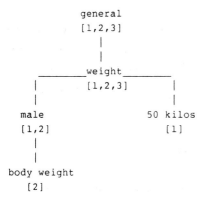

```
                    general
                    [1,2,3]
                       |
                       |
          _____weight_____
         |            [1,2,3]      |
         |                         |
       male                    50 kilos
       [1,2]                       [1]
         |
         |
     body weight
        [2]
```

Figure 4-1:   Example of a Selection Tree

The path back to "general" through the selection tree from the most recent selection is shown to the user every time s/he moves through the graph of items. Additionally, the whole selection tree can be displayed so that the states obtained during unrelated selection sequences can be retrieved. Another related command is "clear", which restores all the records that were available when the session started.

4.2. Displaying selected records

It is necessary to show the items contained within selected records. The ECO browser allows both the printing of complete records and the printing of selected information in records. For example, if someone wanted all the available information about weight in the three example records, the following would be displayed:

```
RECORD 1
weight = 50:kilos
RECORD 2
body weight = 45:kilos
RECORD 3
weight = 100:pounds
```

4.3. Help facility

At any point in the session, a help package can be accessed which describes how to operate the various components of the system. It has been found that the operation of the Browser can be explained using simple conventions – for example, that items shown at a higher level in the path upwards from the current position are more general than those at lower levels – so an inexperienced user need not become bogged down in technical detail when trying to understand how the system operates.

5. An Example of the Browser in Action

A simple test run of the system is shown in figure 5-1. Only the most fundamental operations of the system are demonstrated in this example because of space limitations. The text appears as seen on the screen of a VDU, with italicised annotations at strategic points. User input is shown in boldface.

Note the difference between "searching" and "selecting". One may *search* through the relationship graph by simply typing the choice number in the list of items. This is simply browsing around to see what is there, and has no effect on the records available. One *selects* an item by prefixing the choice number with an "**s**" (eg. **s 3**). Also, when searching or selecting, you may use the name of an item instead of its number. This option may be used to search for or select items which are *not* in currently displayed list of choices (eg. **s sheep**).

At the end of the session, the user has isolated two records, both of which happen to contain parameter values. If judged suitable, these may be then added to the specification of the ecological model using the ECO program. (Alternatively, the records could have contained mathematical relationships or other information which could be used in the model.)

6. Trial Runs With Inexperienced Users

The browser has been tested by five people who had no previous contact with the system. Two of these were familiar with AI techniques; the remainder were final year ecology undergraduates. Before using the browser, they were given a five minute introductory talk and a ten minute demonstration of the system in operation. This was sufficient introduction and they quickly became

```
WELCOME TO THE ECO BROWSER                         ONLY ONE RECORD LEFT
                                                   SELECTED :
If you are unfamiliar with this program, or        a - mammal
become confused at any stage, type "h" for         b - female
information about permitted commands               c - sheep
                                                   ----------------------
YOUR STARTING POINT IS AT THE HIGHEST LEVEL        t - general
(GENERAL)                                            -3 - organism
YOU HAVE 124 RECORDS TO BROWSE THROUGH                 -2 - animal
1 - age                                                  -1 - mammal
2 - sex                                            --------------> sheep <---------------
3 - author                                         NO CHOICES AVAILABLE BELOW THIS POINT
4 - process                                        SELECTION :p I want to see all the information in
5 - equation                                                    the remaining observation
6 - nutrients
7 - habitat                                        THE RECORDS AVAILABLE AT THIS POINT ARE :
8 - geographical location                          RECORD 108
9 - organism                                       [standard,metabolic rate] is 25.7:cal*kg^-1*day^-1
10- numeric variable   I am interested in          sex is female
                       "organism"                  age is adult
SELECTION :9           so I move to choice 9        mammal is sheep

THERE ARE 124 RECORDS LEFT  All the observations    SELECTION :u b   I don't want this information so I
NO SELECTIONS MADE     remain                                        undo my selections back to "female"
                       I haven't selected anything
----------                                         THERE ARE 8 RECORDS LEFT
t - general   I have moved down to "organism"      SELECTED :
------> organism <-----------                      a - mammal   The "sheep" selection is lost from the
          1 - animal                               b - female   current selection history
          2 - plant                                ----------------------
SELECTION :1           I move down to "animal"      t - general
                                                     -1 - sex   I have been automatically moved to "female"
THERE ARE 124 RECORDS LEFT                         --------> female <-------
NO SELECTIONS MADE                                 NO CHOICES AVAILABLE BELOW THIS POINT
----------                                         SELECTION :s cow   I decide to select "cow"
t - general   I am shown a path back to the most                       instead of "sheep"
  -1 - organism   general level so I know where I am
------> animal <------                             THERE ARE 2 RECORDS LEFT
          1 - insect                               SELECTED :
          2 - bird                                 a - mammal
          3 - mammal                               b - female
          4 - fish                                 c - cow
SELECTION :s 3   I want information about "mammal"  ----------------------
                 so I select it                    t - general
THERE ARE 20 RECORDS LEFT                            -3 - organism
SELECTED :                                             -2 - animal
a - mammal   I can see that I have selected "mammal"     -1 - mammal
----------                                         --------------> cow <---------
t - general                                        NO CHOICES AVAILABLE BELOW THIS POINT
  -2 - organism                                    SELECTION :p
    -1 - animal
------> mammal <--------                           THE RECORDS AVAILABLE AT THIS POINT ARE :
          1 - shetland pony                        RECORD 102
          2 - dog                                  [standard,metabolic rate] is 15.2:cal*kg^-1*day^-1
          3 - human                                sex is female
          4 - pig                                  age is adult
          5 - guinea pig                           mammal is cow
          6 - cow
          7 - sheep                                RECORD 96
SELECTION :s female   I know that "female" exists  sex is female
                      so I select it directly      [activity,metabolic rate] is 21.1:cal*kg^-1*day^-1
                                                   age is adult
THERE ARE 8 RECORDS LEFT                           mammal is cow
SELECTED :
a - mammal                                         SELECTION :quit I decide to stop at this stage
b - female
----------
t - general
  -1 - sex
------> female <-------
NO CHOICES AVAILABLE BELOW THIS POINT
SELECTION :s sheep   I remember that "sheep" was
                     available so I select it
```

Figure 5-1: Example Session

accustomed to the display format and effects of basic commands. The only source of confusion was between searching to an item and selecting records which refer to an item. Some of the subjects expected records to be selected automatically whenever a new item was visited but the difference between these actions was accepted without apparent difficulty, when explained by example.

7. Comparison With Other Browsing Systems

Other systems have been constructed which tackle similar browsing problems for different domains and using different approaches. A browser is being developed for the United Kingdom Department of Health and Social Security (as an Alvey Large Scale Demonstrator Project) which allows users to provide a description of the required information by providing values for one or more fields in a standard form [Clark & Pettit 84]. This would be impractical for our application because the number of types of ecological information is extremely large.

The RABBIT browser [Tou et al 82] addresses problems which are more similar to those which the ECO browser faces. It assumes that users will have an incomplete knowledge of the names which they can use in the system to specify their requirements. It also uses "perspectives" which correspond approximately to the "context" information supplied by the ECO browser. However, there are major differences between the approaches used in the RABBIT and ECO browsers. RABBIT relies on finding examples from the knowledge base which match users' specifications and uses these as a means of prompting for further specification details. In other words, the "records" in RABBIT's knowledge base are shown as a prompt for further selection criteria, rather than ECO's method of using relationships between items to drive the selection process and displaying records only upon specific request. This requires users of RABBIT to have some idea, however vague, of what they are looking for when entering the system, in order to access an initial set of examples. The ECO browser starts the user off with a display of the most general items in the knowledge base and offers these as possibilities which may be explored in more detail, allowing the system to be used by people with no preconceptions of the things they are interested in.

The Smalltalk-80 system provides a browser for examining definitions of object classes [Tesler 81]. It distinguishes 4 levels within its classification, each of which is represented within a separate "pane" on a graphics screen. Smalltalk browsing operates on the following principle. First, one item is selected from the list of items at the most general level. The system then displays, in the adjoining pane, a list of children of the selected item. An item from the list of options in the new pane can then be selected. This process is repeated until one item from each level has been chosen, thus defining an individual object description.

The ECO browser differs from the Smalltalk approach in four important ways.

* The Smalltalk browser operates on a comparitively shallow hierarchy, comprising 5 levels. This allows it to display, simultaneously, all the items at each point in the user's path toward a specific object description. The ECO browser must accomodate hierarchies of, potentially, much greater depth. Therefore, it cannot provide all this information at once, for fear of overwhelming the user (see section 3.3).

* Items at a particular level of the Smalltalk classification appear to be mutually exclusive. Thus, selecting one item from a level automatically makes other items at that level unavailable. The ECO browser accomodates records which may contain several items from the same level so the process of selection may entail multiple selections from items of similar status (see section 3.2).

* The only way to move down the Smalltalk classification is by selecting an item from the level above. The ECO browser distinguishes between simply moving around the relationship graph and selecting items of particular interest (see section 3). This allows users to look around before committing themselves to a particular set of choices – an essential feature when browsing through a knowledge base which has connections to observational records at varying levels in the relationship graph (see section 3.1).

* The ECO browser provides a means of returning to previous selection states, thereby freeing users from the tedium of remembering and re-implementing a cancelled selection sequence which they want to retry.

The browser used in Smalltalk is capable of operating successfully, without using complex mechanisms, because it is applied to a comparitively small, rigidly structured knowledge base. The added complexity of the ECO browsing mechanism stems from the need to accomodate a large volume of loosely structured data.

8. Future Additions

8.1. Graphics display

The ECO browser relies heavily on communicating to users their position in the graph. The use of bit-map displays via a suitable graphics interface would allow the meaning of displays to be more obvious to the user. For example, the tree of previous selections could be drawn on the screen using lines for arcs and boxes for nodes, rather than the current method of indenting the name on each line according to its depth in the tree.

8.2. Permitting complex choices

Currently, the browser operates on the assumption that users will be capable of making definite selection choices. This was the case in our short trial sessions but some users may want to make imprecise selections. For instance, in the example in figure 5-1 one might have wanted to say "I am probably interested in cows but might be interested in sheep" instead of selecting cows alone or sheep alone. A mechanism is needed for allowing selections with associated degrees of certainty, combined with the existing definite choice mechanism.

Another browser prototype is being developed which selects records by scoring each one according to how closely its constituent items are to nodes in the graph specified by the user as being of interest. In this way, an arbitrary number of criteria, some of which may be exclusive of each other, may be used to find the most suitable records. This scoring system could be extended to allow the user to specify the importance of each item selected and the system could weight the scores accordingly. However, such complicated mechanisms are likely to reduce the speed of selection significantly. Our policy has been to maintain a simple control system which is maximally efficient and easy to understand.

8.3. Guidance for users

At present, the onus is on the user to decide which items s/he is interested in, with no intelligent advice available from the system. This does not seem to be a problem in the context of the ECO program, since the users are assumed to be prepared to search the knowledge base, testing out various selection options. The people who tested the browser found the method quite easy to understand. However, in some circumstances it would be desirable for the Browser to provide advice about which options to choose; shield some of the possible options from the user or make some decisions automatically. Guidance of this sort would depend on on the previous choices made by the user, the current structure of the simulation model which is being built, and/or information about the user's purpose in entering the system. This implies an initial phase of determining the user's needs. It seems likely that this type of control could be built on top of the current system and work along these lines may take place soon.

9. Conclusions

The ECO browser uses a simple search strategy and display format which is designed to facilitate easy operation of the system. Users with no notion of the type of information they require should be able to select at a general level at first, progressively refining their description as they move through the relationship graph. This approach differs from that of existing large knowledge base browsers, such as RABBIT, which rely on matching examples to users' initial specifications and use these examples as cues for further, detailed specification. Small scale experimental trials with inexperienced users tentatively suggest that our specific requirements of flexibility plus ease of understanding have been achieved by our browser. However, the problems of implementing the prototypical browser to suit large knowledge bases have not been resolved.

Acknowledgements

This work was funded by SERC grant GR/C/06226. Austin Tate provided information about knowledge representation methods and helpful comments on earlier drafts. The browser was tested by Diana Bental, Paul Brna and three anonymous Ecology students.

References

[Bobrow & Stefik 81]
Bobrow D. & Stefik M.
The LOOPS Manual.
Technical Report KB-VLSI-81-13, Knowledge Systems Area, Xerox
Palo Alto Research Center, 1981.

[Clark & Pettit 84]
Clark M., & Pettit, P.
The Alvey Large Scale Demonstrator Project for the Department of
Health and Social Security.
In *The Proceedings of the Joint Alvey MMI/IKBS Workshop on
Applications-Driven Research.* 1984.

[Clayton 84]   Clayton B.
Programming Primer: ART (Version 1.1)
Los Angeles, CA, 1984.

[Fahlman 79]   Fahlman, S.E.
NETL: A System for Representing and Using Real-World Knowledge.
The MIT Press, 1979.

[MacGregor 84]   MacGregor D.R.
An Integrated High Performance, Hardware Assisted, Intelligent
Data Base System for Large-Scale Knowledge Bases.
In *Proceedings of the First Alvey Workshop on Architecture for
Large Knowledge Bases.* 1984.

[Tesler 81]   Tesler, L.
The Smalltalk Environment.
Byte 6(3):90 – 147, 1981.

[Tou et al 82]   Tou F., Williams M., Fikes R., Henderson A., & Malone T.
RABBIT: An Intelligent Database Assistant.
In *Proceedings of AAAI-82,* pages 314-318. 1982.
Xerox Palo Alto Research Center.

[Uschold *et al* 84]
Uschold, M., Harding, N., Muetzelfeldt, R. and Bundy, A.
An Intelligent Front End for Ecological Modelling.
In O'Shea, T. (editor), *Proceedings of ECAI-84.* ECAI, 1984.
Available from Edinburgh as Research Paper 223.

A CAD/CAPP EXPERT SYSTEM SHELL

V.I. Kirov,
Software R&D Institute "INTERPROGRAMMA", Sofia,
Bulgaria

Abstract: The CAD/CAPP expert system shell described
consists of an executive level being an extended
PROLOG interpreter and several design knowledge-
based levels, maintaining a design method named
Recursive Decomposition Method (RDM). A conceptual
modelling-based knowledge representation scheme and
RDM-oriented built-in solving mechanisms are
described. This high level programming environment
is intended to be used for implementation of more
flexible CAD/CAPP systems possessing some problem
solving capabilities.

Key words: CAD/CAPP, expert system, PROLOG, knowledge representation, algebraic approach, formal
grammers, structured programming, problem solving,
conceptual modelling, structural synthesis, program
synthesis.

INTRODUCTION

In this paper a CAD/CAM expert system shell is
described, intended to overcome to some extent the most
important shortcomings of the traditional computer-aided
design/computer-aided process planning (CAD/CAPP) systems in
machinebuilding: insufficient universality and portability,
lack of tools for non-numeric problem solving and decision-
making processes maintainance, long time of development, low
level of automation etc.

The tendency of unification, normalization and
standardization of design/manufacturing solutions at lower
levels and the schemes of their composition at higher levels,
taking place in industry at present, serves as an ideal basis
for computer-aided modular design/process planning. The
modular object environment consists of functionally complete,
usually redundant, set of parts and units (conditionally

considered as primitives), which can be combined and composed
in different (but a priori determined) ways in order to
produce potentially unlimited multiplicity of resulting regular structures on the basis of relatively small number of
basic elements (primitives). In this case there exists a
great number of functionally equivalent variant design solutions, varying mainly in their structures and parameters
values.

The synthesis of an object or process structure,i.e.
primitive components selection, corresponding attributes
values determination and setting of all the necessary functional, spacial, temporary, constructive and other relations
and links at the different levels of object/process description (Fig. 1), is considered as a main design/process planning
task. It is supposed to be solved on the basis of analysis and
juxtaposition of the functional requirements towards the
object/process being designed/planned, on one hand, and generalized empirical knowledge about how to use given object
environment components and natural laws to construct/process
and produce new ones, on the other (Kirov 1983 a; Kirov
1984 a).

Therefore, the part of language and program facilities, providing the necessary means for object/process and
design/planning algorithms structural synthesis was distinguished as a kernal of the CAD/CAPP expert system shell.

So far the first version of shell kernel described
in this paper has been implemented by us experimentally.
Further on this version will be enhanced and extended
depending on the results of its trial applications. The
structure and functions of the CAD/CAPP expert system shell
kernal are shown on the fig. 2.

1   CAD/CAPP EXPERT SYSTEM SHELL EXECUTIVE LEVEL

The CAD/CAPP expert system shell executive level
structure is shown in fig. 3. The executive level provides an
interpretation of Basic Programming Language (BPL)
expressions. The BPL is intended mainly for user program

development. The higer levels of CAD/CAPP expert system shell
have been implemented by means of BPL too.

As shown in fig. 3, the extended PROLOG interpreter
is used as a kernal of the executive level. For this purpose
the necessary interfaces to external program modules,informa-
tion bases and input/output devices are provided as well.

The most important PROLOG extensions implemented at
the executive level are the following:

— a control mechanism for external program modules
execution together with some useful language and interpreta-
tive facilities for structured program systems development on
the basis of the top-down strategy;

— nonprocedural 2D graphics facilities;

— flexible user interface design and management facilities;

— some deductive data base functions;

— nonprocedural string operations;

— real nombers operations.

The most significant feature of the above-mentioned
extensions is that they are realized in a declarative
(nonprocedural) and recursive PROLOG style. This allows
easily to construct and execute unrestricted nested PROLOG-
like logical expressions, including besides the standard
PROLOG types any combination of descriptions of external
modular programs, pictures, strings, integer and real numbers
and so on.

All capabilities described have been achieved by
the introduction of a number of suitable algebras allowing to
describe the above mentioned types of compound resulting
objects in the form of structural formulae and to process
them in a manner similar to the number processing. The same
algebraic approach has been applied further for a compound
objects and functions description on the higher levels of the
CAD/CAPP expert system shell. A necessary set of operations
(usually unary and binary, some of which parameterized) - an
algebra signature for description of the corresponding object
type with arbitrary complexity and unrestricted nesting of
the algebraic expressions has been defined for each algebra.

A priori defined sets of primitives of corresponding types
(subsets of the algebras carriers) serve as algebras canonical
representation classes, for example:
— a set of user-definable logical names of some
conventional programs, written in other programming languages
and included in the external library as independent executable
modules, can be combined in the form of algebraic expressions
by means of five operations, each one providing the formation
of the corresponding program composition scheme recommended by
structured programming (Goodman & Hedetniemi 1977; Linger at
al. 1977). The resulting structural formulae, describing the
corresponding modular program structure, can be sent for
interpretation to the subsystem PROMOD which also serves
simultaneously as an external executive monitor returning the
control flow back to the PROLOG interpreter immediately after
the external program execution has been completed.

It is significant to note the possibility to use
program modules of different types in respect to their
functionality: processing (in bach mode) terminal (i.e.
directly executable) modules; checking terminal modules,
producing in dependence of the test conditions an integer
value of the dynamic cyclic parameter besides the other
specific results; inquiring interactive terminal modules
producing an output text message as a question, and assigning
the answer as an integer value to the dynamic cyclic parameter; prompting interactive terminal modules, giving an
instruction or information output text message; nonterminal
(compound) modules, described by a corresponding structural
formulae in the PROMOD nonterminal library.

Note that the modules of interactive type (the
inquiring and prompting modules) are not as a matter of fact
program ones but virtual. To define such a module it is
sufficient just to enter the corresponding message into the
PROMOD text file and to assign to it an user logical name.
Besides their simlicity these virtual modules are considered
to be very useful, because of the possibility to implement
interactive systems without any programming.

In general, the described approach enables the user
to develop and implement complex modular software systems with
flexible (even dynamically changeable) structures and functions. During the earlier stages of system development and use
the software modules not being yet implemented can be func-
tionaly simulated by suitable interactive modules, successively substituted by real modules as far as available, maintaining the global structure of the system on the whole during its
life-cycle.

A special purpose PROLOG-PASCAL data interface
enables the user to extend the BPL with his own external
predicates, functionally combining PROLOG and PASCAL capabilities, without concerning the main BPL interpreter.

— a set of basic 2D pictures (primitives), including
lines, circles, arcs, texts etc., can be combined in the form
of algebraic expressions by means of two binary (OVERLAY and
WITHOUT - analogues of addition and subtraction of numbers)
and some unary (translation, rotation, scaling, reflection,
draw, store etc.) operations, defined upon the set of 2D
pictures. The equivalence and some other relations have been
defined also on the continuum of 2D pictures;

— a set of some basic (concatenation, removal,
substitution, substring, output etc.) and complex (nonterminal
name search etc.) string operations serves as a signature of
the string algebra.

It is significant to note, that the use of the
above-mentioned operations is intended for nonprocedural,
declarative style of programming, i.e. as a manner for some
new objects definition on the basis of already defined ones
by means of the PROLOG specification operator "is".Futhermore,
an arbitrary location of the defined variable names is allowed
in this case. It may be either on the left or on the right
side of the operator "is". Such a typical declarative
representation became possible because of the built-in
resolver of one variable symbolic equations.

In this way the above mentioned algebras become
declarative sublanguages and can serve as PROLOG extensions
and provide the flexible functionality of BPL for CAD/CAPP

applications (Kirov 1983 b), possessing the necessary
mobility and specific problem solving capabilities as well.

   With the purpose of satisfaction of the contempora-
ry requirements to the user interface design and management
(Kirov 1984 b) the CAD/CAPP expert system shell architecture
has been founded on the following principles:

   — a priority of the external over internal dialogue
control;

   — dialogue structure and form declarative representation as specifications in external files;

   — user-specific macrocommands, command files and menus
definition capabilities;

   — some facilities for CAD/CAPP system external
language design in accordance with the problem area specific
terminology to be provided;

   — the user interface is to be easily modifiable by
the user himself, being usually a non-programmer.

   From the standpoint of large deductive data base
maintainance the CAD/CAPP expert system shell software
structure has been designed in accordance with the PROLOG
facts virtual organization principle (Vassiliou at al. 1985).
As a matter of fact the PROLOG program contains the generalized forms of facts representation only. Some build-in
special search predicates are automatically activated each
time a reference to a variable included in the forms takes
place, providing the corresponding value, derived from the
data base.

   The implementation language of the CAD/CAPP expert
system shell executive level is PASCAL.

2. CAD/CAPP EXPERT SYSTEM SHELL HIGHER LEVELS
FUNCTIONS AND IMPLEMENTATION PRINCIPLES

   All the higher software levels (fig. 2, levels 2÷6)
of CAD/CAPP expert system shell, briefly described in this
paper, have been successfully implemented entirely in BPL,
being interpreted by the lower executive level 1.

2.1   Structure descriptions dynamic generation and interpretation tools

The structural synthesis problem considered as the main design/process planning task has been solved by us (Kirov 1983 a; Kirov 1984 a) on the basis of a metha-language description of the empirically derived design knowledge, represented in the form of a generalized structure of a certain class of objects/processes. The declarative knowledge representation in this case is founded on the introduction of design algebras (Kirov 1976; Kirov 1978) and generative formal grammars theory and methods application (Kirov 1977; Kirov 1978; Kirov 1979; Kirov 1984 a) providing in this way a unified mechanism for generation of regular, in respect to their syntax and semantics, structural formulae which are later on evaluated by a special interpreter.

Further the application area of this approach has been extended and at present includes the generation of modular conventional (fig. 2, level 2) and logical (level 3) programs and objects/processes integral functions decomposition (level 5) as well. The programs generated by level 2 and level 3 are directly executed by PROMOD and PROLOG interpreters, correspondingly. The PROLOG program is considered as a basic one and an arbitrary number of PROMOD programs can be included in it in the form of some structural formulae.

The diversity of these successful applications of the above mentioned approach prove its generality and flexibility. Furthermore, the formal grammar being itself a production system of a special type allows a natural and easy representation in the form of PROLOG-like expressions. On the other hand, the possibilities to associate arbitrary complex predicates to relational expressions in PROLOG resolves the conditional pseudo-grammars interpretation problem (Kirov 1977; Kirov 1978; Kirov 1979).

2.2   Knowledge base representation and use

The CAD/CAPP expert system shell levels 4÷6 are

knowledge base structure-oriented (fig. 4). These shell levels
considered as a high level user programming environment were
developed for a maintainance of a design method named by us
Recursive Decomposition Method (RDM). The knowledge
representation scheme and formalisms and the built-in design
task solving mechanism have been chosen in conformity with
RDM specificity. The main idea RDM has been founded on is to
accomplish the object/process structure synthesis on the basis
of an analysis of the function to be performed. Applied
recursively at each current stage of the function decomposition this method takes into account a large amount of generalized design/manufacturing experience represented as metha-
level decision rules rather than as completed solutions. The
emphasis in RDM is placed on the explication of relevant
construction/planning decision rules then applied for bottom-
up object/process structure formation using the lower level
functional components as "building blocks" at the higher
levels. This multi-stage process is function-directed because
the composition operations are allowed only if the "building
blocks" partial functions can be combined in a way providing
the necessary current integral function the latter being
determined at the corresponding level during the global
function decomposition phase.

The two major interrelated design subtasks-required
function decomposition and object/process structure formation
- are intended to be solved simultaneously in the framework
of RDM. The real design reasonning process permanently
switches from one subtask concepts to another and vice versa.
All the functions are considered in respect to the objects
which could be used for their realization and in turns, the
objects are considered only from a point of view of their
possible applications (use) and the specific roles they could
play in the realization of certain functions. These mental
interrelations are reflected in the conceptual model (fig.4)
of the design/process planning problem environment in the
form of closely correlated functional features of the object
environment physical components, on one hand and object
features of the potentially feasible functions, on the other.

We use here the concept of design problem environment to emphasize the consideration of the physical object environment from the point of view of its components functions, i.e. from the point of view of the design task because of existence of a close relationship (duality) between the feasible functions and the corresponding design/process planning tasks consisting in search of effective means for a given function realization. The functions are considered as abstract objects with a number of valences because they become real ones only after some suitable physical objects have been associated to these valences. In turns, the physical objects acquire a utility feature only because of their potential capabilities to accomplish certain functions and are considered as objects with some functional valences too.

From the point of view of the design/process planning task the knowledge about a given object environment consists of:

— an information about the inherent features of the object environment components (data base);

— knowledge (extracted and generalized on a design experiance basis) about the feasible purposeful applications of the real object environment components and phenomena in the form of a set of structured functions with associative valences of the pairs "function-subject", "function-object" and "function-tool" types;

— knowledge about the principal generalized structure of objects of different classes able to perform the corresponding functional roles, represented in the form of a set of constructive operations and condition-dependent rules of their applications.

We found the conceptual modeling to be the most general, flexible and adequate approach to the design/ manufacturing knowledge representation problem. In our knowledge representation scheme (fig. 4) the concept intensions describe the corresponding objects/functions classes at a quality level as a sets of attributes values domains while the concept extensions describe them at a quantity level as a

sets of corresponding attributes values. Each concept belongs
to one of the two metha-concepts (categories) - the category
of objects and the category of functions. The concept extension includes explicitly either all or a part of the number of
instances being primitive or compound components of the object
environment. In general, each object environment component
can be included logically as an instance into the extensions
of different concepts and thus can be considered from different points of view. All the concepts are hierarchicaly
organized on the basis of a set of "is-a" relations, each
concept inheriting the features of its superconcepts. In
addition a generalized structure description, new objects
generating and attributes values estimating procedures are
associated to each concept definition. A set of roles
references are also set thus forming a multi-related concept
network. The design reasoning process consists in moving the
virtual "attention cursor" from one node ("point of view") to
another all over the concept network, searching for suitable
components and activating from time to time the corresponding
object/process structure building mechanisms and decision-
making procedures.

Each function concept specification defines in fact
(explicitly or implicitly) a corresponding "morphological
set (Odrin & Kartavov 1977), i.e. a set of functionally
equivalent pre-prepared solutions, by means of some role
references. Some compound functions may not have such
references. In this case it is necessary to resolve the
function decomposition task by recursive generation of its
multi-level structure description until a feasible role
object is found for each function component. If an object
explicitly specified for a given role is not found, a
decomposition process is also activated or a synthesis of a
new implicitly given object/process is performed. In the
latter case an explicit reference to the new generated object/
process is inserted into the corresponding function concept
role list. This explication process is founded on the
generalized structure description-based generation of new

compound objects and instances attributes values variation in accordance with the limits fixed by the corresponding concept intension. In the worst case an object environment functional incompleteness has been revealed, the system produces an inquiry for a data base expansion.

In general the functions generalized structure description can include some conditions depending on the function realization quality and effeciency provided by the corresponding decomposition rules.

As mentioned above, the function structure descriptions reflect the decompositions of design/process planning tasks supposed to be resolved by means of RDM. This method is maintained by the highest levels of CAD/CAPP expert system shell briefly described in this paper.

Reference list.

Goodman, S.E. & Hedetniemi, S.T. (1977). Introduction to the Design and Analysis of Algorithms, McGraw-Hill B.C.

Kirov, V.I (1976). Algebraic Approach to the Design Process Formalization Problem. Design Algebra, Technical Thought, No. 3, BAN, Sofia, /In Bulgarian/.

Kirov, V.I. (1977). Algebraic Approach to the Design Process Formalization Problem. The Design Synthesis as An Associative Calculus, Technical Thought, No. 4, BAN, Sofia, /In Bulgarian/.

Kirov, V.I. (1978). A Linguistic Approach to the Decision-Making Problem in CAD/CAM, Proceedings of the Int. Conference "Projectowanie III", v. 1, Wroclaw, /In Russian/.

Kirov, V.I. (1979). Algebraic-Linguistic Approach to the Problem of Automatic Forming A Purposeful Behaviour of Integral Robots, Proceedings of the 5th World IFToMM Congress, Montreal, Canada, Published by ASME, USA, N.Y.

Kirov, V.I. (1983). Software and Information Basis of CAD/CAM Systems in Machinebuilding, IPS-83 Final Report, v. 3, SR&D Institute "Interprogramma", Sofia, /In

Russian/.

Kirov, V.I. (1983 b). A Specification of the Basic Functional
       Requirements to Machinebuilding - oriented CAD/CAM
       Interactive Graphics Environment, Proceedings of
       the Conference "RAIT-83", Plovdiv, /In Russian/.

Kirov, V.I. (1984 a). A Formal Grammers - Based Representa-
       tion of the Knowledge about Object Structure in
       CAD/CAM Expert Systems, Represented on the Int.
       Conference "Data Bases in Computer Networks",
       MCNTI, Moskow, February, /In Russian/.

Kirov,V.I. (1984 b). User Interface Design and Management in
       CAD/CAM Systems, Analysis-84, Final Report, SR&D
       Institute "Interprogramma", Sofia, /In Russian/.

Linger, R.C. & Mills, H.D. & Witt, B.I. (1977). Structured
       Programming: Theory and Practice, Addison-Wesley
       Publ. Comp.

Odrin V.M., Kartavov S.S. (1977). Morphological Analysis of
       Systems, Kiev, Naukova Dumka, /In Russian/.

Vassiliou, Y., Clifford J. & Jarke M. (1985). How Dos an
       Expert System Get Its Data, in "Very Large Data
       Bases", IEEE Computer Society Press.

SYMBOLIC UNCERTAIN INFERENCE : A STUDY OF POSSIBLE MODALITIES

Jean-Gabriel GANASCIA
Yves KODRATOFF

Laboratoire de Recherche en Informatique,
UA 410 du CNRS
Université Paris-Sud, Bâtiment 490,
91450 Orsay, FRANCE.

ABSTRACT

In our opinion, one of the drawbacks of present Expert Systems, is that they do not merge correctly uncertain and certain reasonning. Besides, most experts heavily use certain negative information that is difficult to express and use correctly. This work has been done to look for possible solutions to this drawback.
We describe a methodology and tools for symbolic uncertain inference that will be used in an Expert System. Our aim is to show that we need to introduce some elementary distinctions between different kinds of uncertainty : Particularly, we distinguish uncertain data from uncertain inferences.
Uncertainty is represented by higher order quantifiers called "modulations" as opposed to the modal quantifiers of first order modal logics. Modulations are composed during the inference on the clauses; the details of the way the compositions must be made are not in the scope of this paper, while we describe some of their properties.

Key words : Expert Systems, Inexact Reasoning, Resolution, Certainty Factors, Modality.

1. Introduction

Whatever they are called, uncertain, common sense or coarse, there exist reasonings involving with regularities, frequences, general laws, all of them dealing with truth values different from TRUE and FALSE. When wanting to simulate human behaviour in A.I. the risks of combinatory explosion and the need of transparency leads us to model this type of reasoning. However, the use of classical logic alone seems inadequate. This is the reason why modal, fuzzy or multivalued logics were introduced. Thus, in the Expert System field, systems have been built using non classic logics. For instance, MYCIN [Shortliffe 76] uses a logic based on certainty factors. But, whatever be the MYCIN success, the use of certainty factors is not always possible and, when it is, it introduces many kinds of difficulties [Ganascia 83, Kodratoff et Al. 85a, 85b].

Actually, the nature and the meaning of inferences using certainty factors have not yet been completely elucidated. Moreover, adjusting Knowledge Base in building an Expert System is extremely difficult because there does not exist any complete proof procedure able to validate the Knowledge Base content. Last, certainty factors lead to confuse **contradiction**, i.e. uncertainty about validity of reasonings which concatenate elementary inferential steps and put forward hypothesis, and **incomplete data**, i.e. uncertainty of a result obtained by inexact reasoning. Our aim is to present a symbolic model for uncertain reasoning using both the mathematical properties of certainty factors and the resolution principle. In other words we want to show how logic and theorem proving techniques could be used with benefits in the expert system field.

2. Imprecise or Uncertain ?

Let us begin by naming some of the words related to unlogic reasoning : uncertain, imprecise, inexact, rough, common sense, approximate etc... All these terms seem synonymous and denote a margin, a gap between correctness and reasoning. But, what is the nature of this gap ? Is it a gap between reasoning and formal laws or between measurements and real world ? In order to elucidate this point, let us take the example of physics. Hence, at a given state of the development of the Science and for a given theory, laws are exact. In this sense, except for marginal phenomena that may eventually lead the researcher to modify the theory, its strict application exactly reflects reality in spite of the uncertainty inherent to all measurements. Actually, uncertainties are taken into account by physical laws modulo some basic axioms ; in this case, we are dealing with certain reasoning whereas a physicist when solving a problem may use uncertain reasoning in order to find what law to apply, what equations to pose or what strategies to use.

Our purpose is not to take into account these approximations specific of natural sciences, but to underline the existence of particular reasoning in which the laws themselves are erroneous. For instance, let us consider the following assertions : birds fly, men have two legs, weather is hot in Africa. These propositions are false because there are birds which do not fly, one-legged men and montains in Africa. However, it is essential to use such regularities when building common sense reasoning about everyday life. Therefore, when we speak about uncertain imprecise or inexact reasoning, these qualifying direct towards the generality of inference laws, and not the margin of error around values.

3. Precisions about Uncertain Reasoning

The notion of uncertainty is essential in A.I. and more precisely in the Expert System field, however the nature of this uncertainty is not well defined. It may correspond to uncertainty either on the inference rules or on the data. The former corresponds to our ignorance of causal dependence obliging us to use erroneous inference rules, the latter to underconstrain situations where we put forward hypothesis in order to solve the problem under study. This distinction may seem slightly subtle, however it is fundamental and corresponds to different meaning of the word heuristic [Ganascia 85]. Moreover it leads to two different approaches of uncertain reasoning that interpret two very different realities.

3.1. Uncertainty on Inference rules

In the first case, the uncertainty of reasoning is similar to the EMYCIN's. It is modelled by the use of modulations affecting events belonging to the fact base either with a number, *EMYCIN's approach*, or, more generally, with a symbol, *our approach*. Hence, a rule, when triggered, modifies the modulation associated with several fact base events. In addition, rules premises are not concerned with the truth values of the events belonging to the fact base, as these truth values are uncertain, but with the modulation associated with each event. For example, let us assume a fact base containing the events 'Paul comes' and 'it may happen that Robert comes'. Using modulation, this can be translated into : [certain]comes(Paul) and [may happen]comes(Robert). In the same way, we can express an inference rule like 'If there are some chances that Robert comes, then it is almost certain that Mary comes'. We just have to write :

If [some chance]comes(Robert) Then [almost certain]comes(Mary)

In addition to the fact base modulation, reasonings such as EMYCIN's are characterized by the control structure that manages them : All reasonings which could lead to solution of the problem under study are simultaneously built, and then, for each conclusion the modulations obtained by the way of triggering rules are **combined**. Operators devoted to combine modulations have the elementary properties of a likehood logic : Independence from the ordering in which reasoning are built, monotony etc... For more detail see section 4.3.

3.2. Uncertainty on Events

In the second case, the uncertainty corresponds to needed choices between several possible reasonings, some of them being exact but expensive, others inexact but efficient. This choice is prior to conflict resolution because it takes place just before rules premises evaluation. It leads to put forward hypothesis which, as long as no contradiction appears, are assumed as valid. To be more concrete, let us take the classical 'bird' example : Generaly birds fly. This means that, without contradictory information, we can assume that one particular bird flies, but this event, for instance 'Tweety flies' is uncertain. This uncertainty may be taken into account by using a modulation, but in this case modulation affects the inference rule, and not the event, like in the previous section. Therefore, in case of bird example we only have : {generally} If bird(X) Then fly(X)

This modalities can be interpreted as an indication to use the cheapest and more general rule. As we shall see (see section 4.4.) this meaning of uncertainty is very close to the one modelled by default logic [Reiter 80], circumscription [McCarthy 80] or close world assumption [Clark 78].

4. Modelling Uncertainty with Modulations

Considering this, we think that all problems relative to uncertain reasoning may be handle by introducing **modulations**, but keeping the resolution principle as inference schema. This paper is devoted to describe this approach. However, at first, we shall recall some elementary notions about resolution, and then some definitions.

4.1. Resolution

First of all, its basic principle is that theorems can be put under a *normal form*, i.e., one can get rid of the quantifiers by skolemization and write it

$$C_1 \ \& \ ... \ \& \ C_j$$

where & is the logical AND. Each C_i is called a *clause* and has the form

$$P_1 \ \vee \ ... \ \vee P_n \ \vee \ \neg N_1 \ \vee \ ... \ \vee \ \neg N_m$$

where $\vee$ is the logical OR, $\neg$ the logical NOT, and where P_i and N_i are literals.

A theorem and its normal form are not equivalent but it is then easy to prove that a theorem can be inconsistent if and only if its normal form is inconsistent. A theorem or a cunjunct of clauses are defined as inconsistent when one can deduce from them both TRUE and FALSE. One says then that one can deduce the *empty clause* from them. The empty clause plays in Automatic Theorem Proving a role which is quite comparable to the one plaid by 0 in Mathematics.

The elementary step of resolution is the obtention of the *resolvent* of several clauses. For the sake of simplicity we shall always speak here of the resolvent of two clauses.
Let

$$C_1 = P_1 \lor ... \lor -N_m$$
$$C_1' = P_1' \lor ... \lor -N_p'$$

be two clauses. Suppose that predicates P_q of C_1 unifies with predicate N_r' of C_1', i.e., there exists a substitution σ such that

$$\sigma P_q = \sigma N_r'.$$

Let us call C_2 the clause obtained by deleting P_q and N_r' from $C_1 \lor C_1'$. Then, σC_2 is called a *resolvent* of C_1 and C_1'. There may exist numerous other resolvents of C_1 and C_1', the order in which they are chosen during the resolution process is called the *strategy of resolution*.

One has the theorem [Robinson 65] :

C_1 & C_1' *is consistent if and only if* C_1 & C_1' & σC_2 *is consistent.*

The resolution method tests a system inconsistency by trying to find among the set of its resolvents, two of them, one being equal to TRUE, the other one being equal to FALSE.

4.2. Definitions

Definition 1 : We call **Data Base** a set of clauses which contains assertions, *i.e. the fact base*, clauses without positive literals, *i.e. the problems under study*, and clauses with positive and/or negative literals, *i.e. the knowledge base*. Because we use resolution, we can merge the Fact Base, the Knowledge Base and the Problems. This is the reason why we introduced the concept of Data Base with an unusual meaning in the expert system fields.

Definition 2 : A data base is **inconsistent** iff we can derive the **empty clause** by resolution principle application.

Definition 3 : An hypothesis P is **contradictory** iff we can simultaneously prove P and not P.

Definition 4 : A data basis is **uncertain** iff the clauses and/or the literals are modulated.

As we shall see in the 2 following sections, the modulation may be either an atom or more generally a tree. In case of clauses, modulations are within { } and in case of literals, within [ ].

4.3. Literals Modulation

Operator * takes into account the modulation of events belonging to the premise of an inference rule. For instance, consider the two clauses :

[certain] comes(Peter, meeting) :- [generally] comes(Mary, meeting).
                    [seldom] comes(Mary, meeting).

Since we know that [generally] > [seldom], one cannot solve them.
Our definition will take into account this implicit ordering of the modulations.

When the ordering allows rule triggering, we introduce an * operator, that combines the modulations without using the one of the negative part.
For instance, consider the two clauses :

[certain] comes(Peter, w) :- [seldom] comes(Mary, w).
                [generally] comes(Mary, meeting).

Since we know that [generally] > [seldom], one can now resolve them, but the modulation of the result does not depend on the modulation of the condition comes(Mary, w). We shall designate this final modulation by [certain * generally], thus making the hypothesis that the knowledge relative to the modulation of the fact influences the modulation of the conclusion.

More generally, being given two clauses C_1 and C_2 literals of which are modulated :

$C_1 = [M_1^1]P_1^1, [M_1^2]P_1^2, ..., [M_1^p]P_1^p :- [m_1^1]N_1^1, [m_1^2]N_1^2, ..., [m_1^n]N_1^n.$

$C_2 = [M_2^1]P_2^1, [M_2^2]P_2^2, ..., [M_2^q]P_2^q :- [m_2^1]N_2^1, [m_2^2]N_2^2, ..., [m_2^l]N_2^l.$

The resolution principle may be applied, but the modulation of the resolvent is a combination of the modulations of clauses C_1 and C_2. Here, the resolution can be applied only if $M_1^1 \geq m_2^1$ which means that the modulation associated with P_1^1 must be greater than the modulation associated with N_2^1.

Therefore, if there exist σ such that $\sigma P_1^1 = \sigma N_2^1$ and if $M_1^1 \geq m_2^1$ then the modulation of P_1^1 will be used to modulate the conclusion of the inference rule, i.e. the modulation of C_2 positive literal.

The resolvent of C_1 and C_2 is $\sigma C'$:

$C' = [M_1^2]P_1^2, ..., [M_1^p]P_1^p, [M_2^1 * M_1^1]P_2^1, ..., [M_2^q * M_1^1]P_2^q :-$
$[m_1^1]N_1^1, ..., [m_1^n]N_1^n, [m_2^2]N_2^2, ..., [m_2^l]N_2^l.$

operator *

In case of certainty factors, properties of operator * are well defined (Cf. [Hàjek 82]).

1- $1 * P = P * 1 = P$

2- $a * X$ is a monotonous increasing function in X.

3- $\exists s \in [-1, +1]$ such that $\forall a \forall P \ a \leq s => a * P = 0.$

For instance * may be defined by :

a * P = if a $\geq$ 0.2 then Times(a, P)
                        else 0

or by

a * P = if a $\geqslant$ 0.2 then if P $\geqslant$ 0 then Minimum(a, P)

else Maximum(-a, P)

else 0

operator +

As we saw previously, one of the main characteristics of MYCIN is that all proofs are computed and then combined. Operator + is designed here to make this combination possible. In order to do that, it operates with modulations in the following way : Let us assume $[M_1]P_1$ and $[M_2]P_2$ two positive modulated literals. If P_1 unifies with P_2, i.e. $\exists$ σ such that $\sigma P_1 = \sigma P_2$, then we can derive $[M_1 + M_2]P$ from $[M_1]P_1$ and $[M_2]P_2$, where $P = \sigma P_1$.

As operator *, operator + is well defined in case of plausibilities :

1- For all arguments different from +1 and -1 + is associative and commutative.

Intuitive meaning : the order in which plausibilities are combined does not affect the result of the combination.

2- $\forall$ w such that $w \neq$ -1 $w + 1 = 1 + w = 1$

$\forall$ w such that $w \neq$ +1 $w + $ -1 = -1 + w = -1

1 + -1 is not defined.

Intuitive meaning : this property expresses that +1 means definitely true and -1 definitely false.

3- $\forall$ w_1, w_2, w_3 different from -1 and +1

if $w_1 \leqslant w_2$ then $w_1 + w_3 \leqslant w_2 + w_3$

For instance let us assume that p C_+ q is the combination of p and q when they have the same sign. The three following laws possess the above-mentioned properties :

p C_+ q = p + q - p*q (the law used in MYCIN)

p C_+ q = (p + q)/(1 - p*q) (the law used in PROSPECTOR)

p C_+ q = (p + q - 2*p*q)/(1 + p*q)

However these properties could be questionned in some particular situation. For instance, the weight of some argument may depend on the ordering in which they are given and then, the operator + may be not commutative. Our approach consists in keeping explicitly the modulation tree and then, computing it with a modulation solver built as an expert system. Such an expert system will be able to adapt the type of problem and the nature of uncertainty in the expert domain. Actually, the computation of the resulting modulation is not really a central task : ordering modulations is the most important (and can be done without computing them).

Example : Let us assume a data base containing the 5 following clauses, literals of which are modulated:

C_1 = [some chances]agitated(meeting):-comes(Mary,meeting).

C_2=[certain]agitated(meeting):-comes(Robert,meeting),comes(Elsa,meeting).

C_3 = [many chances]comes(Mary,X):-[certain]comes(Robert,X).

C_4 = comes(Robert,meeting).

C_5 = [some chances]comes(Elsa,meeting).

Using resolution for modulated literals we can derive three clauses from this set of clauses :

from C_2 and C_4 we derive C_6 :

C_6 = [certain]agitated(meeting):-comes(Elsa,meeting).

Then from C_5 and C_6 we obtain C_7 :

C_7 = [certain*some chances]agitated(meeting).

By the same way using C_3 and C_4 we have C_8 :

C_8 = [many chances]comes(Mary,meeting).

Which give C_9 with C_1 :

C_9 = [some chances*many chances]agitated(meeting).

Lastly, using the operator + and the derivation from C_9 and C_7, we obtain C_{10} which can answer a question about the meeting :

C_{10} = [certain*some chances + some chances*many chances]agitated(meeting).

4.4. Clause Modulation

Clause modulation indicates the inference rule degree of validity for a given clause. This means that an inference rule may be 'always' true, 'generally' true, 'seldom' true etc... According to the degree of validity of the rules, their conclusions may be either true or a more or less tangible hypothesis.

Using clause modulation allows us to distinguish true conclusions from the others which can be questionned. Moreover it helps us to order hypothesis, and so doing, the way in which they are questionned. Hence, the main principle is the non contradiction principle : an hypothesis is considered true as long as it is not contradicted. However, contradiction is not inconsistency (see definitions 2 and 3) : an hypothesis is contradictory when we can simultaneously demonstrate its validity and the validity of its negation. When putting forward an hypothesis, a special control structure is needed to test for non-contradiction. Thus, we obtain an inference schema similar to that used in Reiter's default logic [Reiter 80]. However, using modulations introduces several modifications to this schema.

In the first place, while inferences are triggered, we keep all the hypothesis making these inferences possible. This kind of data dependence is analogous to Doyle 's justifications [Doyle 79]. They allow to question contradictory hypotheses and their consequences. In order to take into account every data dependences, the modulation of data inferred is followed by the list of hypothesis on which inferences depend. Moreover, we introduce the operator '|' which describes different alternatives. Concerning this operator, it is important to note that although similar to the operator + used in literal modulation combination, it is not identical. Actually, in case of literal modulation combination we have to carry out simultaneously all the proofs which could lead to conclusion. On the other hand, in case of clause modulation, we may proceed sequentially : one proof leading to certainty is sufficient. Hence, the control structure has to define the optimal research ordering to built a proof as fast as possible.

For the sake of clarity, let us give an example of clause modulation. Let us assume we have the following data base :

{generally} fly(X):-bird(X).
{generally} possess_wings(X):-bird(X).
{generally} possess_wings(X):-fly(X).
{almost_forever} fly(X):-aircraft(X).
bird(Tweety).
aircraft(XR23).

Integrating the treatment of clause modulation with the resolution principle, we can derive some conlusions from this data base :

{generally(fly(Tweety))|generally} possess_wings(Tweety).
{generally} fly(Tweety).
{almost_forever} fly(XR23).
{generally(fly(XR23))} possess_wings(XR23).

Using clause modulation introduces another difference with default logic : it gives a gradation that orders hypotheses, and so defines priorities in their choice. Therefore, clause modulations do not introduce formal differences with default theory, except their heuristic meaning which can be used by the control structure.

4.5. Using both Clause and Literal Modulations.

In order to use simultaneously clauses and literal modulation, we have to introduce hypothesis dependences in literal modulation. For that, it is sufficient to introduce data dependences. For instance, let us assume we have the following data base :

comes(Robert,meeting).
{generally} comes(Mary,X):-comes(Robert,X).
{always} [many chances]agitated(meeting):-comes(Mary,meeting).

Which give : {generally} comes(Mary,meeting). and
{always(comes(Mary,meeting))} [many chances]agitated(meeting). which means that when Mary comes to the meeting, we can always assume there are many chances that the meeting will be agitated.

On the other hand, we do not need to introduce literal modulation into clause modulation because clause modulation has only a heuristic meaning : Hypothesis validation being only demonstrated by non contradiction, it is independent of event plausibility and so, of literal modulation.

5. Using modulation in translating inexact inference rules

The distinction we operate between clause and literal modulation may seem a little abstract and theoretical. However, it becomes obvious as soon as we have to translate uncertain inference rules into formal languages. Actually, it allows to take into account some particularity of uncertain inferences which must be taken into account.

For the sake of clarity, we shall present an example using 3 clause modulations 'always', 'generally', 'seldom' and 4 literal modulations 'no chance', 'some
chances', 'many chances' and 'certain'. Let us assume we want translate the
proposition 'usually, when Robert comes, Mary comes.'. Using our formalism, we
may have two translations C_1 and C_2 which are not equivalent :
C_1 = {generally} [certain]comes(Mary):-comes(Robert).
C_2 = {always} [many chances]comes(Mary):-[certain]comes(Robert).

C_1 expresses that generally the rule comes(Robert)=>comes(Mary) may be
applied which implies that the hypothesis comes(Mary) follows the hypothesis
comes(Robert) except when a contradiction appears. For instance, we may
assume that they are married which may explain this rule. On the other hand, in
case of C_2, the fact that Robert comes considerably increases the plausibility
that Mary comes. It may be the case if Mary loves Robert, but in this eventuality
we may have as well another rule saying that if there are some chances that
Robert does not come, then Mary does not come for fear of being disappointed,
or also another one according to which if there were no chances that Robert
comes, then Mary would certainly come. These two rules may be translated in
our formalism by the following way :
{always} [many chances]comes(Mary):-[no chance]comes(Robert).
{always} [certain]not_comes(Mary):-[some chances]not-comes(Robert).

As we see here, this type of modulation make us able to express rules dealing with modulations and not only with hypothesis formation.

6. Conclusion

This article is intended to present a new approach for inexact reasoning in
Expert System.

Our approach works on certain clauses **exactly** in the same way as resolution does (instead of being 'equivalent in the limit', which is not so easy to
achieve, see the discussion of [Farreny-Prade 85] in [Kodratoff et Al. 85]).
Besides, it deals with the difficulties met when certain and uncertain reasonings
are mixed. Inconsistency is dealt with by separating the proof of an assertion
and the proof of its contrary. In all cases, the elementary inference step is that
of classical first order logic, uncertainty and inconsistency are treated as
modifications of resolution strategy leading to a classical proof.

Moreover, we take into account the main results about certainty factors
which made the MYCIN system possible. So, we introduce modulations that generalize certainty factors.

Using classical expert systems techniques and logic we hope both to have a
better intelligence of inexact reasoning and to build efficient mechanisms.
Because the model we propose is close to logic, we can easily program it in PRO-
LOG. These ideas are now under implemention at LRI in C-PROLOG.

References :

[McCarthy 80] J. McCARTHY : *Circumscription : A form of Non-Monotonic Reasoning*, Artificial Intelligence, Volume 13, Numbers 1,2, April 1980.

[Clark 78] K. CLARK : *Negation as failure*, in Logic and Database, Gallaire H. and J. Minker Eds.,Plenum Press, N.Y. 1978, 293-322.

[Doyle 79] J. DOYLE : *A truth maintenance system*, Artificial Intelligence, Volume 12, pp. 231-272, 1979.

[Farreny-Prade 85] H. FARRENY and H. PRADE : *Mécanisation de raisonnement par défaut en termes de possibilités*, Hardware and software components and architecture for the 5th generation, Paris, 5-7 march 1985, in Proc. pp. 353-364.

[Ganascia 83] J.G. GANASCIA : *MIRLITHO : Détection des contradictions et validation des résultats dans les systèmes experts de diagnostic*, Thèsis, Université Paris-Sud, Orsay,1883.

[Ganascia 85] J.G. GANASCIA : *Raisonnement incertain ou incertitude sur le raisonnement ?*, COGNITIVA 85, in Proc. pp. 633-638, Paris, 4-7 june 1985.

[Hàjek 82] P. HAJEK : *Combining functions for certainty factors in consulting systems.*, Artificial Intelligence and information-control systems of robots, 1982, Smolenice, czekoslovakia.

[Kodratoff et Al. 85a] Y. KODRATOFF, H. PERDRIX, M. FRANOVA : *Traitement symbolique du raisonnement incertain*, Hardware and software components and architecture for the 5th generation, Paris, 5-7 march 1985, in Proc. pp. 33-45.

[Kodratoff et Al. 85b] Y. KODRATOFF, B. DUVAL : *Symbolic Uncertain Inference : Tools for a PROLOG-like Approach*, Proc. AI Conference Europa, Wiesbaden 1985.

[Kowalski 79] R. KOWALSKI : *Logic for Problem Solving*, North Holland Elsevier, New York, 1979.

[Reiter 80] R. REITER : *A Logic for Default Reasoning*, Artificial Intelligence, Volume 13, Numbers 1,2, April 1980.

[Robinson 65] J.A. ROBINSON : *A Machine Oriented Logic Based on the Resolution Principle*, Journal of A.C.M. 12, 1965.

[Shortliffe 76] E.H. SHORTLIFFE : *Computer-based medical consultations : MYCIN.*, New York, American Elsiever, 1976.

INFERENCE UNDER UNCERTAINTY

by
Abe Mamdani, Janet Efstathiou and Dominic Pang

Queen Mary College
Mile End Road
London E1 4NS

1 Introduction

Recently much attention has been devoted by the IKBS research community to the representation and the propagation of uncertainty. Some of the underlying issues were highlighted in the meeting of the Special Interest Group on Reasoning under Uncertainty[1,2]. In that meeting it was also suggested that good comparative studies of the techniques for dealing with uncertainties could be a great help to the understanding of the problem.

In the next section we explain why classical logic is inadequate for expert systems which have to deal with more than just the truth values. The various types of uncertainties are described showing that there is no single inference technique that can handle all of them. In section 3, we briefly describe the background literature on the subject of inference under uncertainty.

2 Logic and Uncertainty

2.1 Inference

Inference is the essential part of an expert system. Its purpose is to draw conclusions from the available data and the knowledge about the domain within the knowledge base. Any given inference process will be composed of a chain of immediate inference steps. Such inference steps, when based strictly on classical logic, result in systems that are not meant to handle uncertainty. All the propositions in such systems are either true or false and the inference rules are based on the tautologies of the system. Classical logic by its very nature ignores the problem of uncertain knowledge. Any attempt to deal with uncertainty within a strictly classical logic framework is itself an ad hoc method and does not constitute a sound theoretical framework.

An analysis of what happens within each inference step can be used to develop the taxonomy of the techniques of inference under uncertainty. One must also pay attention to how the inference chain is constructed and its dependence on the knowledge base. If the information in the knowledge base is ordered and that order can affect the overall conclusion, then that also indicates that the system is dealing with some form of uncertainty[3].

2.2 Uncertainty

Expert systems, must of necessity, be able to handle information that is uncertain. There are many sources of such uncertainty. While it is not yet possible to give an exhaustive account of these, some of the key ones that arise in the literature on expert systems are as follows:

- One's **belief** in a given proposition or a piece of knowledge.

- The **likelihood** of a simple, compound or conditional event.

- The **extent** of a proposition concerning a continuous variable.

- The **imprecision** about any information.

- Any **exception** to a general rule.

- The **mandate** for performing some action.

- The **relevance** of one piece of information to another.

To deal with these types of uncertainties, expert systems require techniques other than classical logic which contains only truth-bearing items and truth-preserving inferences. Plausible reasoning allows plausible conclusions to be drawn from evidence which is only believed but not known to be true. Probability theory is the best tool for handling likelihood. However, imprecision itself can be about likelihoods or extents or degrees of belief. It may be expressed as upper and lower limits of a variable or as a fuzzy subset of all plausible values. Most of these techniques use numeric values to represent the degree of uncertainty but this is not always necessary for representing belief. Beliefs, exceptions, mandate, etc. are propositional attitudes and may be represented as modalities of the underlying propositions, so it is important to reason about not just the propositions but also their modalities.

3 Techniques for Inference Under Uncertainty

Such techniques can be broadly divided into those that propagate numerical values through the inference chain and those that contain essentially binary information. More recent literature contains techniques that do not neatly fit into either of these categories [23,29]. Inference from a set of premises to a conclusion may be immediate if only one rule of inference is invoked, or it may be "mediate" if there are several intermediate steps. In the latter case we have a chain of immediate inferences and this chain may be constructed either forward or backwards. Any one of several inference rules may be invoked at each step of such a chain. In rule-based expert systems based on classical logic, the use of the inference rule "modus ponens" may predominate whether the chain is constructed forwards or backwards. This is because the IF..THEN.. rules are usually interpreted as implications.

The important thing is to note what quantity is propagated through such an inference chain from the premises to the conclusion. If binary values are propagated, then it is necessary to ensure that the binary values of all the propositions in the system have the same unique interpetation. If some true propositions are interpreted as known to be true while others are interpreted as just believed to be true, then the semantic validity of the system can no longer be guaranteed. So even binary truth valued inference systems can give rise to confusion.

In several expert systems, a single numerical value between 0 and 1 is propagated through the inference chain. The number is interpreted as probability and the inference step is based on the use of Bayes' theorem. In fuzzy expert systems, a fuzzy subset rather than a single numerical value is sometimes propagated and the inference step is based on the so called "compositional rule of inference". Such systems are meant to handle the uncertainty in the information, but as with binary systems, these too require that the numerical value of each proposition has the same interpretation. Unfortunately this is not easy to guarantee with naive users of such systems.

A useful way of classifying the techniques for inference **under** uncertainty, therefore, is to divide them into those doing inference **with** uncertainty and those doing inference **about** uncertainty. The former are those in which the degree of uncertainty is represented by a measure. The methods using numerical values all fall within this category. Such methods achieve simplicity by sacrificing some of the information about the source of the uncertainty. The latter techniques have to maintain the information about the source of the uncertainty (normally requiring a complex data structure to do so). Notable examples are of such an approach are non-monotonic logic and Cohen's theory of endorsement (see below). Notice that these two methods of inference under uncertainty are not mutually exclusive and may both be present in a given application.

3.1 Non-monotonic Logics

In inference systems employing non-monotonic logics, assumptions are made which may have to be revised in the light of new information. They have the property that at any given stage more than one mutually consistent set of conclusions can be derived from the available data and possible assumptions. However, practical systems such as Doyle's Truth Maintenance System (TMS)[3] only produce one such set at any stage. Such conclusions that are reached may be invalidated as new data is considered as such new data may be incompatible with some the default assumptions made. The inference system requires that the justifications for any conclusions are recorded during the inference process and used for dependency directed backtracking during the revision of beliefs. Non-monotonic logics are particularly useful for reasoning under incomplete information. The reasoning process call for the use of as many assumptions as possible without producing a logical inconsistency.

The first formulation of non-monotonic logic was given by McDermott & Doyle[4]. They introduced a modal operator "M" so that "Mp" is to be interpreted as "the proposition p is consistent with the theory". They also added to classical logic a non-monotonic inference rule to generate assumptions. Their logic, however, has several weaknesses which have been commented upon by several authors subsequently who have suggested various kinds of improvements. For example, in a later paper McDermott himself proposed a non-monotonic modal logic which inherits the axioms of modal logic[5]. There is an extensive mathematical[6] and philosophical[7] literature on Modal logics. Until recently they have not been used at all in expert systems. Their importance is finally being realised as the interest in non-monotonic logics grows. Alternative formulations of non-monotonic logic that overcome the difficulties of the original formulation are given, among others, by Gabbay[8] who bases it on Intuitionistic logic and Moore[9] who uses a different non-monotonic inference rule. Moore calls his logic "auto-epistemic" logic which is meant to model the behaviour of an "ideally rational agent reflecting upon his own beliefs in contrast to the other formulations which model default reasoning. The distinction may be subtle but is important as it shows how careful one has to be in dealing with the various types of uncertainties. The publications cited here also contain numerous references to other literature on the subject of non-monotonic inference.

3.2 Methods using numerical values

It should be noted that the majority of practical expert systems and shells employ inference techniques that propagate numerical values through the inference chain and they are mostly based on statistical methods. Strict statistical inference has a strong mathematical foundation, but its application to rule-based expert systems can be achieved at the cost of weakening this foundation considerably. Fuzzy sets theory too has a good mathematical foundation though it is relatively weaker than that of statistics. However, fuzzy sets theory is more directly applicable for inference in expert systems.

3.2.1 Statistics

The main statistical technique of inference that is usually employed in expert systems is some variant (some may say deviant) of Bayes' theorem. Such expert systems have theoretical weaknesses that have been pointed out by many authors e.g. White[10], who states that the principle difficulties of systems such as PROSPECTOR and MYCIN[11] are:

1. Violation of the assumption of conditional independence

2. Use of "fuzzy logic"

3. The problem of inconsistent prior information

4. General difficulties arising from the the use of subjective estimates of probabilities whose interpretation leads to confusion between likelihood, degree of belief and the degree to which the answer to a question is "true".

Bayes' theorem itself is not suitable for representing the subjective degrees of belief as it cannot distinguish between the lack of belief and disbelief because it requires the relation $P(A) + P(not A) = 1$. Mycin[11], which is based on confirmation theory, uses 2 parameters, MB and MD to represent degrees of belief and disbelief respectively, of a hypothesis. Shafer-Dempster theory does give a useful measure for the evaluation of subjective certainty. Dempster's theory was proposed in 1967[12] and later redefined by Shafer in terms of credibility and plausibility evidence involves a normalisation process that was criticised by Zadeh[14] as suppressing contradiction and can lead to counter-intuitive result.

3.2.2 Expert Systems Application

Early expert systems such as MYCIN and PROSPECTOR[15] all employed techniques dealing with uncertain information. Publications on these systems as well as general books on expert systems explain the reasons behind the use of the techniques that these systems employed. More recent expert system shells such as SAGE, AL/X, MICRO-EXPERT, etc. that are broadly similar in that they may be together described as "variations on the Bayseian inference theme".

It is difficult to apply the Bayesian or Shafer-Dempster inference rule at each step of the inference chain in a rule-based expert system. This is because not only the prior probabilities but also the joint probabilities are required to compute the probability of the hypothesis from the evidence. This calls for an enormous amount of data that, in practical situations, is simply not available. So the inference rules have to be suitably modified. When statisticians investigate expert systems that make use of some form of statistical reasoning they often conclude, as does White[10] that the "..solution seems to be to give up altogether the goal of attempting to encode the knowledge of the experts directly into an expert system.." and "..that we are better off without windows (human ones that is) if they are obtained at the cost of distorting that which is seen through them°'" Practical expert systems therefore should be considered as employing ad hoc inference techniques because such techniques have been derived by considerably weakening the theoretical foundations of the original techniques.

3.2.3 Fuzzy sets

Fuzzy sets are usually interpreted as representing imprecision in the extent of a continuous variable. The inference step in fuzzy set theory is known as the "compositional rule of inference". The prior information is the fuzzy sets corresponding to the possibility distributions of the evidence. Joint possibility distributions are not required. This makes its use in rule based expert systems attractive. There is an extensive literature on fuzzy set theory which also discusses some of the problems with this theory[16, 17, 18,19,20]. Griffiths et. al. give a survey of techniques which use fuzzy sets in expert systems[21].

Zadeh has also extended fuzzy set theory to deal with fuzzy quantifiers and fuzzy probabilities e.g. most, many, a few, etc. This makes it possible to deal with different types of uncertainty within a single conceptual framework. Much of Zadeh's recent work is concerned with the theory of dispositions[18]. A disposition is a proposition which is preponderantly, but not necessarily always true. Much of the knowledge used in expert systems is in the form of dispositions. Dispositions refer to default inferences that are permissible unless evidence to the contrary is available. Zadeh, therefore, shows another way of dealing with default reasoning instead of non-monotonic logic. Dispositional statements contain uncertainty which is seldom explicitly stated. They can mislead unless the hidden uncertainty is reintroduced by the use of fuzzy quantifiers such as most, almost all, almost always, usually, etc. Thus for example, "Professors are not very rich" should be expressed as "Most professors are not very rich". McDermott & Doyle[4] refer to such statements as "normic" statements i.e. statements that are normally true.

3.3 Other Methods

There are several other papers on reasoning under uncertainty that do not fall within the strict framework of either probability or fuzzy mathematics. Some advocate a combination of the two mathematical approaches. Phelps[22] classifies uncertainty into two types: uncertainty about likelihood of occurrence of events and uncertainty about similarity between concepts. He suggests that probability theory is suitable for the former type and fuzzy theory for the latter. Rollinger[23] represents uncertain knowledge as a point in a two dimensional evidence space. This approach is similar to the two-valued numerical method of reasoning such as Shafer-Dempster theory. Rollinger uses the "compatibility" of evidence and the antecedent of an implication rule in the evidence space as a measure of the "quality" of verification of a premise.

There are other papers that employ various ad hoc methods for reasoning under uncertainty. Bundy[24] is concerned with the meaning of numbers used in the various reasoning mechanisms. He believes that numbers interpreted as probabilities must satisfy the properties of probability theory. He argues, that a purely numerical mechanism should not be used and proposes the use of "Incidence Calculus" which also takes into account the dependency between formulae. Bundy's paper is a response to the widespread belief that uncertainties should not be represented by a single numeric value. It provides a partial solution by representing probability by incidence. We believe that some kinds of uncertainty cannot be represented as probabilities and his mechanism cannot be applied to all kinds of uncertainties.

Fox[25] believes that "belief terms" should be represented qualitatively with an explicit semantics rather than as fuzzy subsets of numeric unit interval. He takes a set of belief terms from the English vocabulary and establishes a semantic hierarchy for them. The belief of a proposition can then be described qualitatively such as "corroborated", "ambiguous", definite", "unlikely" etc. This allows knowledge to be expressed in a more intelligible way.

Cohen and Grinberg[26] describe a theory of reasoning about (as opposed to "with") uncertainty based on a representation of states of certainty called endorsements. The theory of endorsements is a departure from numerical methods of reasoning. Instead of propagating numbers, knowledge about the uncertainty itself is propagated. This knowledge includes strength of evidence, whether the evidence is for or against, provability, etc. Instead of combining all uncertainties into a number, the theory allows domain dependent heuristics to do the ranking and discounting of uncertainty.

Quinlan[27,28] believes that if the information provided to the system is inconsistent, this fact should be made evident along with some notion of alternative ways that the information could be made consistent. This means that Quinlan objects to any method of combining inconsistent information. He insists that the inconsistencies be reported so that corrections may be made in the input information by the user. Our feeling at present is that the user should not be forced to correct inconsistencies, instead the knowledge about contradictions should be propagated over the inference. After all, experts can sometimes cope with contradicting evidence and this knowledge should be captured by the expert system.

Finally, Friedman[29] describes a system based on Polya's[30] Plausible Inference which employs four rules of inference i.e. Modus Ponens, Modus Tollens, Confirmation and Denial. Most expert systems use only Modus Ponens and/or Modus Tollens. Polya's rules of Confirmation and Denial are not present in "standard" logic but are employed by most people during reasoning. The rule of Confirmation is similar to the idea proposed in "Logic and Uncertainty"[2] of "more than a conditionality but not quite a biconditionality".

4 Discussion

A formal system of logic can be created from the collection of inference rules that are to be used. One must then test if the theory obtained is sound. But for such a theory to be applied to practical problems, it is also necessary that the inference process is computationally tractable (i.e. there is an efficient decision procedure for proving a proposition within it), and that its processes are understandable by the ordinary users of the system.

The semantics of standard binary logic assume complete truth functionality of all the logical operators. This means that for any logical operator o (AND, OR IMPLY etc.)

$$v(A \ o \ B) = f[v(A), v(B)]$$

where $v(X)$ is the value of the proposition X. The formal deductive system of binary logic, expressed as a collection of rules of inference, does not require this complete truth functionality, if we adopt a strict interpretation that only the propositions that are PROVABLE may have the value TRUE. Under this interpretation the premises of a theory are neither TRUE nor FALSE. What this means is that a proposition and its negation may both be false without contravening the rules of inference[31]. Thus standard logic, by giving the premises of a theory the value TRUE also gives them the status of PROVABILITY. Standard classical logic opts for complete truth-functionality so as to make the computation tractable, but in doing so it effectively postulates that there is no incompleteness in the information provided. One can therefore, turn this argument on its head and state that one hallmark of a logic that deals with uncertainty arising out of incomplete knowledge is that its operators do not exhibit complete truth-functionality.

In probability theory we know that the p(A OR B) is not truth-functional as it depends upon p(A AND B). Apart from dealing with the probabilities this theory also demands that a complete knowledge about joint probabilities is also available. One reason why fuzzy logic is criticised is that its operators are all truth-functional. In non-monotonic logic, the premises have the value BELIEVED rather than TRUE. This logic contains not only premises but also "assumptions". Assumptions have the value BELIEVED only if their negation do not have this value. Present conclusions have only local belief values as they depend upon what else is believed at present. So in a sense there is no complete truth functionality in this system.

Lack of truth-functionality indicates that the logic in question is not topic neutral and that domain dependant information is necessary to resolve the uncertainty. In non-monotonic logics, it is necessary to state explicitly which and when default assumptions may be made. In probability theory it is necessary to know the extent to which the variables are mutually dependant. These are very similar concepts. We believe that uncertainty of information in expert systems primarily arises out of incompleteness. Numerical information can be useful to resolve further such uncertainty. However, we suspect that in most cases where numbers are used in an ad hoc way, the intention is to express the partial order of the available options. The use of numbers implying a linear order, obscures this intention and gives rise to a set of additional problems concerning the meaning of these numeric values and the grounds for discriminating the neighbouring values.

Acknowledgements

We are indebted to our colleagues at Queen Mary College, John Bigham and Dave Griffiths, for useful suggestions they have made in the preparation of this paper.

This work has had the support of SERC/Alvey in the form of funding a workshop on inference under uncertainty at Queen Mary College in May 1984 and more recently in the form of a research grant that would allow us to study this subject further. The aim of this research is to produce a better understanding of the different inference techniques that have been proposed in the literature and to study the question of **inference** under uncertainty and attempt to bring about a reconciliation with inference in classical logic. In order for us to fulfill these aims we will greatly appreciate the help from any reader of this paper by communicating to us his own or some other work that may appear to be relevant to this research.

5 References

1. Efstathiou, H.J. "Report on the SIG on Inference under Uncertainty, IKBS mailshot, 1984

2. Mamdani, E. H. "Logic and Uncertainty" SIG on Inference under Uncertainty, IKBS Mailshot, October 1984.

3. Doyle, J. "A Truth Maintenance System", Artificial Intelligence, vol. 12, pp. 231-272, 1979

4. D. McDermott and J. Doyle, "Non-Monotonic Logic I", Artificial Intelligence, vol. 13, pp. 41-72, 1979

5. McDermott, D., "Non-Monotonic Logic II: Non-monotonic modal Theories", Journal of ACM, vol. 29, No.1, pp 33-57, 1982.

6. Hughes, G. E. and Cresswell, M. J., An Introduction to Modal Logic, Methuen and Co., London, 1972.

7. R. Bradley and S. Swartz, Possible Worlds: An Introduction to Logic and its Philosophy, Basil Blackwell, Oxford, 1979

8. Gabbay, D. M., "Intuitionistic Basis for Non-monotonic Logic", Artificial Intelligence, vol. 25, No. 1, pp. 75-94, 1985.

9. Moore, R. ᴄ. , "Semantic Considerations on Nonmonotonic Logic",

10. White A.P. "Inference Deficiencies in Rule-Based Expert Systems" Birmingham University - ~~To be~~ presented at the BCS Expert Systems meeting, Dec. 1984.

11. Shortliffe, E. H. & Buchanan, B. B., "A Method of Inexact Reasoning in Medicine", Mathematical Bioscience, vol. 23, pp.351 - 379

12. Dempster, A.P., "Upper and lower probabilities induced by a multi-valued mapping", Ann. Math, Stat., vol. 38, pp325-329,1967

13. Shafer, G.,A Mathematical Theory of Evidence, Princeton University Press, 1976

14. Zadeh, L. A., "On the Validity of Dempster's Rule of Combination of Evidence", Electronic Research Memorandum No. UCB/ERL 79/24, University of California, Berkeley, CA.

15. Duda, R. O. Hart, P. E. & Nilson, N. J., "Semantic Network Representation in Rule-Based Inference Systems", Pattern Directed Inference Systems, pp. 203 - 221, Academic Press

16. Zadeh, L. A., "A Theory of Approximate Reasoning", Machine Intelligence, vol. 9, pp. 147 - 194.

17. Zadeh, L. A., "A Computational Approach to Fuzzy Quantifiers in Natural Languages", Comp. & Math. with Appl., vol. 9, No. 1, pp. 149 - 184, 1983

18. Zadeh, L. A., A computational Theory of Dispositions", Proc. 1984 Int. Conf. of the Assoc. for Computational Linguistics

19. Mamdani, E. H., & Efstathiou, H.J., "Logic & PRUF - A Survey, Higher Order Logics for Handling Uncertainty in Logics", To appear in the Int. J. Man-Machine Systems, 1985

20. Efstathiou, H. J. & Tong, R., "A Critical Assessment of the Truth Functional Modifications and its use in Approximate Reasoning", Journal of Fuzzy Sets & Systems, vol. 7, pp.103-108, 1982

21. Griffiths D.G., Mamdani, E.H. and Efstathiou, H.J. "Fuzzy sets and Expert Systems" - To appear

22. Phelps, B., "Fuzzy Sets, Probability and the nature of Uncertainty", Internal Report, Brunel University

23. Rollinger, C., "How to Represent Evidence - Aspects of Uncertain Reasoning", Proc. 8th IJCAI, 1983, pp.358-361

24. Bundy, A., "Incidence Calculus: A Mechanism for Probabilistic Reasoning", University of Edinburgh, Department of Artificial Intelligence Research Report no. 216

25. Fox, J. "Linguistic Reasoning About Beliefs and Values", ICRF internal Memo

26. Cohen, P.R. and Grinberg, M.R., "A Framework for Heuristic Reasoning About Uncertainty", Proc. 8th IJCAI, 1983, pp.355-357

27. Quinlan, J.R., "Inferno: A Cautious Approach to Uncertain Inference", Computer Journal, vol. 26, 1983

28. Quinlan, J.R., "Consistency and Plausible Reasoning", Proc. 8th IJCAI 1983, pp.137-144

29. Friedman, L., "Reasoning by Plausible Inference", Proc. 5th Conf. on Automated Deductions, pp. 126-142

30. Polya, G., "Patterns of Plausible Inference", Princeton University Press, Princeton, N.J. 1954

31. McCawley, James D., Everything that Linguists have Always Wanted to Know about Logic (but were ashamed to ask), Basil Blackwell, Oxford

Machine (Object) Structure

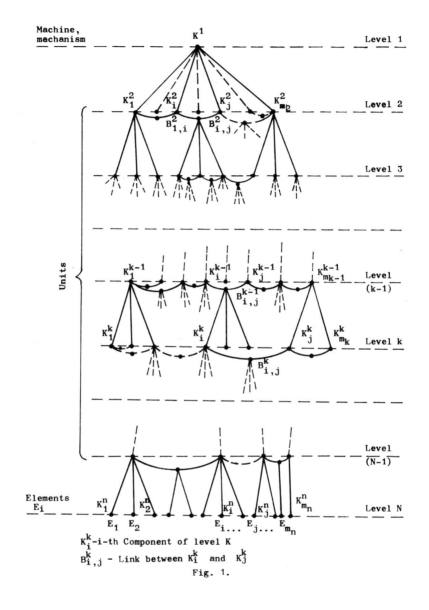

K_i^k-i-th Component of level K

$B_{i,j}^k$ - Link between K_i^k and K_j^k

Fig. 1.

CAD/CAPP expert system shell general structure

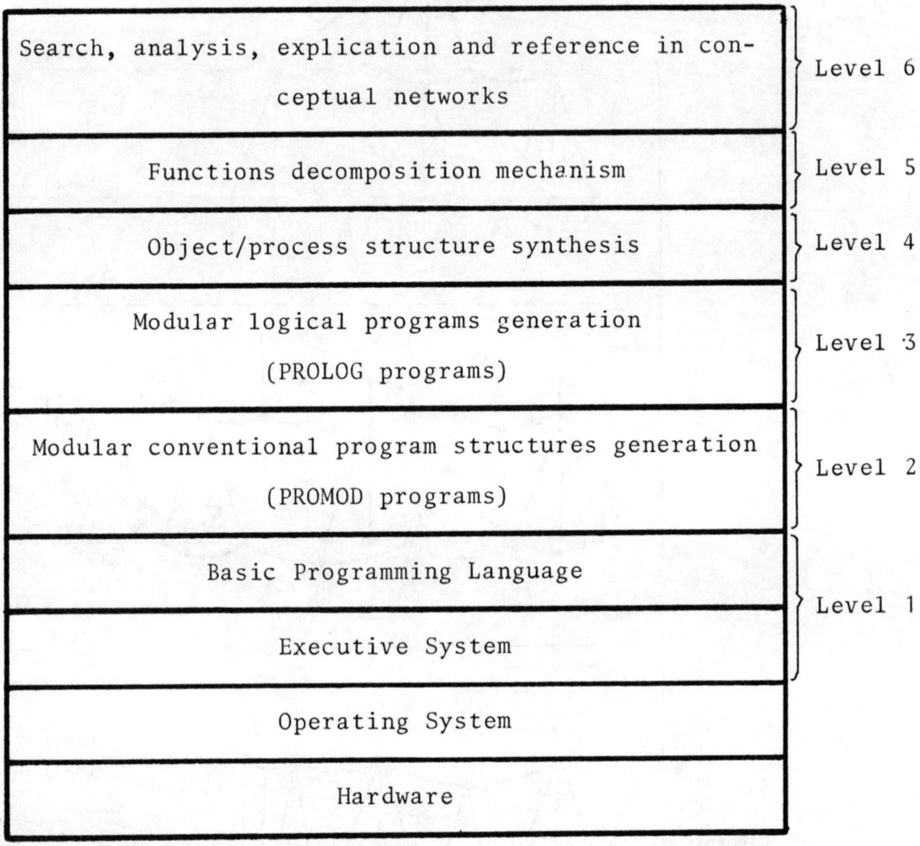

Search, analysis, explication and reference in conceptual networks	Level 6
Functions decomposition mechanism	Level 5
Object/process structure synthesis	Level 4
Modular logical programs generation (PROLOG programs)	Level 3
Modular conventional program structures generation (PROMOD programs)	Level 2
Basic Programming Language	Level 1
Executive System	
Operating System	
Hardware	

Fig. 2.

Executive level structure

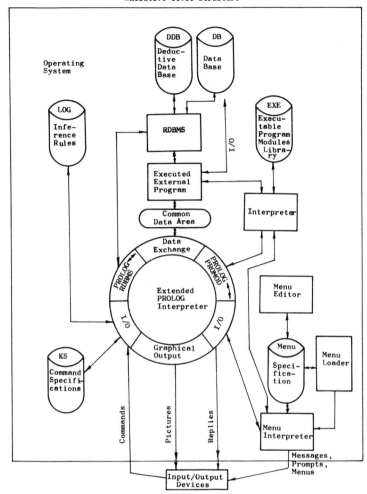

Fig. 3.

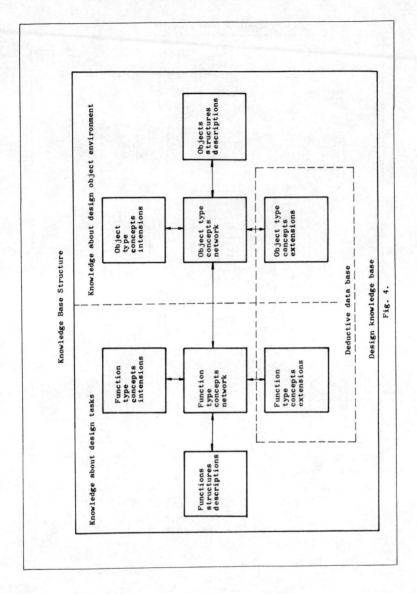

Fig. 4.

SOJA : A DAILY WORKSHOP SCHEDULING SYSTEM
SOJA 's system and inference engine

Claude LEPAPE

Laboratoires de Marcoussis
Centre de Recherches de la C.G.E.
Route de Nozay
91460 Marcoussis
FRANCE

Abstract

We have implemented in the **Laboratoires de Marcoussis** - in Franz-Lisp - a daily scheduling system called SOJA. Given the state of the shop in the evening, SOJA builds a scheduling plan for the next day. This implies :

- selecting the operations to be performed over the day

- scheduling them and computing a time-table for each machine.

Both selection and scheduling processes use an inference engine that has been specially designed for SOJA. We describe this engine and the solutions we have implemented to make it efficient :

- combination of forward and backward chaining

- preservation of partial instances of rules

- compilation of rules.

SOJA will soon be run on real data, coming from an **Alsthom-Atlantique** sheet-iron workshop.

Keywords : scheduling system, constraint-directed search, forward and backward chaining, activation tree.

SOJA : A DAILY WORKSHOP SCHEDULING SYSTEM

1. INTRODUCTION

In 1984 and 1985 and as part of a contract with Alsthom-Atlantique (AA), we have been working on the application of Artificial Intelligence techniques to daily scheduling problems.

Daily scheduling involves two distinct problems :

— the first one deals with computing a "good" scheduling plan for the next day every evening. A scheduling plan provides time-tables for the different resources (machines, tools, ...) used in the shop ; a "good" one makes a compromise among conflicting criteria concerning due-dates, costs, productivity, stability, stocks. Therefore, the "phases" (a phase is a sequence of operations, concerning a given lot of pieces, and to be excuted on the same machine with the same setting) to be performed over the day should be chosen according to these criteria, and the same goes for ordering these phases on the machines. We have implemented an expert system prototype that deals with this problem : it is called SOJA.

— another problem is the real-time reaction to unpredictable events : machine breakdowns, power failures, bugs in numerical control software ... When confronted to such incidents, local changes of the plan become necessary. This will be part of our future research.

Two planning steps are distinguished in SOJA : Selection and Scheduling.

— Selection is done according to the state of the shop and the orders to be completed. Selection rules are used to build a tagged graph, which nodes are phases. Each arc is tagged according to a reason for selecting its extremity, and valued in order to measure the significance of this reason. Then SOJA examines this graph and the resources requirements to decide which phases should be scheduled.

— As M.S.Fox [Fox 1983] we consider scheduling as a constraint-directed reasoning task. SOJA generates constraints and satisfies them by iteratively constraining an initial scheduling plan.
Each constraint is regarded as a disjunction of several facts and each scheduling decision consists in choosing - with the help of scheduling rules - one of these facts. The latter is then forced and its propagation reduces some existing disjunctions or creates new ones. The plan may then become over-constrained, in which case a backtrack process is invoked to undo part of the plan by rejecting a previous scheduling or selection decision.
When all generated constraints are satisfied, the system gives its solution for each machine : phases to be performed - with their arrival, start and departure times - and tool changes that may occur between them. If the total load of the shop is too low, the system may select new phases and schedule them without rejecting its previous decisions.

The next sections will more thoroughly describe the selection and scheduling processes used in SOJA.

2. SELECTION

2.1. The selection graph

The interest of selecting a phase strongly depends on the state of the shop and on the other phases. Therefore such dependencies should be considered and evaluated before selecting the phases.
But the set of lots that are ready to be selected is generally much more important than the set of phases one can expect to process during a day. Consequently it would be unuseful to take into account the dependencies between all the phases ; that is why we have decided to build a "selection graph" $G(X,U)$.

X is a set of nodes containing :
- a root R,
- particular phases that have been "pre-selected".

U is a set of valued tagged arcs. An arc (PH_1, PH_2, VAL, TAG) means that if PH_1 is selected, then the selection of PH_2 is interesting with respect to the criterion TAG. VAL is a positive integer which quantifies the interest of the selection of PH_2 ; when $VAL \geq 20$, the selection of PH_2 is regarded as forced by the selection of PH_1.

2.2. Building the graph

Selection rules are used to build this graph. Each rule is a weighted production of the form : if "conditions" then "pre-selections".
Conditions are relevant to the state of the shop, the pre-selected phases or the phases in general.
Pre-selections consist in adding new vertices and arcs in the graph.

Here are some examples :
- $R1$: if PH has to be performed before the end of the week,
  then add PH and an arc $(R, PH, 17,$ *due-date-requirement*$)$ to the selection graph. (weight : 17).
- $R4$: if PH has been started,
  then add PH and an arc $(R, PH, 20,$ *started-phase*$)$. (weight : 20).
- $R6$: if PH_1 and PH_2 are pre-selected phases using the same machine M and tool T, and if the set-up of T on M is costly,
  then add $(PH_1, PH_2, 12,$ *no-tool-set-up*$)$. (weight : 18).

The initial graph just contains R. At each iteration of the selection process, a rule instance having the highest weight is applied. For example, the following graph is build by successively applying :
- $R4$ with $PH = P1-1$,

- $R1$ with $PH=P2-1$,
- $R6$ with $PH_1=P1-1$ and $PH_2=P2-1$.

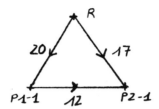

This process ends when the size of the graph reaches a limit depending on the capacity of the workshop.

2.3. Selection

Selection is handled with the following algorithm :

While there are under-loaded machines (a productivity margin is given for each machine) :

Select an arc $R \rightarrow PH$ (several combination functions of arc valuations can be used).

If PH can be selected without over-loading its machine, then :

- select it
- record the tag of the arc
- replace each arc $PH \rightarrow PH$ ' by an arc $R \rightarrow PH$ ' (without changing neither its tag, nor its weight)
- get PH out of the selection graph.

Selected phases are then taken into account by the scheduling process which generates constraints to be satisfied, and builds a scheduling plan concerning these phases.

3. CONSTRAINT-DIRECTED SCHEDULING

A scheduling plan has to satisfy many constraints : operation precedence, sharing of resources, tool requirements, ...

However an acceptable schedule has additional qualities concerning :

— the ability to meet due-dates
— the number of tool changes
— the flow of lots in the shop
— the number of lots coming back to the central stock between successive phases
— the shop stability ...

In ISIS [Fox 1983] these qualities are represented as additional - but relaxable - constraints. In SOJA, they are translated into scheduling rules that guide the satisfaction of the constraints.

Section 3.1. describes the mecanism we have implemented in order to manipulate and satisfy pure constraints and section 3.2. deals with scheduling rules.

3.1. The scheduling process of SOJA

Each constraint in SOJA appears as a conditionnal disjunction of "basic facts", among which a choice is necessary. A decision consists in choosing and propagating one of these facts.

The propagation is fulfilled with the help of a "scheduling graph", which nodes are the selected phases - there is a special node B representing the beginning of the day - and which valued arcs embody time inequalities such as : $start\text{-}date(PH_i) + VAL \leq start\text{-}date(PH_j)$.
These inequalities lead to a contradiction if and only if there is a positive circuit in the graph. Also at any given moment of the scheduling process some facts are banned because they would lead to such a contradiction.

Six categories of constraints are taken into account by SOJA :

— each phase has an earliest start date that depends on the time that is necessary to convey the lot on the machine and to change the tool (if it is not already set on the machine). Such a constraint consists in only one fact and only one arc : $B \rightarrow PH$.

— each selection decision implies that the selected phase should be executed before the end of the day. Again there is only one fact in the disjunction and one arc : $PH \rightarrow B$.

— precedence constraints are disjunctions of only one fact (*precedes* $PH_1 \ PH_2$). Such a fact brings an unique arc which valuation depends on several parameters such as the machines used to perform PH_1 and PH_2, tool set-up times ...

— resources are shared ; consequently, if two phases PH_1 and PH_2 use a common resource - for example, the same machine - they must satisfy the disjunction : $[(precedes \ PH_1 \ PH_2) \ or \ (precedes \ PH_2 \ PH_1)]$.

— Between two successive phases concerning the same lot and to be performed on two different machines M_1 and M_2, the lot may either be sent back to the central stock of the shop or wait near M_1 or M_2.

A third solution consists in delaying the first phase.
SOJA regards such a problem as a disjunction of three facts called "return", "wait" and "stick". Decisions concerning "return" or "stick" add new arcs in the graph. "Wait" does not but it generates new constraints concerning the waiting areas of the machine.

— The number of locations used to stock lots beside the machines is limited. For exemple, only two places per machine are available in the AA shop. Consequently every lot that "waits" between two phases has to reserve a waiting area. This implies new constraints about the sharing of waiting areas.

At any given moment of the scheduling process, four states are distinguished for each constraint :

— satisfied : one of the facts of the constraint is implied by previous decisions.

— impossible to satisfy : each fact belonging to the disjunction is banned.

— imperative : only one fact belonging to the disjunction is not banned.

— disjunctive : at least two facts can be chosen to satisfy the constraint.

The scheduling algorithm is based on the following principles :

— When a constraint becomes "impossible to satisfy", a selective backtrack procedure is called. It selects a decision to be rejected, undo the effects due to this decision and to decisions that have followed - note that this decision is either a scheduling decision, or a selection decision -. The corresponding fact is then banned and the scheduling process restarts.

— When a constraint becomes "imperative", the only remaining fact is immediately asserted and propagated. This consists in adding arcs to the graph, banning facts and generating new constraints.

— If there is no "impossible to satisfy" or "imperative" constraint, the system chooses a fact - with the help of scheduling rules - to satisfy a remaining disjunctive constraint. This fact is then asserted and propagated.

— If all constraints are satisfied, a scheduling solution is inferred from the scheduling graph.

3.2. The use of scheduling rules

Scheduling rules are available to select a fact from all the facts in disjunctive constraints.

Some of these rules concern the scheduling criteria. For

example, the following one is used to spare tool changes :

> If $F=(precedes\ PH_2\ PH_3)$ belongs to a disjunctive constraint
> and if PH_1, PH_2, PH_3 use the same machine
> and if PH_1 and PH_2 use the same tool and PH_3 another one
> and if $(precedes\ PH_1\ PH_3)$,
>
> then assert F.

Other rules are used :

— to favour some constraint categories : for example, sharing the machines can be viewed as the most important problem

— to postpone some constraints : when conveying durations are small compared with phases durations, some "return", "wait" or "stick" constraints can be postponed and considered at the end of the scheduling process

— to activate heuristic functions, which are evaluated in order to find the "best" fact to assert.

SOJA's scheduling rules proceed from two expert fields :

— one is concerned with Operations Research heuristic rules that are known to be useful to rapidly build scheduling plans having particular properties

— most of the rules had been written with the help of people working in the AA shop : they concern the specific problems and criteria to be taken into account in this shop. We believe that taking this particular knowledge into consideration is very important to build scheduling plans. This is SOJA's main interest.

SOJA'S INFERENCE ENGINE

An inference engine has been built specially for SOJA. In forward chaining, it activates production rules that modify a LISP environment containing frames. The aim of this chapter is to describe the typical features of this engine.

1. RULES CONTAINING LISP

In a real industrial case, machine and phase characteristics would be found in a database. SOJA is only a prototype, so we decided to represent machines, lots and phases as frames that can be viewed as tuples from a relational database.

Selection and scheduling rules frequently refer to these tuples, to their slots and to whole relations. Therefore natural syntax and efficient access are necessary.

This leads to an implementation in which :

— the system knows the relation schemata and the frame slots that point out frames from other relations.

— frames corresponding to a given relation are collected in a list ; its name is the name of the relation.

— the variables used in a rule are declared : a declaration (*X relation-name*) means that *X* represents a frame from *relation-name* ; (*X list-name*) means that *X* can be matched with any member of the list *list-name* ; (*X variable*) means that *X* belongs to no particular list or relation.

— the request (*slot-name X*) brings back the slot *slot-name* of frame *X*.

SOJA's rules are used to make decisions that are propagated. These propagations imply a big amount of computation. To be efficient, these propagations are done in LISP. Consequently SOJA's rules embody LISP function calls in conclusion.
Some conditions can also be evaluated directly in LISP. In particular, compilation of rules transforms all the slots requests into LISP functions. Therefore, to know if a lot *LOT* has to be finished within three days, SOJA evaluates (*lessp* (*difference* (*due–date LOT*) (*date*)) 3) where *due-date* - a slot from *LOT* - has been replaced by a LISP function.

2. SOJA'S RULES

2.1. Slots of the rules

SOJA's rules are represented as frames containing nine slots :
— *ref* is a rule identifier ; during the compilation, an atom named of "ref" is bound to the rule.
— *information* contains sentences explaining the rule ; when the interactive mode is on (cf 5/), they are used to inform the user.
— *weight* is a positive integer, or a LISP function computing a positive integer ; rules having a high weight have priority when the system has to choose among a set of active rules.
— *variables* is used to declare the variables that appear in the rule.
— *conditions* and *conclusions* are the lists of *conditions* and *conclusions* of the rule. They are described in section 2/2/.
— the use of *category*, *partial-instances* and *total-instances* is discussed later (cf 3/ and 4/).

2.2. Conditions and conclusions

The aim of this section is to describe what the conditions and conclusions of SOJA's rules are, i.e. what our inference engine is able to process.

We call "frame-term from relation R_0" every expression T that satisfies one of the following properties :

• T is a variable, representing a frame from R_0,

• $T=(slot\text{-}name\ X)$ and X is a frame-term from a relation R_1 which slot *slot-name* points out a frame from R_0.

We call "frame-term" every T that is either a frame-term from a given relation R_0, or an expression $(slot\text{-}name\ X)$ where X is a frame-term from a relation R_1 having a slot *slot-name*.

We call "evaluable term" every T that satisfies one of the following properties :

• T is a frame-term

• T is a variable

• T is an atom which belongs to the current LISP environnement

• $T=(F\ T_1\ T_2\ \cdots\ T_p)$ where $T_1 \cdots T_p$ are "evaluable terms" and F a LISP function.

We call "positive term" - respectively "negative term" -, an expression $(P\ T_1\ \cdots\ T_p)$ - respectively $(not\ (P\ T_1\ \cdots\ T_p))$ -, where $T_1 \cdots T_p$ are "evaluable-terms" and P a predicate that is **not** a LISP function.

A rule condition is either an evaluable term or a positive term. An evaluable term is verified when the result of its evaluation is different from *nil*. A positive term must be proven with the help of other rules.

A rule conclusion is either an evaluable, a positive or a negative term.

2.3. Conclusion

SOJA's rules include terms that can be evaluated in a (LISP + Frames) environment.
However predicates can be defined by the system's user. Positive and negative terms are then incorporated as conditions or conclusions of the rules.

In this way, the following rules enable to use the "available" predicate. - *(pred PH)* points out a phase that precedes *PH* to complete the same order. -

```
(rule
    ref          R1
    variables    ( (PH phase) )
    conditions   ( (null (pred PH)) )
    conclusions  ( (available PH) )
    )
(rule
    ref          R4
    variables    ( (PH phase) )
    conditions   ( (pre-selected PH) )
    conclusions  ( (available (succ PH)) )
    )
```

It's not useful in SOJA to apply such rules in forward chaining and for every possible instance. That is why SOJA combines forward and backward chaining. The next section deals with this combination.

3. FORWARD AND BACKWARD CHAINING

3.1. Rule categories

There are three rule categories in SOJA :

— forward rules : they are used by the system to modify the (LISP + Frames) environment.

— backward rules : they are called in backward chaining to prove positive terms that appear in conditions of other rules. When a demonstration fails on a positive term, the system records the term. Later, when the term is asserted, the demonstration is resumed in forward chaining.

— demon rules : the first condition of a demon rule is a positive term but the system does not try to prove it. It considers that the condition must **become** true to activate the rule : its activation results from the application of other rules.

3.2. Backward chaining and instanciation

Let us consider a forward rule R, a list or relation $L=(l_1, \cdots, l_p)$, a variable V declared as belonging to L, a predicate P and a condition $(P\ V)$. To find which members of L satisfy $(P\ V)$, we can either call backward rules that conclude about $(P\ V)$ without binding V or successively try to prove each $(P\ l_i)$.

In SOJA we decided to bound variables as soon as possible, except when the user of a predicate defines it and specifies term ranks to be instanciated as late as possible.

Example :

```
(rule
  ref
  category      RPRED_:=
  variables     backward
  conditions    ( (OBJECT variable) )
  conclusions   ( )
  informations  ( (:= OBJECT OBJECT) )
)                ( "trick" )
```

```
(predicate
  ref
  late_ranks    ( 1 )
)                      :=
```

To evaluate the condition (:= M (*machine PH*)), - PH represents a phase and *machine* is a slot from *phase* relation -, SOJA successively :

— binds PH to each possible phase - satisfying previous conditions -
— evaluates $m = (\textit{machine PH})$, and binds *OBJECT* to the result m
— concludes (:= $m\ m$)
— binds M to m.

```
(rule
  ref          R1
  category     backward
  variables    ( (PH phase) )
  conditions   ( (null (pred PH) ) )
  conclusions  ( (available PH) ) )
)

(rule
  ref          R2
  category     backward
  variables    ( (PH phase) )
  conditions   ( ( = (set-tool (machine PH)) (tool PH))
                 (available PH))
  conclusions  ( (available-without-tool-change PH) )
)

(rule
  ref          R3
  category     forward
  variables    ( (PH phase) )
  conditions   ( (available-without-tool-change PH) )
  conclusions  ( (pre-select PH RACINE 18 nil)
                 (pre-selected PH) ) )
)

(rule
  ref          R4
  category     demon
  variables    ( (PH phase) )
  conditions   ( (pre-selected PH)
                 (succ PH) )
  conclusions  ( (available (succ PH))
                 (princ (succ PH))
                 (princ "becomes available.")
                 (terpri) )
)
```

```
(phase
  ref       P1-1
  pred      nil
  succ      P1-2
  machine   M1
  tool      O1
)

(phase
  ref       P1-2
  pred      P1-1
  succ      nil
  machine   M2
  tool      O2
)

(phase
  ref       P2-1
  pred      nil
  succ      P2-2
  machine   M1
  tool      O3
)

(phase
  ref       P2-2
  pred      P2-1
  succ      nil
  machine   M2
  tool      O4
)

(machine
  ref       M1
  set-tool  O1
)

(machine
  ref       M2
  set-tool  O2
)
```

Figure 1

3.3. Example

Let us consider the rules and data given in figure 1.

There is a unique forward rule : $R3$. For each phase, $R2$ is called by $R3$, its first condition is evaluated and for $PH=P1-1$ and $PH=P1-2$, $R1$ is called. (*null* (*pred* $P1-1$)) evaluates to t, so (*available* $P1-1$) and (*available-without-tool-change* $P1-1$) are true. (*null* (*pred* $P1-2$)) evaluates to *nil*, so (*available* $P1-2$) and (*available-without-tool-change* $P1-2$) are not proven.

$R3$ is then applied with $PH=P1-1$. Consequently, the demon rule $R4$ is active and applied. (*available* $P1-2$) is proven, and $R2$ - with $PH=P1-2$ - is immediately applied in forward chaining ...

Note that (*available* $P2-1$) is true but has not been proven : it is unuseful.
That is the main interest of backward chaining in SOJA : unuseful facts are not considered, even if they can be proved. This is very important to solve a combinatorial problem like scheduling.

4. PARTIAL AND TOTAL INSTANCES

When including LISP functions within rules, the following problem - this is a part of the famous frame-problem [Raphael 1971] - is raised : is it necessary to redo the whole pattern-matching at each engine cycle ?

Using add-lists and delete-lists [Fikes & Nilsson 1971] would imply the exclusion of LISP functions and the filling of a working memory containing any relevant information. Building the initial working memory would have been, in SOJA's case, very costly.

Another solution consists in maintaining a relation between the rules and LISP, while specifying among rule conclusions the changes of an implicit working memory.

SOJA's user can choose among two pattern-matching processes :

— the "naive" process : the whole pattern-matching is made again at each cycle ;

— a process in which LISP functions are only used for rigid knowledge ; evolutive information is then represented with the help of predicates - positive terms - ; therefore, rule conclusions have to specify every modification of the truth values of these terms. This process is used in SOJA because many relevant pieces of information are static.

To implement SOJA's process, we decided :

— to record partial and total rule instances : an ith level partial instance is a substitution of variables for which the first $(i-1)$ conditions are verified ; a total instance is a substitution satisfying all the rule conditions.

Of course, ith level partial instances are not recorded when the ith condition is static (note : partial and total instances are viewed as nodes of an activation tree as described in [Descotte 1981]).

— to propagate positive and negative terms - appearing among applied rule conclusions - through these instances. Unification and "partial instance extension" algorithms are used ; in particular, they enable the system to resume demonstrations that have previously failed.

5. THE PARAMETERS OF THE ENGINE

SOJA's engine is called with five parameters :

— *rule-list* is a list of rules.

— *stop-test* is either *nil* - the engine works as long as there are active rules - or a LISP function ; in this case, the engine stops as soon as *(stop-test rule-list)* does not evaluate to *nil*.

— when *inter* is different from *nil*, we are in an interactive mode : then, the user can get information concerning the rules used by the system and confirm or refuse their conclusions - except for rules which weight is greater than 20 -

— when *trace* is different from *nil*, the system prints all its conclusions.

— if *naive* is different from *nil*, the pattern-matching is completely restarted at each engine cycle - propagation is only done for the first conditions of demon rules - ; since SOJA calls its engine with *naive = nil*, partial and total instances are recorded and positive and negative terms are propagated at each cycle : this enables to restart interrupted demonstrations.

6. COMPILATION OF RULES

We have implemented a rule compiler. This compiler :

— modifies each variable and name of declared predicate : this ensures that no confusion will occur between these objects and LISP atoms or functions.

— transforms frame-terms by LISP macros.

— creates evaluation functions for predicates : this is possible if all the backward rules that conclude about this predicate only contain evaluable terms as conditions.

At present, we are considering other transformations :

— A positive or negative term, appearing as a rule conclusion, can be replaced by a LISP function call. This call will insure the propagation of the term.

— Demon rules can also be replaced by LISP function calls.

7. CONCLUSION

SOJA provides a scheduling plan that makes compromises among antagonist criteria.
To build such a plan both selection and constraint-directed scheduling processes use rules.

SOJA contains its own inference engine. It has been specially designed for problem solving techniques that take into account much information while modifying a small part of it.
SOJA's rules contain predicates and LISP functions : this avoids, on the one hand to build a working memory, on the other hand to redo the whole pattern-matching at each cycle.

SOJA is implemented in Franz-Lisp and runs on a VAX-780. With 18 machines it takes five minutes to select and schedule 42 phases - for a four-hour-period - and twenty to select and schedule 83 - for an eigth-hour-period -. The average machine loading time is nearly 70%.

We will soon try to run SOJA with real data coming from the AA shop. Between 100 and 150 phases will be scheduled.

8. FUTURE RESEARCH

The aim of our future research is to deal with the real-time reaction to unpredictable events.
This implies :

— extending SOJA's capabilities to represent and handle various constraints : a more general tool has to be designed in order to propagate constraints and specify possible relaxations.

— evaluating the quality of a scheduling plan with respect to each criterion : this will allow to diagnose poor solutions and decide on criteria to favour.

SOJA makes us believe that a good constraint and criterion representation will be very useful to solve the real-time reaction problem.

REFERENCES

Descotte, Y. (1981).

Représentation et exploitation de connaissances expertes en génération de plans d'actions. Thèse de troisième cycle. Institut National Polytechnique de Grenoble.

Fikes, R.E. & Nilsson, N. (1971).

Strips : a new approach to the application of theorem proving to problem solving. Artificial Intelligence, 2, pp.189-208.

Fox, M.S. (1983).

Constraint directed search : a case study of job shop scheduling. PhD Thesis. Carnegie-Mellon University.

Le Pape, C.M. (1985).

Description du système SOJA : Système d'Ordonnancement Journalier d'un Atelier. Laboratoires de Marcoussis.

Raphael, B. (1971).

The frame problem in problem-solving systems. In Artificial Intelligence and Heuristic Programming. American Elsevier.

REAL TIME MULTIPLE-MOTIVE EXPERT SYSTEMS

Aaron Sloman

Cognitive Studies Programme, University of Sussex,
Brighton, BN1 9QN, England

Abstract. Sooner or later attempts will be made to design systems capable of dealing with a steady flow of sensor data and messages, where actions have to be selected on the basis of multiple, not necessarily consistent, motives, and where new information may require substantial re-evaluation of plans and strategies, including suspension of current actions. Where the world is not always friendly, and events move quickly, decisions will often have to be made which are time-critical. The requirements for this sort of system are not clear, but it is clear that they will require global architectures very different from present expert systems or even most AI programs. This paper attempts to analyse some of the requirements, especially the role of macroscopic parallelism and the implications of interrupts. It is assumed that the problems of designing various components of such a system will be solved, e.g. visual perception, memory, inference, planning, language understanding, plan execution, etc. This paper is about some of the problems of putting them together, especially perception, decision-making, planning and plan-execution systems.

Introduction: designing intelligent actors

We already know something about how intelligent systems may be able to select or construct plans and execute them. Current AI planning systems can cope with a goal given by the user, together with a database of relevant constraints and factual information. A suitable plan may either be retrieved from a database or synthesised using plan formation techniques, whose details need not concern us now. (Standard textbooks on AI describe planning systems, e.g. Boden (1977) Winston (1984). See also Tate (1985) for a recent overview.)

Some systems can also execute plans, for instance in controlling a robot, managing a refinery or playing a game. It is not always possible simply to execute the plan, once it has been chosen or constructed: execution may have to be interleaved with further planning. It has long been known that a plan may have to be changed or gaps filled in during execution, for instance because not all the required information is available initially, or because the assumptions on which the plan was based may not remain true during execution.

There is nothing conceptually difficult about this. If suitable perceptual mechanisms are available, it is possible to insert into a plan at various points instructions to survey the scene and check assumptions or collect new information, after which the planning module may be invoked to modify or extend the current plan if necessary. Let us call this the 'regular re-assessment' strategy.

Quite apart from the difficulties of designing perceptual systems, planning mechanisms, inference mechanisms, managing databases of plans, controlling actions, etc., there are several problems with this as a general model of intelligent planning and action. The problems are concerned with the global organisation of the system: its macro-architecture. By analysing the requirements for intelligent action we shall see the need for a number of asynchronous parallel sub-processes with complex interactions between them. The major problems derive from incomplete knowledge, other resource limitations and the need for speed. Further complications arise out of the fact that intelligent systems may have multiple, not necessarily mutually consistent, independent sources of motivation.

The need for concurrent monitoring

The first problem arises because the environment does not buffer its information until we are ready to examine it. The regular re-assessment strategy assumes that new information can be collected at various discrete convenient pre-assigned steps during plan execution, whereas usually there is a continuous, or at least very rapid, flow of potentially relevant new information. If the information is ignored except at points where plans allow for new information to be considered, then information may be lost. This means that (at least conceptually) the perceptual process of absorbing new information and assessing its significance should go on in parallel with plan execution. In fact this is clearly how humans and animals work, as do interrupt-driven computer operating systems.

This will be called 'concurrent monitoring'. It could be simulated on a fast enough single processor, using polling or interrupts, but that does not affect the conceptual point that logically there are distinct parallel processes: acting and perceiving.

The need to be able to interrupt execution

The perceptual process might simply produce an internal database of information which would be accessed from time to time by the plan execution process, if the plan specified occasions for considering whether relevant new information has arisen. In some cases, however, new information will indicate that it is not worth continuing the current sub-action, since its preconditions are already known to be violated, like finding that the train you planned to catch has been cancelled. Equally the new information may indicate that the whole current plan is misguided, for instance because the conference you were travelling to has been cancelled.

Either way, waiting for the next pre-programmed break in the current plan could involve wasted effort, risky delay, or even worse consequences.

To complicate matters further, in intelligent systems there may be many different co-existing goals, not just one goal provided by the user. For instance, one of the very high priority goals may be to preserve oneself, or other agents from fatal damage. New information acquired by continuous monitoring processes may indicate that there is an urgent need to abandon the current action and take steps to avoid some new danger or pursue some important new opportunity: for instance learning that the field you are about to cross is mined, or discovering that a movie you have long wanted to see is coming to town just after you had planned a trip.

This means that not only should the perceptual processes go on in parallel with current actions, but in addition there needs to be a process of comparing new information with existing long and short term goals and preferences. We could regard this 'goal evaluation' process as part of the concurrent monitoring process. However, goal evaluation may need arbitrarily complex reasoning, for instance to work out the implications of some new information for a current goal, and therefore either the goal evaluation needs to run concurrently with both the action and continued monitoring processes, or else, if it interferes with one of the other processes, then it must use rule-of-thumb heuristics which are guaranteed to give a quick (but potentially fallible) result.

We therefore have, at least conceptually, three parallel processes, action (plan execution), monitoring and goal evaluation. The result of the goal evaluation process must be capable of causing the current action to be interrupted (or modified) if necessary.

Systems in which one process is capable of interrupting another whether the second is ready for it or not are anathema to mathematical computer scientists, since it is very difficult to prove properties of such systems. An algorithm cannot be proved to produce a certain result if some portion of it it is capable of being interrupted or redirected at an arbitrary time. My view is that this flexibility is essential for intelligent systems and, if necessary, the analytical techniques will have to be extended rather than restricting the design of programming languages to rule this out. As we'll see, the feasibility of formal analysis of intelligent systems will be further undermined because of the need for speed, which dictates the use of rule-of-thumb heuristics at crucial stages.

Interrupting vs modifying

Sometimes new information can generate a need for existing actions not to be abandoned or suspended but to be modified. For example if you discover evidence that the bridge you are walking over is unsafe, you may start treading more lightly and watching out for evidence that it is about to collapse. While asking someone questions in an interview you discover he has recently had a bereavement: you may go on with the questions originally planned, but alter your manner and perhaps some of the phrasing.

Human beings are able to modify execution of a plan without interrupting it. There are many different sorts of modification, for instance speeding up or slowing down the action, changes of style, changes of route, attending to more of the details, choosing sub-actions with more care, using a different sort of monitoring process, moving more smoothly or evenly, using different materials or sub-actions.

Current plan formalisms and plan executing systems will need to be extended to be able to permit such variation in performance of the same action. This paper does not discuss modification of actions in any depth, as the main points we are interested in can be made in connection with suspending or aborting actions. A full investigation would require analysis of different forms of modification of an ongoing action, the circumstances under which they are useful, and the mechanisms which make them possible. (Sloman 1978 chapter 8 includes some examples.) To simplify discussion in the remainder of this paper I shall merely talk about 'interrupting', though in many cases 'interrupting or modifying' would be more appropriate.

Rule-of-thumb strategies

We have just seen an example of a general point. Many of the comparisons, or decisions, which are discussed in this paper are capable in principle of requiring indefinitely lengthy processes of analysis and inference, and possibly also new physical actions in order to collect new information or experiment with tools or plans before making a decision. It will often not be possible to permit such processes to continue at length: a decision or result has to be computed fast, or without disturbing some other ongoing activity. It may then be useful if rules or mechanisms are available which produce a decision quickly, even if it is not always the right decision. In the extreme case, where information is totally inadequate but a decision has to be taken urgently (e.g. whether to take the left or the right fork in order to escape from a dangerous pursuer), it may be better to choose at random than to think about the choice.

In less desperate situations there may be fragmentary evidence or quick calculations which provide some basis for choosing but may yield a wrong conclusion. An example would be a rule of thumb which says 'If choosing X in other situations has proved successful, then choose X now'. This rule may be useful for a range of problems even though in some cases deeper investigation would show that Y was a better alternative than X. That is not of much use if doing the deeper investigation takes so long that you lose the opportunity to choose either X or Y, e.g. because the delay has enabled something to injure you, or has enabled both X and Y to flee. Even if an alternative more reliable method is quick, it is no use if the only way to apply it is to interrupt something else which would prove disastrous. For instance, the driver of a fast-moving heavy truck should guess whether to take the next turn rather than take her hands off the wheel to consult a road-map.

So the selection of a quick but unreliable method may be enforced by either resource constraints or time limits.

Where it is certain that delay or interruption of an action will be disastrous, it may be best to use a quick method which is not certain to produce the right result in all cases – as long as it sometimes produces a good result. This may be called the 'Rule-of-thumb' strategy. We shall see that it may need to be employed by several different components of an intelligent system with time constraints and limited knowledge or resources. This is, in principle, no different from the well-known need for heuristics in planning or problem-solving systems, i.e. rules of thumb which cut down search spaces or processing time, possibly with a loss of soundness or completeness.

Among the key issues in the design of intelligent systems using rule-of-thumb strategies from time to time, is where those strategies should come from, how they can be evaluated, and how their use may be controlled. In some cases, as indicated in the above example, they may be derived by simple inductive inferences from previous experiences. The mechanisms required for this sort of learning may be different from other sorts of learning mechanisms, e.g. mechanisms concerned with formation of new concepts, or creation of new explanatory theories, or development of problem solving skills. (There is a vast philosophical literature on whether any strategy for inductive learning can be rationally defended without circularity. For engineering purposes it may not be necessary to produce a totally general and provably correct solution. The same applies to explaining actual human and animal abilities.)

The need for concurrent priority comparisons

In its simplest form concurrent perception and goal evaluation, together with an interrupt mechanism, allows the receipt of new relevant information to cause the execution process to be interrupted so that new planning may be done, either to achieve a new high priority goal, or in order the better to achieve the original top-level goal.

Both the regular re-assessment model and this concurrent monitoring model assume that when new information shows that some re-planning is required, action can be suspended for as long as is necessary for the re-planning to be completed. In some cases, as we have seen, planning, or re-planning, may require arbitrarily complex and lengthy processes of inference, collecting new information, consulting experts, doing experiments, etc. Often it will not be possible to wait for such a re-planning process to be completed. Death or disaster may come first.

It may not be possible even to start the re-planning process, for instance if new information becomes available during the course of executing some extremely dangerous and difficult sub-operation which cannot temporarily be abandoned or suspended without risk to life and limb. Alternatively, pausing to consider a new goal or to plan a different strategy may lose forever an opportunity to achieve the current goal, while the other could have waited. So, sometimes, instead of being done quickly using rule-of-thumb methods, a new activity may have to be totally suppressed.

Occasionally, the risk of ignoring the new information will be even greater than the risks of interfering with the current action, for example where the new information concerns some terrible unforeseen danger, or a marvellous unexpected new opportunity. Thus we see that in some cases the current action must not be interrupted on account of new information, whereas in other cases it is more urgent that the replanning be done.

In principle it would be possible to continue with the current action whilst alternative plans are synthesised and evaluated in parallel, in the light of the new information. This may sometimes be feasible and at least in the case of human beings is often done, for instance if you continue driving along a route whilst considering whether you ought to revise your route in the light of new information about congestion ahead. Planning alternatives in parallel with plan execution makes it unnecessary to interrupt execution.

Sometimes it is not possible to do both in parallel, either because the computational load required for both activities cannot be supported, or because the new planning process requires physical activity in order to collect new information or experiment with new tools, etc. A physical system cannot be in two places at once, and eyes or cameras or hands cannot be directed in two directions at once. Thus computational resource limits and physical resource limits may make it impossible to complete the new planning without interrupting the old action. But, as already indicated, this could be disastrous.

So, although in general actions need to be interruptable and modifiable, some actions should not be disturbed except for more urgent tasks. This suggests that concurrent monitoring needs to be supplemented with a 'priority comparison' mechanism which decides whether new information is sufficiently important and urgent to warrant interrupting current plan execution. This could be part of the goal evaluation mechanism, e.g. if every new goal is compared with currently active goals to decide whether they are important enough to generate an interrupt. Alternatively, if new goals are put into some sort of queue, it may be possible for yet another independent process to compare them with existing goals (Croucher 1985).

The need for rule-of-thumb priority comparisons

A problem with any attempt to evaluate new information or to compare new goals with old ones is that it may not be immediately evident whether the new information is or is not more urgent, since assessing the implications of new information, or comparing the implications of two courses of action, may itself be an arbitrarily complex task. If the task requires getting new information, performing elaborate deductions, or in any way using resources required for the current activity, then deciding whether it would be desirable to interrupt the current activity may not be possible without actually interrupting it! This means that the priority comparison mechanism must be capable of running in parallel with the main plan execution, just as perceptual· monitoring does, and secondly that it must be capable of taking resource-limited decisions. I.e. where comparing alternatives in detail would interrupt a high priority process, or where concurrently working out which priority is higher would take a long time, there must be a way of doing the comparison quickly, with the inevitable consequent loss of reliability.

An implication of this rule-of-thumb strategy for comparing priorities, is that sometimes the main action may be disturbed by this interrupt mechanism when it should not be. Elsewhere it has been argued that this is one source of emotional states in intelligent systems. (Sloman and Croucher 1981, Croucher 1985.)

The need for 'reflex' responses

I have talked about several processes that may be arbitrarily complex and time-consuming which go on in parallel since none has the right to dominate the rest. Several different forms of decision making are involved. But they are all relatively slow, involving explicit, conscious or unconscious deciding, or planning, or inference. In some cases the need for speed may be met by making the processes use the rule-of-thumb strategy. However, in other cases even this will be too slow. If you put your hand down on a red-hot plate, then by the time you have worked out whether having it burnt is more serious than taking some weight off your legs, your hand will be badly damaged. Avoiding that sort of possibility requires certain sorts of new goals to trigger action directly, without going going through any decision making process. These may be called reflexes.

Reflex triggering can be done in several different ways, including fairly direct electro-mechanical circuits which cause a reaction without any high level processes intervening, or the use of software driven interrupts. We could call these 'hard' and 'soft' reflexes.

A measuring device may be able to trigger an action as soon as a threshold is exceeded. The human body seems to have many such "hard" reflexes. Other reflexes may be triggered by the addition of some new assertion to a store of beliefs, or even by the formation of a certain description at a low level in the perceptual process. These "soft" reflexes may be the result of learning, or, more precisely, training, like the boxer's automatic responses to some of his opponent's movements, or the expert pianist's sight-reading capabilities, which seem to involve temporarily switching on a set of sophisticated reflexes. This sort of thing could be implemented using a 'software demon' mechanism.

The design of a system which allows reflex actions triggered by new information rapidly to take control, poses many problems about how to deal with sudden interruptions of a very large number of different processes at different levels. In existing computing systems it is possible to cause a process to abort completely or to freeze and go into some kind of 'break' mode for debugging purposes. But where the interrupt requires a complete new action to be initiated very rapidly, possibly including the control of several physical mechanisms guided by ongoing analysis of sensory input, then significant advances in AI and Computing Science will be needed.

Internal vs external actions

The discussion of the need for parallel monitoring and goal evaluation, and the possibility of interrupts and reflex responses, is applicable both to internal and external actions. For example, someone who is confronted with making a difficult choice may have a plan for thinking the problem through and may carry out that plan without performing any external action. Playing chess or trying to remember where you might have lost your bag are examples of internal actions. Monitoring of new information may proceed in parallel with an internal action too: for instance watching the clock while trying to decide. And the internal process may have to be interrupted if some new information turns up, like the discovery that making a decision is urgent whether or not the analysis has been completed. Alternatively, some far more important goal may be triggered by the arrival of new information, such as that your house is on fire.

Internal processing may have to be monitored too. For example, the mathematician thinking about an equation may have to be on the lookout for transformations in which she divides both sides by zero; and a plan synthesisor may have to monitor the consistency of sub–plans or the relations between the plan being constructed and the constraints, such as expense or resources available. If checks are made only whenever a complete plan has been formulated, the search for a good plan is likely to be defeated by a combinatorial explosion.

Meta-level motivators

There is a great deal more to be said about where goals come from and how they are compared. Some are subgoals of a prior goal and are generated by the planning process. Some are responses to new information, such as wanting to know what is happening outside as a result of hearing a loud noise. A full discussion would need to describe various kinds of motive generators, motive generator generators, etc.

Similarly, since not all the goals generated may be mutually consistent, and even the consistent ones may not be simultaneously attainable, various sorts of motive comparators will be required for deciding which of two incompatible goals should be rejected, or which of two compatible goals should be pursued first, etc. Motive comparators may themselves be subject to modification, or new ones may be created in the light of experience by 'motive comparator generators'.

Research is needed on how to design generally useful motive generators, motive comparators, and higher-level generators which can be thought of as one type of learning system (Sloman & Croucher 1981). Research will also be needed on types of global architecture which will enable such things to function in resource limited systems which need to be able to store and process enormous amounts of information.

Two sorts of parallelism

The kind of parallelism required for the reasons given here may be called macro-parallelism, and distinguished from micro-parallelism of the type supposed to characterise fifth generation computers. Macro parallelism concerns the division into relatively few, possibly quite complex sub-systems which compute in parallel and send one another messages, perhaps interrupting or modifying one another's behaviour. Each sub-system might be very like a single conventional computer, or it might be a highly parallel system with a micro-parallel architecture. Micro parallelism concerns the construction of very large numbers of processors amongst which any sort of programming task may be shared, for example under a data-flow regime. There is plenty of evidence that the brain uses micro-parallelism, though the processing units seem quite unlike the units employed in computers, including highly parallel computers. What may not be so obvious is that for the reasons we have been analysing, there is a need for macro-parallelism in animal brains too.

My own view is that for the design of truly intelligent systems it is more important for us to understand forms of macro-parallelism than micro-parallelism.

Conclusion

The space of possible computing systems is enormous and very varied, and we have barely begun to explore it. There has been some impressive progress, but overall the achievements of many animals and very young children outstrip even the most sophisticated computing systems of our time. Natural intelligence still shows many sorts of creativity and flexibility unmatched by artefacts. I have tried to draw attention to a type of flexibility which has not received much attention in the AI and Expert Systems literature, and I have pointed towards mechanisms which might help achieve it.

Current research is mostly concerned with the design of relatively simple systems which perform one sort of task — and quite rightly so, since we must learn to walk before we run, or fly. Sooner or later, however, the components will have to be assembled. There may be many different ways of putting things together for different purposes. We have noted some of the constraints relevant to assembling systems which are resource-limited, yet driven by multiple and changing goals in a fast-moving and not always friendly environment.

Some of those constraints point to the need for macro-parallelism and the ability of some sub-processes to interrupt or modify others. Some of the constraints imply that not all important decisions (e.g. whether a current action should be interrupted) can be left to the highest level inteligent processes: at the time such a decision should be taken, the high-level process may have been single-mindedly pursuing a task which does not expose it to the need for reconsideration.

The need for speed or the need to avoid diverting resources from important ongoing activities may enforce a rule-of-thumb strategy for many of the components, so it cannot be expected that such systems will always behave optimally. The experience of AI researchers hitherto suggests that when large knowledge stores and powerful inference mechanisms are available it will always be necessary to use fallible heuristics to enable decisions to be taken quickly. A system with so many fallible components in key positions may be expected to be almost human. The inevitability of familiar types of fallibility should be a matter of concern to those who hope that important decisions can be taken very rapidly by machines in the not too distant future.

Acknowledgements

This work is supported by a fellowship from the GEC Research Laboratories, and a grant from the Rennaisance Trust. The ideas have benefited from discussions over several years with Monica Croucher, and reading her draft thesis.

BIBLIOGRAPHY

Boden, M.A. (1977). *Artificial Intelligence and Natural Man,* Harvester Press and Basic Books.

Croucher, Monica. (1985). *A Computational Approach to Emotions,* Draft Thesis, University of Sussex, 1985

Simon, H.A. (1967). 'Motivational and Emotional Controls of Cognition', reprinted in *Models of Thought,* Yale University Press, 1979.

Sloman, A. (1978). *The Computer Revolution in Philosophy: Philosophy Science and Models of Mind, Harvester Press and* The Humanities Press.

Sloman, A. and M. Croucher. (1981) 'Why robots will have emotions' in *Proc. 7th IJCAI* Vancouver, p. 197-202.

Tate, A. (1985). 'A review of knowledge-based planning techniques' in *The Knowledge Review,* vol 1 no 2, British Computer Society.

Winston, P.H. (1984). *Artificial Intelligence,* Second Edition, Addison Wesley.

O-PLAN – CONTROL IN THE OPEN PLANNING ARCHITECTURE

Ken Currie & Austin Tate

Artificial Intelligence Applications Institute
University of Edinburgh
South Bridge
Edinburgh

ABSTRACT

This paper gives an overview of O-Plan - Open Planning Architecture. This is a prototype, computer based AI planning system. The design strategy aims to provide clear functional interfaces to the parts of the planner to allow for experimentation and integration of work underway in several aspects of knowledge based systems which together are an implementation of an opportunistic planner. The planner is part of an overall system for command, planning and control. As well as an overview of the O-Plan system, this paper concentrates on the control structure of the planner.

1. Introduction - the lead up to O-Plan.

The roots of O-Plan are to be found in earlier planning work on NONLIN by Tate [1] who investigated means of helping a user in the process of constructing project networks. In turn that work was based on the early hierarchical planner NOAH [2] which spawned a new generation of non-linear planning systems. NONLIN identified the problem areas of domain representation and the capture of the "intent" of actions within plans.

The problem of domain representation led to the development of a high level language, called Task Formalism, for specifying the activities within a task domain and their more detailed representation as a set of sub-activities and ordering constraints on them. A detailed plan is formed by chosing one suitable "expansion" of each high level (abstract) activity in the plan and including the relevant set of more detailed sub-activities. Any necessary ordering constraints are then imposed to ensure that the "effects" of some activities satisfy the necessary "conditions" before any activity can be used. The detailed descriptions of activities, called Schemas, describe how the planner should go about satisfying and maintaining each required condition within the schema by using "typing" of the conditions.

The main condition types are

supervised   satisfied by a sub-activity within the same overall
                  activity.

unsupervised   satisfied outwith the overall activity by some outside agent
                  (possibly another contractor working earlier or in parallel)

usewhen   satisfied by environmental information about the cases in
                  which it is meaningful to use the activity.

The capture of the "intent" of the actions within the plan was achieved by
a "Goal Structure" Table (GOST) [3] which records the condition(s) necessary for any action in the plan and the points in the plan where the
effects to satisfy the condition have been asserted. GOST records the
"scope" or "holding period" of these effects (possibly only one) which must
extend at least as far as the condition. GOST therefore provides a mechanism for the detection of interactions between parallel activities.

The O-Plan planner builds on the concepts of NONLIN Task Formalism and GOST
but within the framework of a totally new, more flexible architecture.
This paper will give an overview of the O-Plan system, concentrating on the
planner's control structure.

2. Objectives of the O-Plan Prototype.

O-Plan is intended to be part of a system for command, planning and control
of tasks such as project management, job scheduling and vehicle control.
Figure 1 shows how the O-Plan planner integrates into an overall system
comprising

- a "workstation", which is the interface between the various types of
   user (human planner, domain specialists, etc) and the AI planner.

- the O-Plan AI planning system and resource allocation module.

- the plan execution and monitoring system.

The prototype O-Plan is based on the Task Formalism (TF) and GOST concepts
introduced in NONLIN but improves on many features found in NONLIN and
other planners.

The O-Plan planning process proceeds by gradual restriction of choices in
the plan by the propagation of symbolic constraints (for example the restricting or binding of a variable in the plan) hence enabling some decisions to be made "later" in the planning process than in earlier systems.
This allows the planner to find solutions to problems would have had many
failure paths if choices of variable binding, for instance, were forced
without reason. The implication of this is that there will be more information in the plan about why decisions were made.

O-Plan also copes with planning in temporal domains hence requiring management of time window information (earliest and latest start or finish times
on activities), durations of activities and delays between successive
activities in the plan. Allowing time to be expressed in a plan's domain
clouds the definition of "beforeness" of activities in the partial order

activity graph ("procedural net" in NOAH terms) so complicating the recording of Goal Structure and the answering of questions about the facts that
hold at some point in a plan (in the question-answering module). The O-Plan
temporal constraint propagation algorithms (Bell & Tate [4]) extend those
of the DEVISER planner (Vere [5]).

Resource usage reasoning in O-Plan guarantees that a restricted class of
resource constraints are satisfied. Several resource types have been identified (Bell [6]). Of these, two types are handled in O-Plan: "strictly
consumable" and "single item re-useable" resources. Strictly consumable
resources are those for which there is an initial stockpile which can only
be depleted or untouched by any action in the plan and the management task
is one of guaranteeing that the level of the stockpile never falls below
zero. Re-usable resources can be reserved by an activity for a particular
time period, during which the resource is not available to others, but
after which the resource is returned to being available for use. Here the
management task is one of ensuring that the use of a resource by competing,
parallel activities do not exceed the amount of that resource at any
instant. "Incremental" approaches to reasoning about these resource types
are used in O-Plan. These allow up-to-date information about the validity
of the resource constraints to be examined after any choice made by the AI
planner.   Other types of resource management are dealt with after the generation of the plan using algorithms from Operations Research.

3. How O-Plan will develop.

The present O-Plan prototype, or "early" O-Plan, provides a skeleton for
further research and development. The following are active areas of
development in the prototype:

(i)   User Interaction or Manual Control.

(ii)   A rule based system for the control of the choices made by the
        planner (at its meta-level) to replace the present procedure which
        acts as the scheduler.

(iii)   Interfacing to various sub-systems, specifically information sub-
        systems and special purpose sub-planners (for route finding,
        geometric manipulation, etc.)

(iv)   The handling of scheduled and triggered events (for example, "the sun
        will rise at 6am", or "if A & B then C"). Events may be used in for-
        wards or backwards search to contribute towards the triggering or
        achieving of an effect.

(v)   Clearly identifying the planner's use of its underlying database.
        This work centres on the "functions in context" data model (Tate
        [7])*.

---

* The "functions in context" data model provides a data
store which holds entity/relationship data as statements with values which change in "context" and which
can be inherited in various ways. The basic statements
are of the form

4. Full O-Plan.

The "full" O-Plan design allows for dependency directed search and will   at
any stage retain only one solution (NONLIN and early O-Plan use a heuristic
search strategy and keep many partial plan solutions spawned at each   decision point).   The action on plan failure in full O-Plan will be guided by
decision dependency information, recorded at choice points earlier in   the
plan. The work is based on that of Hayes [8] and Daniels [9]. This will
enable the failed, singly-retained solution to be "repaired" to remove   the
failed components. Then planning will re-start by re-making a choice at an
appropriate previous decision point, allowing the planning process to continue hopefully to a solution. The planner will be restartable in the sense
that it will be willing to receive back a partially executed plan for
repair, and able to use the successful parts of the plan as the basis of
its new starting point.

5. Main Areas of Research on the O-Plan Project.

The four main areas of research and development on the O-Plan project are
obvious from Figure 1, namely:

(i)   AI Planner Design

(ii)   Domain Knowledge Elicitation, including Task and Goal   representation
       and User Interface.

(iii) Execution and Monitoring system and Replanning on Failure.

(iv)   Realistic Trials

The work and ideas on these areas will now be presented in the following
sections in sufficient detail to present a complete view.

6. Planner Design.

O-Plan is an abbreviation for "Open Planning Architecture" as the overall
design is intended to provide a flexible base for AI planning work. The
planner is being implemented as a co-operative venture, rather than the
work of an individual, so the design reflects the use of formal software
engineering techniques. Emphasis has been placed on independent modules
with a well specified set of functional interfaces allowing for rapid prototyping of minimally operating modules in order to quickly provide a

---

$$f(arg1, arg2, ...) = <value> \text{ in } <context>$$

The context mechanism provides efficient storage of a
(rapidly) changing database by layering alterations
made to earlier states of the database. These changes
can be fully or partially ordered within a graph of
layers, or contexts, of the database. The model also
allows for the retrieval of partially specified items
in the database at some point in the graph.

complete system. This modularity allows for experimentation within modules to achieve maximum efficiency, even to the extent of implementation of essential modules in hardware - at least one module has been designed with this in mind.

The design is data structure centred and at the heart of O-Plan there are a set of well defined data structures and some globally accessible data areas.

6.1. The Plan State.

The main data structure in the plan state is a graph of nodes reflecting the activities so far included in the plan, and a set of agendas which hold a list of pending tasks. Each pending task must be carried out by some method for the plan to be acceptable as a result. The current plan being developed and its associated information is called a "plan state". A building block of a plan state is the Pattern record as all statements in the database are of the form:

$$f(arg1, arg2, ...) = <value>$$

These are expressed in pattern form as for example in

$$\{on\ a\ b\} = true$$

Partial specification is possible within the pattern (except on the first, fixed word which is the function or relation) and the value hence the expression

$$\{on\ ?x\ b\} = ??$$

would be permissible and indicates that it will match any specification which matches the fixed words "on" and "b", the restriction on the variable "?x" and any value. Patterns occur in many different structures within O-Plan.

Early O-Plan employs three agenda lists which hold the following structures:

Agenda 0   As with NONLIN, the early prototype O-Plan saves partial plan states, along with the alternative choice(s), whenever a decision is taken in the planning process. These are kept on Agenda 0. Full O-Plan will record decision dependencies (e.g. why a variable was bound to a certain value to achieve a condition), to be used for the repair of the single partial plan state instead of using this alternatives agenda.

Agenda 1   This is the main task agenda, or posting area, for pending activities. These are operations which must be carried out for the plan to be valid. It may record failures to be repaired as well as normal steps to be taken to develop the plan to the level of detail required. Only task agenda records which refer to fully instantiated items (i.e. no variables) will be found on Agenda 1.

Agenda 2   The agenda for pending tasks which contain some non-fully bound
                variables in patterns. Only fully bound agenda 1 records are
                used in the planning process so the records on this agenda must
                become fully bound, by plan state variable instantiation, and
                then moved over to agenda 1 before being processed.

Other important structures in the plan state include:

- the detail of the activity nodes within the graph, recording temporal
  and resource information, activity type (normally "action" or "dummy")
  and pattern, and its successor and predecessor activities (to form the
  graph).   Start and finish time windows, resource usage levels and other
  constraints are held as (minimum, maximum) pairs of numbers which
  represent numeric bounds on the (possibly symbolic) values of these
  entities.

- Variables, which can be specified within the Task Formalism schemas to
  permit a generic description of domain activities (e.g. (put ?x on top
  of ?y) is a description of a "put-on" action for a robot arm involving
  any two objects). When the activity is used within the plan then a
  choice of binding or restriction of the variable will be imposed and any
  further use of that variable will inherit this binding or restriction.
  Variables local to the TF schemas which do not get fully bound when the
  activity is used appear in the plan state as globally accessible variables awaiting further restriction and eventually binding. An agenda
  record is posted to ensure that a binding is eventually chosen - if it
  does not get fully instantiated. This plan state variable may be shared
  and hence restricted by many structures in the plan.

- The agenda records themselves which hold an identifier and type field, a
  pattern record, type specific information (e.g. that this is an "effect"
  (on a b) — true to be asserted at activity node 5 in the current plan
  state network) and a scheduling information field for the particular
  record. Figure 2 shows this structure.

With the exception of Agenda 0 (which is only present in early O-Plan) all
the plan state structures, the values of items in the database and the plan
state variables are "context layered". In early O-Plan these context layered plan states can be very deeply layered with many small changes between
layers. In full O-Plan, the context layering will only be used for local
hypothetical exploration of alternatives.

6.2. Globally Available Information.

The domain dependent information derived from the Task Formalism has the
"schema" as its main structure. This is compiled into an internal data
structure which holds information about the way in which the schema can be
used (e.g. that it expands some action or achieves some effects), information on the requirements of the use of the schema and details the way in
which it expands the activity network when used. Resource usage and
activity time window information is also contained within a schema. Key
"expand" or "achieve" patterns within the schema are used to index into a
hash table for quick access to find relevant schemas. Schemas are also

used to represent primitive actions, which cannot be further expanded out, and also to specify the initial conditions, or state of the world, in the application domain.

7. Agenda Lists and the Dymanics of O-Plan.

During the planning process the pending tasks are recorded on the agendas. These agenda records contain task specific information, including the task type and scheduling information (currently based on the agenda type, choice branching factor and various heuristic estimates). Associated with each agenda type is a "handler" which can act on an agenda record of the appropriate type and process that record. In doing so it may change the plan state and generate, modify and record new or existing agenda entries. The priority of triggering of these handlers on a particular agenda record is determined by the scheduling information of the agenda records on agenda 1 and the type associated with the agenda record.

The agenda records themselves are therefore the mechanism by which the system is driven in a "best-first" processing manner. The agenda priorities put forward the "next-best" candidate which, at present, is picked up by a very simple controller which then invokes the appropriate handler for the agenda record type, with the type dependent information passed on as a parameter. Figure 3 shows the Controller Cycle of early O-Plan.

This approach has some similarities to Blackboard Architectures (e.g. see Hayes-Roth [10]) except that there is a difference in the dynamics of the problem solving process. Problem solving in O-Plan proceeds as a sequence of cycles, each of which is capable of generating new entries within the agendas. The handlers, or Knowledge Sources, are driven by the agenda records which hold the scheduling information determining the next best. The selected knowledge source then executes - possibly creating new, prioritised agenda records or modifying existing records. These events may even cause agenda priorities to change (e.g. by removing a record from an agenda, or by variable restriction or binding). This differs from full blackboard architectures in that they have greater flexibility on which knowledge sources are executable - changes to the triggering information being dynamically evaluated. However both systems support an opportunistic approach to problem solving.

The early O-Plan scheduling system is fairly rigid in its assignment of priorities to agenda records but full O-Plan will include a rule based system which will allow the scheduler to better reflect the understanding of the problem and how it relates to the applicability of the knowledge sources.

One interesting aspect of O-Plan's agenda record driven system is the ease with which the user can interrupt the process to take control. The cycle controller checks for user attention and adds a very high priority agenda record on to the agenda 1 list. This in turn drives the system in exactly the same way as any other record in that it calls a "user" handler or knowledge source to be executed. The user may then wish to query the system, control the next few cycles or whatever. Other handlers can also request user assistance by a similar mechanism.

The cycle controller also has the capability of adding agenda records to the agenda list via a "diary" mechanism, which may do things such as "print a representation of the plan state every 10 cycles" or "review the satisfied conditions every minute of planning" or even modify some detail of an agenda record (e.g. up the priority or prune a tree of suggested arcs to be linked into the activity graph).

Knowledge sources have the power to "poison" any plan state if it is known that no solution can be found from the current plan state. In early O-Plan an agenda 0 record would then be used to go back to an earlier partial plan state and to choose an alternative to the decision made at that point. In full O-Plan a "repair" agenda record will be scheduled to use the assumptions recorded at decision points and to repair the plan state to allow the planning process to continue. If a plan state has been poisoned and there are no further agenda 0 records (or no relevant dependencies in full O-Plan) then there is no solution to be found within the specified domain and given constraints. A solution has been found when there are no further tasks outstanding on agenda 1 (and by implication agenda 2), however there may be further solutions to be found if there are still any agenda 0 alternatives left.

8. Knowledge within Plans.

An O-Plan solution for a planning task contains more information than simply the graph of activities with perhaps critical path information. From the Goal Structure Table (GOST) and the related Table of Multiple Effects (TOME) it is possible to extract information about why actions are inserted into the plans, specifically the conditions they contribute towards, and where effects are asserted which contribute to the satisfaction of conditions these actions require. Also it is possible to query the "context", or known state of the world, at any point in the plan. Hence it is possible to play through, or simulate, the operation of a plan - the potential here is enormous.

9. Domain Knowledge Elicitation.

The human planner or domain specialists interface to the AI planner through the TF Workstation [11]. This workstation communicates with the domain specialists or experts to elicit their knowledge about the application domain or with the human planner to build a description of the goal task or to show the resulting plan. The aim of the workstation is therefore to provide a natural, ergonomic interface for the creation of the structured Task Formalism and the presentation of plan results.

The current prototype TF Workstation provides a demonstration of the functions to be included in the user interface. It provides separate regions for structured text editing, using a TF-knowledgable editor, and for graphical editing of activity orderings within schemas. Control of operations within this graphics centred workstation is effected by mouse and pop-up menus. Figures 5a and 5b show typical sessions at the workstation's main window when editing a schema and viewing results respectively.

Consideration has been given to the imposition of a requirements analysis methodology onto the user interface to impose structure on the knowledge elicitation process. The use of Systems Designers' CORE methodology has been considered (on an M.Sc project [12]) as this has much in common with the structures used in the present Task Formalism. There is a clear over-lap between knowledge elicitation for a planning domain and the specifica-tion of modules in a software engineering environment.

10. Plan Execution, Monitoring and Re-planning

Goal Structure is a high level representation of information about a plan which states the relationship between the individual actions in the plan and their purposes with respect to the goals or sub-goals they achieve. This information is used by the O-Plan planner to detect and correct con-flicts when higher level plans are refined to greater levels of detail.

Goal Structure also represents information on which an execution monitor can operate effectively. The Goal Structure statements represent precisely the outcome of any operation which should be monitored. If lower level failures can be detected and corrected while preserving the stated Goal Structure, the fault need not be reported to a higher level. The implica-tions of any propagated failure are computable and corrective action can be planned.

The techniques are equally applicable to the generation of plans and the monitoring of their execution for fully automated or fully manual situa-tions as well as the more usual mixed environment. Intelligent sensors can be instructed as to what to monitor and by when to report. Hence we are suggesting an overall organisation within which individual modules for planning or control can operate. We have published a paper (Tate [13]) describing the proposed execution monitoring framework.

11. Applications of AI Planning.

O-Plan is being tested via the development of domain descriptions in the enhanced Task Formalism for various applications. The automatic generation of plans for representative tasks is being undertaken in these domains. The applications of interest to us at present include:

- small batch manufacturing and assembly systems

- logistics, command and control

- project management (such as in civil engineering and software produc-tion)

- spacecraft mission sequencing

Early O-Plan has generated simple plans (of between 30 and 60 activities) in house building and software production project management domains. The spacecraft mission sequencing example will use the published domain description given to the NASA Jet Propulsion Laboratory DEVISER planner (itself based on our own earlier NONLIN system). This will provide an early realistic trial and comparative data.

We are also engaged in an Alvey Community Club project (PLANIT) to show the benefits of manipulating pre-existing plans. This will provide detailed information on three domains:

- back axle assembly at Jaguar Cars

- a software production project at Price Waterhouse

- a job shop problem at Harwell Atomic Engergy Authority

The PLANIT project will also be of value in providing realistic data on which to try out the automatic production of plans in these domains (a development assumed by the Alvey Community Club project).

We are also concerned with the specification of suitable interfaces to an AI planning system from higher level management, design and aggregate (or capacity based rough-cut) scheduling software and to lower level detail planners, instruction generators, resource smoothing packages, intelligent sensors and robotic devices.

12.   Conclusion.

This paper gave an overview of the O-Plan (Open Planning Architecture) project and the important concepts it builds on. These concepts are essential for domain and task description for input to the new planning system and for manipulating "knowledge-rich" information in the resulting plan.

The design approach, centred round clear functional interfaces to modules, was explained and an insight into the dynamics of the system, driven by the current plan state and its agenda lists, was given in enough detail to present a complete description of the system. O-Plan is currently operating at about the level of the earlier NONLIN planner although the potential which will be achieved in the near future will allow planning in more varied and realistic domains.

13.   References

[1]   Tate, A. (1977) Generating Project Networks, in IJCAI-77, Cambridge, MA, USA.

[2]   Sacerdoti, E.D. (1977) "A Structure for Plans and Behaviour" Elsevier-North Holland.

[3]   Tate, A. (1984) Goal Structure - Capturing the Intent of Plans, in ECAI-84, Pisa, Italy.

[4]   Bell, C. and Tate, A. (1985) Using Temporal Constraints to Restrict Search in a Planner. Third Alvey IKBS Planning SIG Workshop, Sunningdale, UK. Also in AIAI-TR-5, Artificial Intelligence Applications Institute, University of Edinburgh.

[5]   Vere, S. (1981) Planning in time: windows and durations for activities and goals. IEEE Trans. on Pattern Analysis and Machine Intelligence,

Vol. PAMI-5, No. 3, pp. 246-267, May 1983.

[6] Bell, C. (1985) Resource Management in Automated Planning, Fourth Alvey IKBS Planning SIG Workshop, Essex, UK. Also in AIAI-TR-7, Artificial Intelligence Applications Institute, University of Edinburgh.

[7] Tate, A. (1984) Functions in Context Data Base. Paper for the Second Alvey Workshop on Architectures for Large Knowledge Bases, Manchester University, July 1984. Also in AIAI-TR-1, Artificial Intelligence Applications Institute, University of Edinburgh.

[8] Hayes, P.J. (1975) A Representation for Robot Plans, in IJCAI-75, Tbilisi, USSR.

[9] Daniels, L. (1983) Planning and Operations Research, in Artificial Intelligence: Tools, Techniques and Applications (eds O'Shea and Eisenstadt).

[10] Hayes-Roth, B. (1983) The BlackBoard Architecture: a general framework for problem solving? Heuristic Programming Report HPP-83-30 Computer Science Dept. Stanford University

[11] Tate, A. and Currie, K. (1985) The O-Plan Task Formalism Workstation. Third Alvey IKBS Planning SIG Workshop, Sunningdale, UK. Also in AIAI-TR-6, Artificial Intelligence Applications Institute, University of Edinburgh.

[12] Wilson, A.C.M. (1984) Information for Planning, M.Sc Thesis, University of Edinburgh.

[13] Tate, A. (1984) Planning and Condition Monitoring in a FMS. Proceedings of the International Conference on Flexible Automation Systems. Institute of Electrical Engineers, London, UK, July 1984. Also in AIAI-TR-2, Artificial Intelligence Applications Institute, University of Edinburgh.

Figure 1: Overview of the 0-Plan System

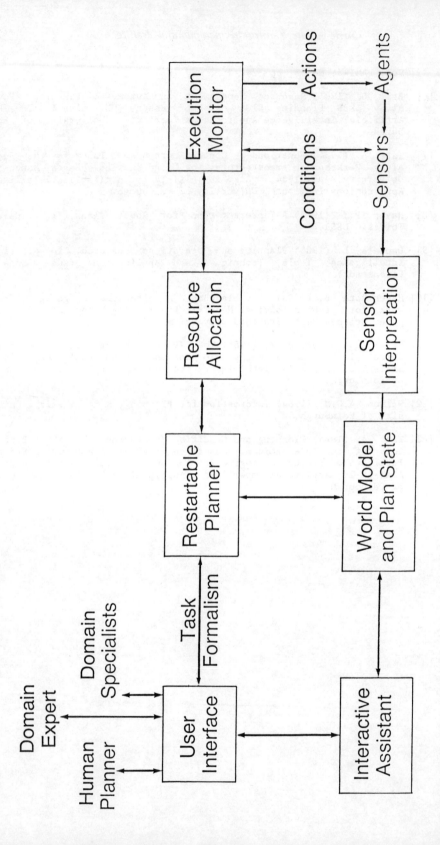

O-Plan Agenda Record

agenda identifier
agenda type
pattern/value/ variable dependency
scheduling information
agenda information specific to type OR list of agenda info

Figure 2: An Agenda Record.

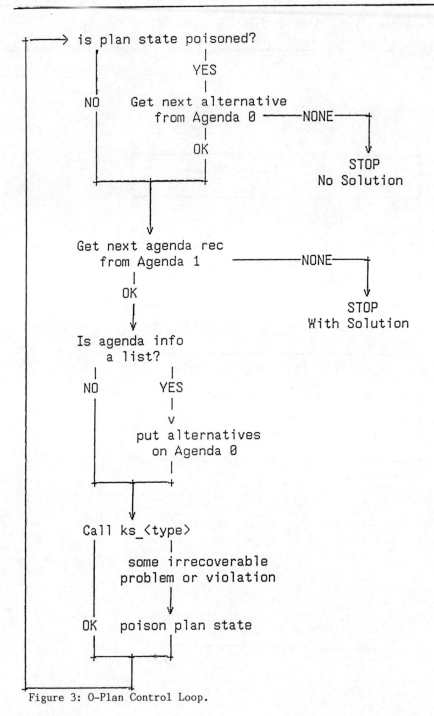

Figure 3: O-Plan Control Loop.

0-Plan Plan State

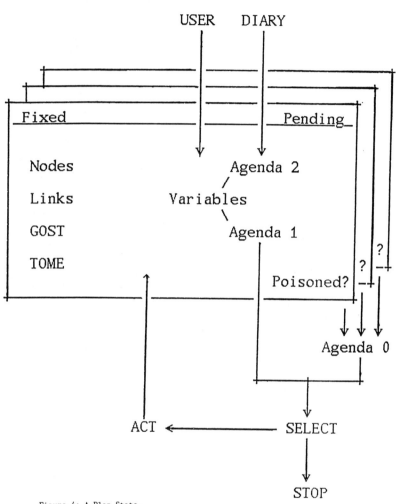

Figure 4: A Plan State.

Figure 5a:

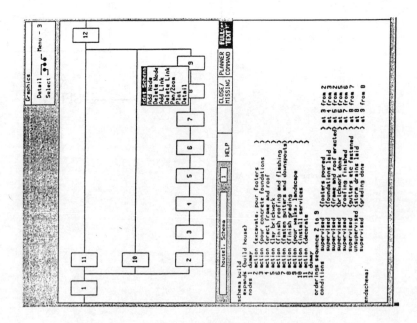

Figure 5b:

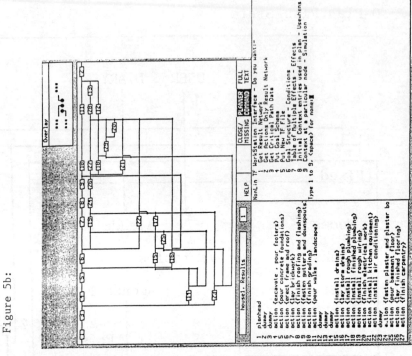

AN EXPERT SYSTEM FOR EFFICIENT OFFICE OBJECT MANAGEMENT

K.L. Mannock
C.H.C. Leung
Department of Computer Science, University College London,
Gower Street, London WC1E 6BT, England

Abstract. An expert system for the efficient management of
objects in an electronic office is described. The major
features of the system include the integration of diverse
search strategies/criteria, the use of conceptual and fuzzy
information, and the automatic classification of office
objects. The manipulation algorithms and organization of the
prototype Office Object Management System (OOMS) are discussed
in detail. The system consists of several interacting
processes which provide: a user interface of the window
manager/natural language type, an object identification
module, a query parser/optimizer providing template and fuzzy
language facilities, secondary storage manager, a rule and
concept based indexing module which incorporates non-monotonic
reasoning, and reorganization and archival facilities.

1. INTRODUCTION

In the electronic office environment a basic requirement is
for an effective and efficient storage and retrieval tool. In order to
retrieve specific information, the office system must provide the means
for searching the stored objects on the basis of textual content,
attribute values, concepts, document type and fuzzy values. There do not
appear to be any existing systems which can effectively cope with these
differing search criteria; more specifically, they require (i) the
identification of concepts, (ii) classification of objects, (iii)
integration with existing management functions, (iv) provision of fuzzy
queries, and (v) the ability to adopt varying search strategies and
inference mechanisms. In this paper we present the architecture of an
experimental system which is able to fulfil these requirements based upon
a synthesis of database, artificial intelligence and information retrieval
techniques.

Existing management systems have generally concentrated on at
most a combination of three out of the above five criteria. The principal
choices have been between the electronic filing cabinet [Seybo81,Seybo83]
and boolean retrieval approaches. Within boolean retrieval there appear

to be two main alternatives: (i) systems based upon binary signatures for the text (e.g. superimposed coding techniques (SC) [Rober79,Tsich83] and [Rabit84]) and (ii) information retrieval systems (IR), generally based upon inverted file structures and vector models [Rijsb79,Salto83] and [Buell81]. There have been attempts to utilize database management techniques, but they have not been able to substantially increase the system functionality, apart from the integration of content and attribute data [MacLe80,Kowar82,Crawf81] and [Schek82,Croft82,Porte82,Sacco84]. The system presented in [Tsich84] integrates text, graphics, pictures and audio and provides efficient searching mechanisms for text and attribute data [Falou84]; it does not consider the effects of contextual information, fuzzy queries or the use of varying search strategies, however.

Techniques that are based upon inverted file structures are unlikely to provide the functionality desired, although they are effective for content based searches (despite being somewhat inefficient with respect to space and time considerations). The clustering techniques in IR are based upon statistical criteria and therefore lose the context information [Salto78,Schko77]; however, it can lead to the development of appropriate synonyms and has been used in the automatic construction of thesauri [Mazur79]. A major difficulty with IR clustering routines is the need to provide either the maximum number of clusters, or the number of members of each cluster in advance of the clustering process [Harti75]. In [Salto83a] a scheme has been suggested that integrates the inverted file and vector approaches of IR. They do not however integrate attribute or concept data into their system.

The use of conceptual information has been investigated in the Cyrus system [Schan80,Kolod83] which processes selected news stories and answers natural language queries about specific individuals. The major differences when compared with our approach are: (i) the absence of any conclusive membership functions for the concepts, (ii) concentration on emulating the human memory behaviour, (iii) the indexing scheme and memory organization are not as concerned with the data management aspects. The basic FACT structure [McGre84] is quite similar to our own tuple structure except that their membership criteria and searching algorithms are much simpler as they are working with non-fuzzy data and they do not apply their scheme to modelling concepts. Mozer [Mozer84] has suggested a scheme based upon inductive search but the inhibition levels are purely numerical and there is no attempt to introduce conceptual information.

In combining logic and nets, the study [Deliy79] is prominent for its use of first order predicate logic and semantic nets. Other notable papers based upon net type approaches are Minsky's **Frames** based system [Minsk75], Generalization Hierarchies [Winog75] and Saaty's work on fuzzy logic and hierarchies [Saaty78]. A major problem with the implementation of any of these net approaches is the number of pointers that have to be stored, although they are obviously a powerful representational mechanism.

The notion of using fuzzy membership functions to model the concepts associated with various office objects is initially appealing on three fronts: (i) it is able to provide the grades of membership [Zadeh65], (ii) the fuzzy set approach appears to be appropriate for manipulating and constructing hierarchies based upon concepts [Mamda81,Wagne81], (iii) it provides a framework for the classification problem [Clanc84,Garla83]. There has been considerable research into fuzzy sets and logic, and [Robin81,Bezde74,Prade83,Radec79,Tahan76] are especially relevant to our problem. In [Buckl82] an example application is described where fuzzy methodology is applied to relational databases. There are objections to its use for concept hierarchies involving the semantics of the results [Smith82,Cohen84], although attempts have been made to apply it to such problems [Saaty78,Wagne81].

The MYCIN system provided an early attempt to reason with uncertainty [Bucha84]. For conjunction operations they used a fuzzy type Minimum function, and for disjunction a bayesian form. The major criticism being that it appears to be an ad-hoc solution and does not provide sufficient flexibility in its search strategy selection mechanism. The PROSPECTOR system uses a form of fuzzy set theory to manipulate logical relations, the fuzzy set primitives being used to determine a value for hypotheses constructed out of logical relations [Goasc79]. In the REVEAL system [Jones84] an additional data type is provided, that of the fuzzy set. The characteristic (or membership) function there requires the specification of three values: (i) the upper and lower bounds (standing for no degree and full membership), and (ii) a value that represents fifty percent membership. If a function cannot be represented in this way it is possible to enter a numerical value instead.

In the following sections we present the architecture of our prototype system and briefly describe its implementation.

2. SYSTEM ARCHITECTURE

The management system consists of a set of asynchronous processes that communicate via message passing [Byrd82]. The system is implemented on a VAX-11/750 running 4.2bsd UNIX using the POPLOG development environment [Sloma83]. The Natural Language Interface is written in PROLOG using an extended form of the basic grammar rules, whilst the Window Manager is implemented in C using the Curses and Inter-Process Communication(IPC) routines [Arnol81,Jacob84,Leffl83]. The Query Handler/Parser is written using a PARLOG implementation based on POP-PROLOG [Clark84] which allows "pseudo" parallel processing to be carried out on the rule base, thus avoiding some of the inefficiency inherent in implementations of PROLOG. The Query Handler optimizes the queries based upon heuristics derived from the concept hierarchy and knowledge base. The retrieval module is a combination of PROLOG, POP-11 and C utilizing the common structures of POP-11 and POP-PROLOG [Melli84]. The Grid File implementation of the knowledge base is being carried out in POP-11 but this may have to be changed to C in order to improve system performance. The separate modules are implemented as either (i) POPLOG processes communicating via POP message passing techniques, or (ii) by Unix processes using the 4.2bsd IPC routines.

The basic architecture of the system is shown in Figure 1. The Object Manager module coordinates the activities of the system. It communicates with the User Interface which provides a window type interface supplemented by a natural language interface (NLI), based upon a restricted grammar to a fuzzy language [Zadeh78]. There are two main modes of operation: filing and retrieval. The Filing module communicates with the Object Identification, Indexing and Storage Manager processes, of which the Object Identification module is responsible for determining the type of object and performing the decomposition. The Indexing process then extracts the appropriate terms returning the information to the Filing module which constructs the rules and entries for the concept hierarchy. A subset of this data and the source object are then passed to the Storage Manager which allocates and organizes the secondary storage.

The retrieval mode interacts with the Query Handler/Parser, Indexing mechanism and Storage Manager in recalling the relevant object(s). The Query Handler/Parser decomposes the query according to a combination of (i) a type of "query-by-example" interface [Zloof77] and (ii) the NLI. The decomposed query is then passed to the Filing module which interacts with the Indexing module in interrogating the concept

Figure 1. Architecture of the OOMS

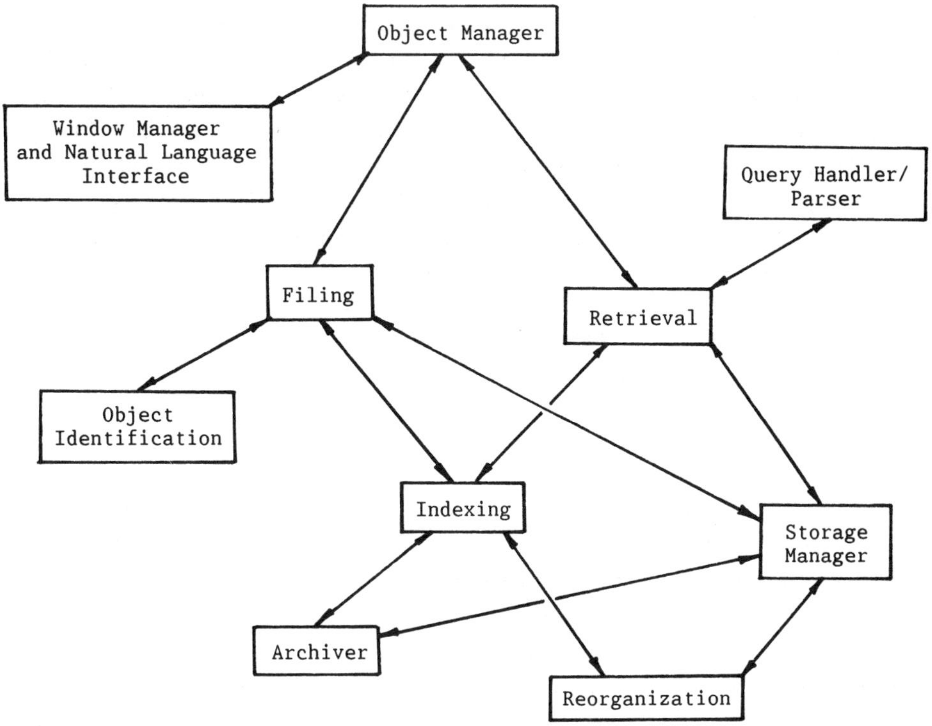

hierarchy and rule base; the objects are then recalled from secondary storage by the Storage Manager. As the query mechanism is based upon a feedback cycle the interaction just described is a somewhat simplified view of the actual operation but serves as an indication of the system procedures.

The reorganization and archival processes run autonomously with respect to the main system functions, although they both communicate with the Indexing and Storage Manager processes. The Reorganization Module is responsible for reorganizing the concepts and rule base whilst the archiver manages the ageing of objects and transition between storage states.

In the following sections the above components of the system are described in detail, with particular attention being paid to the storage organization, concept hierarchy, rule base and the associated manipulation algorithms.

3. MEMORY ORGANIZATION AND SECONDARY STORAGE CONSIDERATIONS

There are a number of criteria that have to be considered when designing the memory organization. It should be able to: (i) deal with attribute-based data and queries (e.g. the relational model) [Codd70], (ii) establish relationships between entities (e.g. semantic nets) [Tsich82], (iii) incorporate generalization and specialization information [Smith77], and (iv) enable the manipulation of data and meta-data in a uniform manner [Gibbs82,Ahlse84]. In our system we have adopted a structure that fulfils these requirements:

Tuple Id.	Object	Relation	Value or Object	Age

This tuple structure is similar to existing "simple" fact retrieval systems, most of which are implemented in VLSI([McGre80,Johns84,Azmoo84] and [McGre83,Marti84]). The major difference between our approach and theirs are the "age" component and the manipulation of, and semantics accorded to the structure. Our method, being software based, has to call upon slightly different techniques. The method adopted in our system is the Grid File structure [Nieve84] which is based upon the compression of a large sparse matrix and allows multikey access to records. The major advantages of the structure are: (i) an upper bound of two disk accesses for a single record retrieval, (ii) the ability to handle range and partial match queries, and (iii) it adapts smoothly to insertions and deletions.

3.1.1. Obtaining the Concept Terms.

A vital aspect in the construction of the system is the decision of descriptors for the objects. This problem can be approached from two viewpoints: (i) the syntactic approach which is based upon traditional information retrieval techniques and is effectively a statistical criteria [Salto78a], or (ii) the semantic approach which uses the context of the terms to decide upon which concept clusters the new information should join [Kolod83a]. The approach adopted in our system is a combination of the two perspectives, utilizing the frequency of terms in addition to their relationship to information associated with the object. The automatic term extraction process is based upon the algorithm in Figure 2. In [Yu82] it is shown theoretically that term frequency combined with term relevance is the optimal weighting function for IR; however, it does require relevance judgements for every

Figure 2. Syntactic Term Extraction Algorithm

Divide the text into words.
(The definition of a word being text characters bounded by space)

For each word in the text
   remove the text features (bolding, italics, accents etc.),
   ignore all characters other than alphabetics and digits,
   if the wordsize < 2 skip to next word
   fold characters to lowercase,
   if the word is in the stoplist then skip to next word
   strip prefix and suffix using an appropriate stemming algorithm,
   the resulting term indexes the document.
End

item in the document collection and is therefore not a sufficiently viable approach for our purposes.

     3.1.2. Concept Categories.   Once a set of index terms have been extracted they are allocated to the correct concepts in the hierarchy by posing the insertion as a query to the already existing structures. A bi-directional search upon the concept hierarchy is performed until a structure (or set of structures) is found that almost match the query, the differences between the query and structure then being used as a basis for storage. The main alternatives are: (i) an item exists with sufficient correlation that the incoming object can be stored there, or (ii) no item exists with those index terms. In the latter case a new node is constructed using the differences as the main indexing feature. When sufficient branches exist out of the same concept cluster they are then coalesced to form (possibly several) new cluster nodes, the information propagating through the hierarchy. We have treated concept clusters and objects in a uniform manner, so simplifying the traversal and concept verification algorithms.

     3.2. Storage of Objects
     There are two main approaches to the management of secondary storage for the documents (rather than the items and rules): (i) decompose into blocks consisting of text, graphics, pictures etc. [Wong82], or (ii) use an object format header and retain the single block structure [IBM84]. Here we have decided to use the latter as it simplifies the storage and retrieval operations. Within this approach there are various strategies as to the placement of the objects in store: (i) on a first-come first-served basis (sequential allocation), or (ii) according to some clustering algorithm. With the former, any information which may suggest that two

documents are similar would be ignored, and the possibility of reducing the number of disc accesses by anticipatory fetch strategies is lost (This is ignoring the fact that apparently adjacent locations in virtual store may be dispersed in physical store due to fragmentation etc.). Of the several different criteria upon which to base the clustering, we have used the concepts as they suggest inter-relationships between objects (e.g. invoices should be clustered consecutively according to number). This will either result in large holes being left in the store or necessitate frequent reorganization. We have chosen to use another grid file to map those details into secondary storage due to its flexibility and efficiency. The disadvantage of this approach is when accessing the object with a variable number of concepts, but as we are ignoring the importance factors of the concepts by using them as terms we can use superimposed coding techniques to circumvent that difficulty.

4. THE RULE BASE

A way to partially solve the uncertainty within data and query that is inherent in our application is to incorporate the physical nature of the relationship between documents and descriptors [Mozer84], which can be represented as a set of rules. A query then evolves as the set of terms stated in the query triggering various descriptors in the knowledge base. Those triggered descriptors are associated with various other objects which are "most likely" relevant to the query. If we then allow those documents to trigger the terms that they are associated with and continuely repeat that process, then the activation will echo through the system, as illustrated in Figure 3. This process could carry on indefinitely (or until the system is saturated), therefore some thresholds and inhibition factors have to be enforced in order to keep the system in control. This method is an inductive approach rather than deductive, as the resultant set contains information based upon premises that were not

Figure 3. The Induction Process

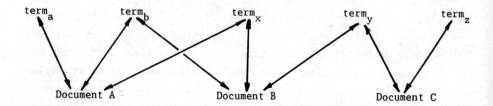

included in the original query.

-          If we extend the basic principle of induced retrieval to include concepts and their associated rules we have the potential to retrieve a set of documents that would otherwise not have been considered, thus improving the potential recall of the system. We also have to consider entry at any point of the concept hierarchy and traversal mechanisms based upon the inductive approach. Therefore simple backward or forward chaining strategies will not suffice. It is also unlikely that any one of the naive AI searching techniques (alone) will be able to solve the problem as the potential state-space is too large. It also does not correspond to the type of problem that can be solved by classification algorithms as they depend upon a fixed set of alternatives [Garla83]. In trying to solve this problem we are led to the use of fuzzy logic and non-monotonic reasoning within the concept system in order to control the inhibition levels (EMYCIN [Melle79], F.R.I.L. [Baldw83], Reveal [Jones84], etc). A mechanism for selection of the correct combination of strategies for the traversal of the search space is then required [King80] and our research into this area has suggested the algorithms presented in section five of this paper. From this analysis we can see that we require several different types of rule: (i) the fuzzy concept rules; (ii) the queries; (iii) the negation information; and (iv) object rules.

4.1.1. Fuzzy Concept Rules. At system startup a set of rules is specified as a guideline for concept construction. The rules consist of a membership function for the concept composed of various terms and possibility values. New concepts are therefore created once two concepts have a number of terms in common. An optimal threshold for this "merger" has still to be determined, so as an interim measure we have adopted strategies similar to node merging criteria in tree type data structures. Once a new concept has been created a new fuzzy membership function is formed out of the sub-concept functions (or basic term rules). Those functions are then altered to include a reference to the new concept rule, so reducing the amount of rule storage required. This also simplifies execution of the search algorithms by enabling the use of negations at a higher level.

4.1.2. Queries. The queries are represented as rules consisting of standard boolean or fuzzy operators in addition to various fuzzy language terms [Zadeh78]. The general form of the rule is:

query → (term$_a$,fuzzy term),boolean|fuzzy op,.....

and

$$query\_result \rightarrow doc_a, \ldots, doc_n$$

the amount of information to store concerning the query results is still
being investigated.

4.1.3. Negation.   In common with non-monotonic systems and
in contrast to traditional databases we integrate negations into the
retrieval process and effectively support different belief systems which
leads us into an open rather than closed world view of data [Galla84].
This approach means that we not only store facts that disprove hypothesis
but also cater for interpretations that deal with uncertainty [McDer80].

4.1.4. Object Rules.   Object rules are simply a shorthand
way of improving the performance of the inductive process as they could be
derived from the knowledge base but for efficiency reasons are stated
explicitly.   The form of a document rule is that of a fuzzy rule
consisting of the terms found within the document together with their
importance factors.   In many respects this resembles a document vector
from the IR domain:

$$doc(obj\ id) \rightarrow (term_a, weight_b) \ldots (term_m, weight_n)$$

The difference from the weighted IR approach is the way in which the rules
are interpreted and the integration of negations.   The importance factors
are then used as guidelines for the membership values [Lumle83] thus
allowing the correct importance to be allocated to specific terms.   As the
documents age, the object rules are modified by the queries that act upon
them, indicating the increased (or decreased) belief in the particular
terms relevance to the object in question.

5. THE ALGORITHMS

5.1. Search

The combination of search algorithms to traverse the knowledge
base (KB) are shown in Figure 4.   In each case the decision of which
search strategy to follow depends upon the presence (or absence) of:
attribute values, text terms, concept terms, fuzzy values, and similar
queries.   In Table 1 the search strategy selection criteria are shown.
The major problems arise when there are only concept terms present in the
query and they do not match any of the directly accessible features,
implying that an entry point into the system has to be derived.   At that
point the conceptual structure breaks down and some rather cumbersome
heuristics have to be applied.   The (present) alternatives are: (i) use

Figure 4. Search Algorithm

```
repeat

        if algorithm A or B or C or F selected
        then
             access attributes
             retrieve object numbers
        endif

        if algorithm A or D or E or F selected then
             access concepts
             set loose leashed level search
        endif

        if algorithm A or B or D or G selected then
             sift on text
        endif

        rank on fuzzy rules
        present to user
        modify query?

    until user satisfaction;
```

the concept terms as a query formulation on the textual content of the database (transform them using SC), or (ii) to ask the user for more information.

A fundamental part of this mechanism of interacting search strategies and algorithms is that the fuzzy rules (leashing levels) are continuously modifying the triggering criteria. In order to avoid combinatorial explosion search situations three basic levels of inhibited search are available: (i) leashed, (ii) semi-leashed, and (iii) unleashed, and they determine how the fuzzy rules are interpreted and how quickly the

Table 1. Search Strategy Selection

Search Criteria			
Attributes	Text	Concept	Algorithm Selected
x	x	x	A*
x	x		B+
x			C*
	x	x	D+
		x	E-
x		x	F+
	x		G+
all dependent upon the inhibition level of induction.			
*		leashed	
+		semi-leashed	
-		unleashed	

search is closed. There are three basic types of tuple: (i) specializations, (ii) concepts, and (iii) terms, and the search algorithm modification depends upon the combination of leashing and type of tuple, as shown in Table 2.

As with other information retrieval systems a dialogue is carried out with the user to determine the relevance of the material so far retrieved [Yu76] modifying the query in one of several ways:

- the user can accept a retrieved object (with or without comment),
- they can reject a retrieved object (again, with or without comment),
- they can refine the query so that it is more appropriate for their needs (which may mean that they make the query less effective as they have mis-interpreted the way in which the search is being conducted by the system).

This information is then combined into the query mechanism.

5.2. Insertion

The insertion process acts as a search on the document collection. The terms and attributes are extracted from the document and the importance factors are applied as membership values to the knowledge base. This leads to the creation of: (i) attribute tuples, (ii) doc-type tuples, (iii) term and weight tuples, (iv) document rules, and (v) an insert-query rule. The first four are self-explanatory. The last is effectively the document rule posed as a query. The primary difference between (iv) and (v) is that the former may have some terms replaced by concepts and can be modified (as described above).

During the insertion process several clusters may need to be merged as they are found to be inappropriate or need generalizing. This

Table 2. Leashing Criteria

Tuple Type			
Specials	Concepts	Terms	Leashing Level
x	x	x	leashed
x	x		unleashed
x		x	semi-leashed
	x	x	semi-leashed
	x		unleashed
		x	semi-leashed
x			semi-leashed

leaves us with two alternatives, either update the concepts in situ, or mark them as requiring modification deferring the operations for the reorganization routines. The former is initially appealing as in a dynamic environment it would be extremely useful if the clusters were consistent avoiding the need to check a list of "updates to be carried out" in order to confirm the validity of an hypothesis. The difficulty being the amount of time and space required to perform the modification procedures. The approach we have adopted is to insert the new details and to decrease the belief in the old data which has the advantage that inappropriate cluster modifications can be altered "on-the-fly".

5.3. Deletion

The deletion process is called in two ways; either by the user (using search and delete confirmation), or by the archiver. In either case it is debatable as to how much associated detail should remain within the system. A solution to this dilemma is to use a "dustbin" for all recently deleted material, and to mark the appropriate rules and clusters so that the search handler is aware that the information it is dealing with has no physical basis. The reorganization routines can then be used to "clear out" the dustbin, so that accidentally deleted material can be retrieved with the minimum of inconvenience.

5.4. Reorganization

The reorganization operations are delegated to two processes that periodically restructure the concept hierarchy. In many respects they can be considered similar to garbage collectors common in many symbolic languages, whilst avoiding the poor performance associated with those routines. They are essential to maintain system efficiency at an acceptable level and to check dynamic performance deterioration over time. The processes are chiefly concerned with: (i) clearing out the wastebin, (ii) reorganizing the concept hierarchy, (iii) maintenance of the grid files (where appropriate) and of the secondary storage files, and (iv) simplification of the rule base and maintenance of the belief systems. These processes are run as daemons.

6. SUMMARY AND CONCLUSIONS

We have presented an expert object management system for an electronic office environment. The architecture of the system consists of a set of asynchronous interacting processes which communicate by means of message passing. An Object Manager module is responsible for coordinating the two main activities of the system: retrieval and filing. The

Retrieval Module interacts with a Query Handler/Parser to produce a query derived from the template/fuzzy language interface. The query is then passed to the Indexing and Storage Manager Modules which negotiate a solution with the user based upon the concept hierarchy and flexible rule base. The Filing Module communicates with the Object Identification, Indexing and Storage Manager Modules to determine the object type and appropriate index entries and storage location. In addition, two reorganization Modules are run as daemons responsible for restructuring the concept hierarchy and refining the various rules.

The principal advantages of the system include: (i) the integration of a variety of search criteria, (ii) use of concepts and fuzzy values/language, (iii) the automatic selection of appropriate (and modifiable) search strategies, (iv) the automatic classification of objects, and (v) the attainment of high recall whilst maintaining efficiency. The chief contribution of this work is that is represents a concrete synthesis of Information Retrieval, Database Management and Artificial Intelligence techniques which has not been undertaken before; it should be of practical interest to expert systems architects and those engaged in the design and implementation of office automation systems.

ACKNOWLEDGEMENTS

This research on Office Object Management is supported by the U.K. Science & Engineering Research Council, under Grant no. 83303949.

REFERENCES

Ahlse84.   Ahlsen, M., Bjornerstedt, A., Britts, S., Hulten, C., and Soderlund, L., "An Architecture for Object Management in OIS", ACM Transactions on Office Information Systems Vol. 2(3) pp. 173-196 (July 1984).

Arnol81.   Arnold, K.C.R.C., "Screen Updating and Cursor Movement Optimization: A Library Package", Unix Manual Volume II (1981).

Azmoo84.   Azmoodeh, M., Lavington, S.H., and Standring, M., "The Semantic Binary Relationship Model of Information", Proc. of the 3rd Joint BCS and ACM Symposium, pp. 133-151 (July 1984), Research and Development in Information Retrieval.

Baldw83.   Baldwin, J.F., "F.R.I.L. - An Inference Language Based on Fuzzy Logic", Expert Systems 83, pp. 163-173 (1983).

Bezde74.   Bezdek, J.C., "Cluster Validity with Fuzzy Sets", Journal of Cybernetics Vol. 3(3) pp. 58-73 (1974).

Bucha84.   Buchanan, B.G. and Shortliffe, E.H., Rule-Based Expert Systems, Addison-Wesley (1984), The MYCIN Experiments of the Stanford Heuristic Programming Project.

Buckl82.   Buckles, B.P. and Petry, F.E., "A Fuzzy Representation of Data for Relational Databases", Fuzzy Sets and Systems Vol. 7 pp. 213-226 North-Holland, (1982).

Buell81.   Buell, D.A. and Kraft, D.H., "A Model for a Weighted Retrieval System", Journal of the American Society for Information Science Vol. 32(3) pp. 211-216 (May 1981).

Byrd82.   Byrd, R.J., Smith, S.E., and Jong, S.P. de, "An Actor-Based Programming System", Proceedings ACM SIGOA Conference on OIS, pp. 67-78 (1982).

Clanc84.   Clancey, W.J., "Classification Problem Solving", Proc. of the 4th Nat. Conf. on AI, AAAI-84, pp. 49-55 (1984).

Clark84.   Clark, K.L. and Gregory, S., "Parlog: Parallel Programming in Logic", Research Report DOC 84/4, Department of Computing, Imperial College of Science and Technology (April 1984), (Revised June 1985) To appear in ACM Transactions on Programming Languages and Systems.

Codd70.   Codd, E.F., "A Relational Model of Data for Large Shared Data Banks", CACM Vol. 13(6) pp. 377-387 (June 1970).

Cohen84.   Cohen, B. and Murphy, G.L., "Models of Concepts", Cognitive Science Vol. 8(1) pp. 27-58 (1984).

Crawf81.   Crawford, R.G., "The Relational Model in Information Retrieval", Journal of the American Society for Information Science Vol. 32(1) pp. 51-64 (January 1981).

Croft82.   Croft, W.B., Wolf, R., and Thompson, R., "A Network Organization Used for Document Retrieval", SIGIR Forum Vol. 17(4) pp. 178-188 ACM, (1982).

Deliy79.   Deliyani, A. and Kowalski, R.A., "Logic and Semantic Networks", Comm. of the ACM Vol. 22(3) pp. 184-192 (1979).

Falou84.   Faloutsos, C. and Christodoulakis, S., "Signature Files: An Access Method for Documents and Its Analytical Performance Evaluation", ACM Transactions on Office Information Systems Vol. 2(4) pp. 267-288 (October 1984).

Galla84.   Gallaire, H., Minker, J., and Nicolas, J-M., "Logic and Databases: A Deductive Approach", ACM Computing Surveys Vol. 16(2) pp. 153-185 (June 1984).

Garla83.   Garland, K., "An Experiment in Automatic Hierarchical Document Classification", Information Processing and Management Vol. 19(3) pp. 113-120 (1983).

Gibbs82.   Gibbs, S.J., "Office Information Models and the Representation of Office Objects", Proceedings ACM SIGOA Conf on OIS, pp. 21-26 (1982).

Goasc79.   Goaschnig, J., "Prospector: An Expert System for Mineral Exploration", pp. 47-65 in Introductory Readings in Expert Systems, ed. D. Michie," Gordon and Breach (1979).

Harti75.   Hartigan, J.A., Clustering Algorithms, John Wiley & Sons, New York (1975).

IBM84.   IBM,, "Document Content Architecture", Technical Report No. SC23-0758-0 (1984).

Jacob84.   Jacob, R.J.K., "User-Level Window Managers for UNIX", Proc. UniForum International Conference on UNIX, pp. 123-133 (1984).

Johns84.   Johnson, R.G. and Martin, N.J., "Triples as a Substructure for More Intelligent Databases", Proc. of the First Workshop on Architectures for Large Knowledge Based Systems, Alvey IKBS Special Interest Group, (22-24 May 1984), Manchester University.

Jones84.   Jones, P.L.K., "REVEAL: An Expert Systems Support Environment", in Expert Systems: Principles and Case Studies, ed. R. Forsyth," Chapman and Hall (1984).

King80.   King, J.J., "Intelligent Retrieval Planning", Proc. of the 1st. National Conference on Artificial Intelligence, AAAI-80., pp. 243-245 (1980).

Kolod83.   Kolodner, J.L., "Maintaining Organization in a Dynamic Long-Term Memory", Cognitive Science Vol. 7(4) pp. 243-280 (1983).

Kolod83a.   Kolodner, J.L., "Reconstructive Memory: A Computer Model", Cognitive Science Vol. 7(4) pp. 281-328 (1983).

Kowar82.   Kowarski, I. and Lopez, M., "The Document Concept in a Database", ACM SIGMOD, International Conference on Management of Data, pp. 276-283 (June, 1982), Orlando, Florida..

Leffl83.   Leffler, S.J., Fabry, R.S., and Joy, W.N., A 4.2BSD Interprocess Communication Primer, University of California, Berkeley (1983), Computer Systems Research Group, Dept. of Engineering and Computer Science.

Lumle83.   Lumley, J., "Planning in a Prolog Expert System", Expert Systems 83, pp. 63-69 BCS Expert Systems Specialist Group, (1983), Churchill College, Cambridge.

MacLe80.   MacLeod, I.A., "The Relational Model as a Basis for Document Retrieval Systems Design", Technical Report No. 80-96, Department of Computing and Information Science, Queen's University, Ontario (1980).

Mamda81.   Mamdani, E. H. and Gaines, B. R., Fuzzy Reasoning and Its Applications, Academic Press (1981).

Marti84.   Martin, N.J., "The Construction of Interfaces to Triple Based Databases", BNCOD 3, pp. 151-172 BCS, (1984).

Mazur79.   Mazur, Z., "Properties of a Model of Information Retrieval System Based on Thesaurus with Weights", Information Processing and Management Vol. 15 pp. 145-154 (1979).

McDer80.   McDermott, D. and Doyle, J., "Non-Monotonic Logic I", Artificial Intelligence Vol. 13 pp. 41-72 (1980).

McGre80.   McGregor, D.R. and Malone, J.R., "The Fact Database: A System based on Inferential Methods", Proceedings of the 1st BCS-ACM Conference on Information Retrieval, pp. 203-217 (1980).

McGre83.   McGregor, D.R. and Malone, J.R., "The Fact Database: An Entity-Based System using Inference", pp. 537-562 in Entity-Relationship Approach to Information Modeling and Analysis, ed. P.P. Chen," North-Holland (1983), from the 2nd. International Conference on the Entity-Relationship Approach, Washington, 1981.

McGre84.   McGregor, D.R. and Malone, J.R., "An Integrated High Performance, Hardware Assisted, Intelligent Database System for Large-Scale Knowledge-Bases", Proc. of the First Workshop on Architectures for Large Knowledge Based Systems, Alvey IKBS Special Interest Group, (22-24 May 1984), Manchester University.

Melle79.   Melle, W. Van, "A Domain-Independent Production Rule System for Consultation Programs", Proc. of the 6th Int. Joint Conf. on AI, pp. 923-925 (1979).

Melli84.   Mellish, C. and Hardy, S., "Integrating Prolog in the POPLOG Environment", pp. 147-162 in Implementations of Prolog, ed. J.A. Campbell," Ellis Horwood Ltd., UK (1984).

Minsk75.   Minsky, M., "A Framework for Representing Knowledge", in The Psychology of Computer Vision, ed. P.H. Winston," McGraw-Hill (1975).

Mozer84.   Mozer, M.C., "Inductive Information Retrieval Using Parallel Distributed Computation", Technical Report No. 8406, Institute for Cognitive Science, Center for Human Information Processing, University of California San Diego (June 1984).

Nieve84.   Nievergelt, J., Hinterberger, H., and Sevcik, K.C., "The Grid File: An Adaptable, Symmetric Multikey File Structure", ACM

Transactions on Database Systems Vol. 9(1) pp. 38-71 (March 1984).

Porte82.   Porter, M.F., "Implementing a Probabilistic Information Retrieval System", Information Technology Vol. 1 pp. 131-156 (1982).

Prade83.   Prade, H., "Databases with Fuzzy Information and Approximate Reasoning in Expert Systems", IFAC/IFIP Symposium on Artificial Intelligence, pp. 113-119 Pergamon Press, (October 1983).

Rabit84.   Rabitti, F. and Zizka, J., "Evaluation of Access Methods to Text Documents in Office Systems", Proceedings of the 3rd joint BCS and ACM symposium on Information Retrieval, pp. 21-40 (1984).

Radec79.   Radecki, T., "Fuzzy Set Theoretical Approach to Document Retrieval", Information Processing and Management Vol. 15 pp. 247-259 (1979).

Rijsb79.   Rijsbergen, C.J. van, Information Retrieval, Butterworths, London (1979), (2nd edition).

Rober79.   Roberts, C.S., "Partial-Match Retrieval via the Method of Superimposed Codes", Proc. of the IEEE Vol. 67(12) pp. 1624-1642 (December 1979).

Robin81.   Robinson, E.J. and Turner, S.J., "Improving Library Effectiveness: A Proposal for Applying Fuzzy Set Concepts in the Management of Large Collections", JASIS Vol. 32(6) pp. 458-462 (November 1981).

Saaty78.   Saaty, T.L., "Exploring the Interface between Hierarchies, Multiple Objectives and Fuzzy Sets", Fuzzy Sets and Systems Vol. 1 pp. 57-68 North-Holland, (1978).

Sacco84.   Sacco, G.M., "OTTER - An Information Retrieval System for Office Automation", Proc 2nd ACM-SIGOA Conf on Office Information Systems, pp. 104-112 (June 25-27, 1984), also SIGOA Newsletter Vol.5 Nos.1-2.

Salto78.   Salton, G. and Wong, A., "Generation and Search of Clustered Files", ACM Trans on Database Systems Vol. 3(4) pp. 321-346 (December 1978).

Salto78a.   Salton, G. and Waldstein, R.K., "Term Relevance Weights in On-Line Information Retrieval", Information Processing and Management Vol. 14 pp. 29-35 (1978).

Salto83a.   Salton, G., Fox, E.A., and Wu, H., "Extended Boolean Retrieval", Comm. of the ACM Vol. 26(11) pp. 1022-1036 (Dec. 1983).

Salto83.   Salton, G. and McGill, M.J., Modern Information Retrieval, McGraw Hill International Student Edition (1983).

Schan80.   Schank, R.C., Kolodner, J.L., and DeJong, G., "Conceptual Information Retrieval", Proc of the 1st BCS-ACM Conf on Information Retrieval, pp. 94-116 (1980).

Schek82.   Schek, H.-J. and Pistor, P., "Data Structures for an Integrated Database Management and Information Retrieval System", Proc. of the 8th VLDB Conf, pp. 197-207 (1982), Mexico City.

Schko77.   Schkolnick, M., "A Clustering Algorithm for Hierarchical Structures", ACM Trans on Database Systems Vol. 2(1) pp. 27-44 (March 1977).

Seybo81.   Seybold, J., "Xerox's Star", The Seybold Report Vol. 10(16)(1981).

Seybo83.   Seybold, J., "Apple's Lisa - A Personal Office System", The Seybold Report on Office Systems Vol. 6(2)(24 jan. 1983).

Sloma83.   Sloman, A.A. and Hardy, S., "A Multi-Purpose Program Development Environment", Information Technology: Research and Development Vol. 2(1983).

Smith82.   Smith, E.E. and Osherson, D.N., "Conceptual Combination and Fuzzy Set Theory", Proc. of the 4th Annual Conf. of the Cognitive Science Society, (1982), Ann Arbor, MI..

Smith77.   Smith, J.M. and Smith, D.C.P., "Database Abstractions: Aggregation and Generalisation", ACM Trans. on Database Systems Vol. 2(2) pp. 105-133 (June 1977).

Tahan76.   Tahani, V., "A Fuzzy Model of Document Retrieval Systems", Information Processing and Management Vol. 12 pp. 177-187 Pergamon Press, (1976).

Tsich82.   Tsichritzis, D. and Lochovsky, F., Data Models, Prentice-Hall (1982).

Tsich83.   Tsichritzis, D., Christodoulakis, S., Economopoulos, P., Faloutsos, C., Lee, A., Lee, D., Vandenbroek, J., and Woo, C., "A Multimedia Office Filing System", Proceedings of the 9th VLDB Conference, (1983).

Tsich84.   Tsichritzis, D., Christodoulakis, S., Gibbs, S., Faloutsos, C., Economopoulos, P., Thanos, C., Rabitti, F., Bertino, E., and Fedeli, A., "Design Issues of a File Server for Multimedia Documents", Pilot Project NR 28, Brussels (September 1984), First Esprit Technical Week.

Wagne81.   Wagner, W., "A Fuzzy Model of Concept Representation in Memory", Fuzzy Sets and Systems Vol. 6 pp. 11-26 North-Holland, (1981).

Winog75.   Winograd, T., "Frame Representation and the Declarative/Procedural Controversy", in Representation and Understanding, ed. A. Collins," Academic Press (1975).

Wong82.   Wong, K.Y., Casey, R.G., and Wahl, F.M., "Document Analysis System", IBM Journal of Research and Development Vol. 26(6) pp. 647-656 (Nov. 1982).

Yu76.   Yu, C.T., Luk, W.S., and Cheung, T.Y., "A Statistical Model for Relevance feedback in Information Retrieval", Journal of the ACM Vol. 23(2) pp. 273-286 (April 1976).

Yu82.   Yu, C.T., Lam, K., and Salton, G., Term Weighting in Information retrieval Using the Term Precision Model. 1982.

Zadeh65.   Zadeh, L.A., "Fuzzy Sets", Information and Control Vol. 8 pp. 338-353 (1965).

Zadeh78.   Zadeh, L.A., "PRUF: A Meaning Representation Language for Natural Language", International Journal of Man-Machine Studies Vol. 10 pp. 395-460 (1978).

Zloof77.   Zloof, M.M., "Query-by-Example: A Data Base Language", IBM Systems Journal Vol. 12(4)(1977).

COMPREHENSION BY MODEL-BUILDING AS A BASIS FOR AN EXPERT SYSTEM

Jonathan Cunningham
Cognitive Studies Programme
University of Sussex

Abstract. This paper describes how a program designed to build a model (in the formal logical sense) can be used as the inference component of an Expert System. The paper briefly introduces "model building", then gives some details of an existing program which does it. This program also includes features which form the basis for a non-numerical handling of uncertainty.

Keywords: Inference, Uncertainty, Default, Reason/Truth Maintenance, Logic.

1. *Introduction.*

Although this paper discusses a program which works with logic, it is *not* a paper about theorem proving. There are definite advantages to be gained from using formal logic as the basic representation language of an expert system. These lie chiefly in the well-defined semantics for formal logic, which would allow clean interfaces between the inference component of an expert system, and other parts of the system: the natural language interfaces and the control component. Other systems (such as automatic planning, or theorem provers) could also be cleanly interfaced.

Use of logic in the control component of the system allows the elimination of the ad-hoc numerical computations at present performed by most expert systems. Again, the well-defined semantics allows clear expression of exactly how uncertain knowledge is being handled by the system. This extra clarity will be illustrated by a distinction made in section 3.4.2.

This paper describes how a program to perform a certain logical task - model building - may be used as the inference component of an expert system. Model building is distinct from theorem proving, and this paper describes the model building problem in section 1. In section 2 the paper describes a program to build models of the kind described in section 1.

Section 3 compares the features needed for an expert system, and relates them to the existing program described in section 2.

1.1 *The Model Building Problem.*

This section starts with a very brief and *informal* description of the nature of a logical model. For a formal description of a model, see any introduction to symbolic logic, for example [Tap76].

A model, in the sense used by this paper, can be viewed as a small database. This database must have two properties: firstly, all the facts in the database must satisfy a set of constraints, and secondly, the database must be complete enough that it would be impossible to add any new facts to the database which violated the constraints without directly contradicting facts already present in the database. The contraints are expressed as logical formulae (full first order logic, as opposed to the restricted subset used in *current* "logic programming" languages, is a more expressive language than most common knowledge representation formalisms, so this is an advantage – for arguments in favour of logic, see e.g. "In defence of logic" [Hay77]).

To illustrate what I mean by "directly contradicting", and as an example, suppose that a database contains facts of the form "X is male" or "X is not male" or "X is female" or "X is not female" (where X stands for either of the names "Mary" or "Lesley"). Further, suppose that the only constraint is that someone can not be both male and female. Now, we will consider three possible databases:

(1) "Lesley is male"
    "Lesley is female"

This could not be a model, because it violates the constraint.

(2) "Mary is female"
    "Lesley is not female"

This does not violate any constraints but it is not a model because it is possible to add another fact, e.g. "Mary is male", which does not directly contradict a fact already in the database but does violate the constraint. However, it is possible to extend the database (2) to give:

(3) "Mary is female"
    "Mary is not male"
    "Lesley is not female"
    "Lesley is male"

This database does not violate the constraint. Facts such as "Mary is male" which would violate the constraint are explicitly contradicted by facts already present in the database (in this case "Mary is not male".)

With this informal definition, the model building problem is to take a set of formulae (constraints) and an initial database, and to extend the database until it is a model, as the example (2) was extended to give (3). Notice that it was necessary to restrict the possible values of "X" in the description of allowable facts, otherwise it would still have been possible to add facts to violate the constraints. For example we could have added the facts "John is male" and "John is female".

The set of possible values for variables is called the "universe". In a first order logic with only a finite number of non-logical symbols, if the universe of some model is finite, then the model itself is finite. For some sets of formulae no finite model exists – even though there may be infinite models. This possibility lends intuitive plausibility to the following (true) assertion "Determining whether an arbitrary set of logical formulae is consistent is not a computable problem (not decidable)".

> It is well known that only semi-decision procedures exist for first order logic. i.e. that it is possible to find a proof of a theorem if one exists. but that it is not a computable problem to determine whether a proof exists. Existing algorithms may not terminate for some formulae which are not provable. The assertion above follows from this, since if a theorem is not provable its negation is consistent.

Since the general problem is uncomputable, I have restricted myself to finding finite models for sets of formulae. For any given finite universe this problem can easily be shown to be equivalent to determining consistency in the propositional calculus (since there can only be a finite number of distinct substitutions for bound variables), and is therefore decidable. There are well known algorithms to do this, for example the method of *semantic tableaux* will find a model for a consistent set of propositions. However, the task of finding a model, even when it is known that there is a model, is NP-complete (i.e. it requires at least exponential time). Consequently, for the problems of interest, the search space rapidly becomes enormous and heuristic techniques must be used. In section 2, I will describe a program to do this task for formulae of a sorted logic.

The task of model-building must be contrasted with theorem proving, because although a conventional resolution theorem prover can be used to find model fragments, and this model building program can be used to detect inconsistencies in a set of formulae, the primary emphasis of the two tasks is different.

2. *The Existing Program.*

A program has been built to build a model to satisfy a given (consistent) set of axioms. This section discusses some features of this program; these features are referred to in section 3 — the discussion of using this program as the kernel of an expert system.

2.1 *The Logic.*

The program represents knowledge using a sorted first order logic. The difference between a sorted logic and conventional logic is similar to the difference between a typed programming language and an untyped language. The use of sorted logic allows a given problem to be axiomatised more concisely than in conventional unsorted logic, although it is necessary to specify sort declarations for the function and predicate symbols used in any particular problem. Even so, there is a net improvement in clarity and conciseness for all but the most simple problems. (The program is designed to work with tens of axioms, rather than a few. For such problems the improvement in clarity and conciseness is much greater than for only a few axioms.)

Sorted logics are discussed more fully in, for example, [Coh83], and the particular sorted logic used by the program is described in [Cun85].

This sorted logic is the representation language used internally by the program, that is, it is not reduced to some primitive normal form such as Horn clauses. All the usual logical connectives are allowed, plus some unusual ones (for example, there is a "partitioning" connective, see below). Most connectives are not treated as binary connectives, but have a natural n-ary form. Thus

$$(P <=> Q) \text{ and } (Q <=> R) \text{ and } (R <=> S)$$

may be written as

$$P <=> Q <=> R <=> S$$

If the propositions P, Q, R and S were themselves complex, there would be an even greater computational saving in treating the equivalence connective as n-ary. (Consider also the representation of the above expression in Disjunctive/Conjunctive normal form - even assuming the propositions are atomic.)

Function symbols as well as predicate and relation symbols may be used. This allows a natural representation of one distinction between "the" and "a" in English. Thus a Moslem might say:

Allah = god()

where a Hindu might say

God(Allah)

More specifically, the use of a function symbol is a convenient way to represent that there is only one of something.

This example also illustrates another unusual distinction made in the logic used by this program: there is a distinction made between *constants* and functions of no arguments. Informally, this distinction corresponds to the distinction between two kinds of singular definite noun phrases as made by, for example, Donnellan [Don66].

The constant symbol corresponds to a referential noun phrase, it refers to a known referent: in the program, the constant symbols are the same symbols that are used for elements of the universe. The symbol, used as a formal language symbol, always refers to itself as a universe element. This is a notational and implementational convenience.

The function of no arguments corresponds to an attributive noun phrase, it refers to some unknown referent. This referent must be one of the elements of the universe, but exactly which one is unknown until a model has been successfully built.

This distinction could be helpful in implementing a natural language interface to the program. This point is mentioned again in sections 3.1 and 3.5.

The formalism also allows use of a "partitioning" connective. Hayes [Hay79] calls formulae resulting from this connective "taxonomies" by analogy with classification. I shall refer to such formulae as "partitionings". The partitioning connective (like most of the connectives used in this system) is n-ary. As an example:

P I Q I R I S

is a partitioning of P, Q, R and S, where P, Q, R and S are boolean valued formulae.

The meaning of this example formula is that exactly one of the four sub-formulae holds (is true). If none of them are true, then the partitioning has the value "false". Thus we could have the following "taxonomy":

$$
\begin{array}{ll}
(x). & \text{Vertebrate}[x] \\
<=> (& \text{Mammal}[x] \\
\| & \text{Bird}[x] \\
\| & \text{Reptile}[x] \\
\| & \text{Fish}[x] \\
\| & \text{Amphibian}[x])
\end{array}
$$

2.2 *Program Operation.*

The purpose of the program is to accept a collection of axioms, and to generate a database representing a possible model for the axioms. The program takes as input a specification of the sort information needed to process the axioms, a collection of axioms and, optionally, some initial fragment of the model. Then the program works by ensuring that axioms evaluate to "true". Since a given expression may have different values in different models, it is not possible to infer every value in a model. So the program assumes values for some expressions, when they are not otherwise constrained. It doesn't assume a value for some expression if the value of the whole expression can be determined without it. For example, if, evaluating the expression:

P and Q and R and S

the program discovers that, say, R evaluates to "false" it is unnecessary to evaluate, or assume values for, any of the other sub-expressions.

The checking process is necessarily fairly simple (for efficiency reasons), so this assumption of values can occur even when, theoretically, the value is determined by the requirement for a consistent model. Consequently, it is possible to have two contradictory assumptions. In these circumstances, the program starts reasoning at a "meta-level" about the various assumptions it has made, in order to decide which of them to reject. When it rejects an assumption, a form of "reason maintenance" is necessary [Doy78], because the value of other formulae in the system will be contingent upon the rejected assumption.

For use as an expert system, as well as an obvious goal that the program should be reasonably efficient, there is a second constraint: that the system should appear to ask sensible questions. I will discuss the "sensible questions" constraint in section 3.

There is only one important requirement necessary to achieve efficiency: the program should not make incorrect assumptions. To avoid incorrect assumptions, the program can partly rely on heuristics, but must mainly rely on not making any *unnecessary* assumptions. For this reason, the program works in one of four "modes" of operation, switching between them as necessary. The modes are determined by whether or not the program is in a mode in which it is possible for it to make inferences, and whether or not it is in a mode in which it is permitted to make assumptions (thus giving four modes). Naturally, the preferred mode is the mode in which it is able to make inferences, but does not make assumptions. Thus the main efficiency gains could be achieved by evaluating axioms in some optimal order, and also by changing modes optimally. (If it is necessary to know a value for some term but the actual value is unimportant, then it is better to assume some value, which can only be done in two of the modes, than to continue to attempt to infer the value in one of the non-assumption modes.)

2.3 Meta-level Reasoning.

As stated in section 2.2, the program must carry out a form of reason maintenance. However, the reason maintenance in this program is performed by the model building process itself (rather than a "bolt-on" package): the system can switch to a meta-level copy of all its data-structures, in order to reason *about* the problem domain as opposed to reasoning *in* the problem domain. Certain procedures, most notably those controlling the making of assumptions, can access the meta-level in order either to add information (e.g. about a new assumption), or to inspect data-structures (e.g. to guide what assumptions to make).

At present, this mechanism is not used for control decisions, but there would be no difficulty in using the existing mechanisms for this purpose, and an extension to the program of this nature is proposed in section 3.

This meta-level reasoning capability seems likely to be most useful when more realistic expert domains are investigated, which involve different kinds of uncertain knowledge. For example, it may be useful to use "default" axioms before making any assumptions about the values of terms occurring in such axioms, but perhaps "uncertain" axioms should only be used after all other axioms have been considered.

There is also scope for generalising the notion of "model": for example, finding partial models using only the two "non-assumption" reasoning modes. There could be different kinds of axiom: those which are completely satisfied by a model, requiring evaluation in all four modes; and those only used to restrict the model for the first kind of axiom, and evaluated only in the "non-assumption" modes.

The exact status of any axiom would be represented as a meta-level assertion. Since the meta-level works in the same way as the problem level, this representation strategy allows for the status of axioms to be left undefined, and hence assumed by the program.

3. *Comparison of Expert Systems and Model Building.*

The task an expert system must perform can be seen as very similar to the task this model building program must perform. I consider each requirement of an expert system in turn, and relate them to the model building program.

3.1 *Domain Knowledge.*

It must accept general domain specific knowledge in a form conveniently specified by a human expert. In many earlier systems this knowledge is effectively in the form of "IF ... THEN ..." rules, that is, rules with some condition and a consequent action or inference, although these rules may be organised into a network.

The particular sorted logic used here is a convenient formalism in which to express expert rules. Any statement expressible in the full first order predicate calculus is expressible, so the system can accept information in a more convenient and expressive form than most current rule-based expert systems. It is not, of course, immediately suitable for use by someone unfamiliar with formal logic. However, it is a tractable research problem to translate highly domain specific natural language into this sorted logic and the task is made easier by the interactive nature of an expert system. There is a related problem here with natural language output - see section 3.5 below.

3.2 *Volunteered Information.*

It must be able to accept volunteered information about a particular problem within that domain. This volunteered information should be acceptable at any time in the "expert" consultation.

Since the program works by building a model satisfying some initial formulae, there is no difficulty in adding volunteered information to the model before building commences. Once the program is in operation it may make assumptions, either using defaults or as working hypotheses. Volunteered information can conflict with such assumptions, but this is no harder to deal with than conflicts between internally inferred data and assumptions. The existing program mechanisms can cope unchanged.

3.3 *Optional Answering.*

It must ask questions when it would benefit from being given the answer, but it should also be able to continue if no answer is available. Also, it should be able to accept an indirect answer. By this I mean that the user of the system should be able to volunteer information in answer to a question (as specified in point 3.2 above), and if this information makes it unnecessary to obtain a direct answer, it should not re-ask the original question.

In the present version of the program, certain "concepts" (actually, predicate or function symbols) may be marked as "askable". If the program infers a value for a term involving such a concept, it will query the user concering the correctness of this inferred value. The user can either confirm or reject it. If the user rejects a value, then some of the assumptions leading to that value must be wrong. Similarly, if the system needs a value for such a term, but lacks one, it will ask the user to suggest a value (the user need not choose a value, in which case the program will proceed as if that particular term had not been "askable").

3.4 *Uncertainty and Defaults*

3.4.1 - *at use time.* Answers to questions and volunteered information may be uncertain or incomplete. An expert system should allow this, and be able to make sensible use of such information.

The program already distinguishes between known facts and assumptions, thus it already distinguishes between certain and uncertain knowledge. It may be desirable to extend the range of possible "certainties" with which the program works. This could, if desired, be done numerically by associating numerical "confidence" values with the inferred and hypothesised data. A more interesting approach lies in using the system's meta-reasoning capabilities. This was discussed in section 2.3.

3.4.2 - *at development time.* The human expert's knowledge may be heuristic and even inconsistent. In particular, the use of defaults should be permitted. An example default rule is "All people have two legs", which could be disregarded in cases which were exceptions. An expert system with such a default rule should accept a statement like "Long John Silver has only one leg".

 The program distinguishes between two kinds of knowledge. The first kind, corresponding to expert domain knowledge, consists of "axioms". These are well formed formulae in the full sorted logic. (The program also needs to be given information about the sort-structure assumed by these axioms.) The other kind of knowledge corresponds to "facts" about a particular problem within the domain. For the program, this would be a specification of part of the mapping from atomic propositions and terms to the model. At present, the program only allows uncertainty in this second kind of knowledge, and it requires definite "axioms". The modification to the program to enable it to use default axioms, and uncertain axioms, is fairly straightforward.

 There is a real distinction between "uncertain" axioms and "default" axioms. The difference lies in the effect of discovering some fact (or assumption) that contradicts the axiom. As an example, consider the axiom "all birds can fly":

$$(x).Bird[x] => Can\_fly[x]$$

Suppose the universe contains three birds: an owl an eagle and an ostrich. What should be the effect of discovering that the ostrich cannot fly?

 If the axiom is (to be used as) a default, then we simply disbelieve that the ostrich can fly. It is as if the axiom is a concise representation of three separate assumptions: that the owl can fly, the eagle can fly and the ostrich can fly. The assumptions are unconnected, so discovering that one is wrong has no effect on the others.

 If the axiom is uncertain, then discovering one exception may cause complete loss of confidence in *any* inference from the axiom. Suppose we think it possible that "all pigs have wings":

$$(x)Pig[x] => Has\_wings[x]$$

We then encounter Porky the pig, and discover him to be wingless. This could shake our belief in the wingedness of the pigs Pinky and Perky.

When the axiom is quantified over more than one variable, the possibilities get more complex. As a further complication, we may wish to have a spectrum of possibilities between the "default" kind of axiom, and the "uncertain" kind of axiom. Alternatively, the "default" and "uncertain" properties can be considered as distinct notions so that, for example, if we know nothing about whether birds fly, and the first bird we discover is an ostrich, we may postulate an uncertain default axiom:

$$(x).Bird[x] => not\ Can\_fly[x]$$

The notions of uncertain and default axioms need further consideration.

3.5 *Explanation.*

An expert system should be able to explain its reasoning. By this, I mean two things. Firstly, it should be able to provide a justification of any conclusions it reaches (either intermediate or final). Secondly, it should be able to describe what inferences can be made from a particular piece of knowledge, and hence what use might be made of the answer to some question the system has asked.

Both these kinds of explanation should be in a form comprehensible to a human, although it is acceptable that the human has to be expert in the application domain in order to understand the explanation.

In order for the program to have a form of reason–maintenance system, it must record reasons for all of its beliefs. Thus, in order to justify any given assertion to a human user, it is able to refer to the rules, data and hypotheses on which that assertion is based. Ideally, a natural language description of, say, a rule would be generated from the actual sorted logic formula representing that rule. This would be in contrast to most existing expert system technology which requires an "explanation text" to be associated with each rule, although there are exceptions.

3.6 *Credibility.*

When the system asks questions there should appear to be some purpose to them. The system should not appear to be asking unrelated questions. This is clearly an important requirement when the system is being used by a human expert (and hence when a system is being developed), but I am not sure to what extent this requirement would be necessary if the system were being used by someone unfamiliar with the problem domain. (Would a person unfamiliar with a given problem domain be able to understand the point of questions a human expert would regard as relevant? If not, they couldn't be concerned by apparently irrelevant questions, since for them all the questions would seem obscure.)

Making the system ask apparently purposeful questions is perhaps the most challenging part of the task of modifying the existing program. At present the program has a very simple control strategy, and although a simple question asking modification has been added (mentioned in 3.3 above), that will ask a group of related questions for one rule, there is no control over how it chooses rules to consider.

I have already mentioned that when the program discovers an inconsistency in its hypotheses, it starts reasoning at a meta-level (using the same mechanisms as for the original problem). At this level it is reasoning about the assumptions and symbols used for the original problem. It is not until a consistent meta-model has been found for the original problem that the original problem can be resumed. Thus the making of an assumption is determined by procedures working in the problem domain but these procedures can access the meta-level database to determine how to make an assumption. An assumption can only be rejected after doing some meta-level reasoning about that assumption and its relationship with other assumptions.

The natural way to handle control questions in this framework would be for the control decision procedures to be influenced by the facts and hypotheses about the non-logical symbols of the problem domain which are present in the meta-level database. Since the mechanisms used in the meta-domain are the same as those used in the problem domain (implying the existence of a meta-meta-domain), there could be interaction with the user about the meta-domain. Also, the program would be capable of making assumptions *about* axioms from the problem domain. It might even conclude that some default rule should never be used! (Such meta-information, being about general rules and defaults, might even be allowed to persist from one specific problem in the domain to another: thus providing a limited learning capability. These issues are still being investigated.)

I conjecture that a good control strategy, if determined using the meta-reasoning capability mentioned in section 2.3, would also be "sensible" in the sense that it would tend to discover contradictions between assumptions as soon as possible, and hence to ask questions which were related. To do this well might require the ability to switch from evaluation of one axiom to evaluation of another axiom which had terms in common with the first axiom. At present, the program can perform this switch of axioms after doing some meta-reasoning. However, there is no clever method of determining which axiom to consider next: only simple heuristics are used at present.

The system is designed to allow its control strategy to be influenced by its meta-level reasoning.

3.7 *Joint Initiative.*

The system should be able to work in conjunction with a human expert, so that at one stage the system might take the initiative but a human expert could advise the system that it was working on an incorrect hypothesis, and the human could suggest an alternative strategy.

This requirement, for interactive operation and control guidance, is naturally provided by the strategy discussed in section 3.6. The meta-domain is concerned with the relationships between assumptions, rules and facts, and with issues of control. It works in exactly the same fashion as the original problem domain, so the requirement for joint initiative can be reduced to requirement 3.2 (volunteered information) at the meta-level. Notice also that every time a difficulty is encountered with the inference process at the problem level (such as a contradiction between assumptions), a consistent resolution of this must be found at the meta-level. This, as well as resolving the conflict, might very easily result in a different consistent model of the best control strategy for the problem domain. If the system described this consistent control strategy, it would be keeping the user informed of just what it was trying to do - in fact, the user could have been participating in the formation of the control strategy.

4. Conclusion.

It has been shown that there are definite similarities between the inference part of the task that an expert system must perform, and the task of constructing a model satisfying a collection of logical formulae. Whether or not the greater generality of the model building task must impose too great a barrier to efficiency of the system when used as an expert system is an open research question, although the results achieved so far have been promising.

References.

Cohn, A G, (1983), "Mechanising a Particularly Expressive Many Sorted Logic", PhD Thesis, University of Essex.

Cunningham, JL, (1985), "A Methodology and a Tool for the Formalisation of "common sense" (Naive Physical) Knowledge", PhD Thesis, University of Essex.

Donnellan, Keith (1966), "Reference and Definite Descriptions", Philosophical Review LXXV, pp 281-304.

Doyle, J, (1978), "Truth Maintenance Systems for Problem Solving", MIT Artificial Intelligence Laboratory Report 419, January 1978

Hayes, P J, (1977), "In Defence of Logic", in Proceedings of IJCAI 5.

Hayes, P J, (1979), "The Naive Physics Manifesto", Expert Systems in the Micro Electronic Age (ed D Michie), Edinburgh University Press.

Tapscott, B L, (1976), "Elementary Applied Symbolic Logic", Prentice-Hall

ACQUISITION OF CONTROL AND DOMAIN KNOWLEDGE BY WATCHING IN A BLACKBOARD ENVIRONMENT

C.D.B. Boyle
Department of Computer Science and Statistics, Queen Mary College,
University of London, 91 Mile End Road, London, El 4NS

ABSTRACT: *Knowledge Acquisition is a fundamental problem in expert systems. The JOBBES careers advice blackboard system is described as a learning platform. Learning in a hierarchical blackboard structure is investigated, methods for obtaining both domain and control knowledge are presented. Previous work has focused on the expert watching and debugging the system. The opposite approach is taken with a learning program observing the expert.*

1.0 Introduction

1.1 Problem

Acquisition of knowledge has long been recognised as a fundamental knowledge engineering problem. Experts often use more knowledge than they are able to explain during an interview, control knowledge [HR85] is particularly difficult to obtain. Methods of refining a blackboard systems rules by observing an expert are investigated.

1.2 Previous Work

The blackboard model is examined by Erman [ERM80] and Nii [NII80]. Hayes-Roth [HR84b,HR85] created the BB1 domain independent blackboard system capable of learning control heuristics with extensive domain expert interaction. Her approach is to have the expert watch the system and override any incorrect decisions. The program then questions the expert and modify its own rules. Wilkins et al. [WILK84] have presented a method of acquiring domain knowledge by observing the expert in a MYCIN environment. A modified and expanded version of Wilkins system is presented here to learn both control and domain knowledge while taking advantage of the hierarchical structure of the blackboard concept. The program is kept as transparent as possible to minimise the experts effort.

1.3 Platform System

JOBBES (JOb finding Blackboard Based Expert System) has been implemented as a platform system for experimentation with learning techniques. This is briefly described here as a prelude to discussion of the learning system. The author describes JOBBES more fully elsewhere [BOYLE85]. It operates in a careers advice domain receiving data on a persons interests and school abilities and suggests careers as output.

2.0 Description of JOBBES

The JOBBES system does not claim to be an accurate model of the careers advice problem. The knowledge used is based on data from Miller [MILL84]. The method of representing the task serves as an example of how to structure the problem in a blackboard environment. The approach taken here combines subjects personality and abilities to find an appropriate career.

Data arrives into the system at a primitive level and could be obtained by an unskilled interviewer or even the subject.

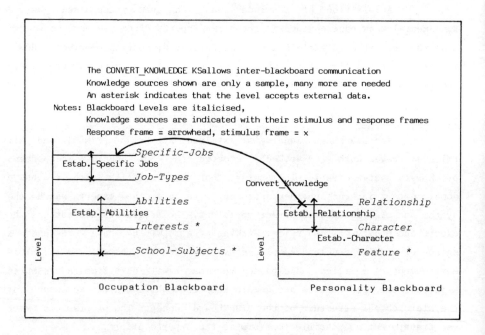

Figure 1. The Jobbes domain blackboards and example knowledge sources

2.1 JOBBES Blackboards

Jobbes has one control and two domain blackboards. Figure 1 shows the domain blackboard structure and some example knowledge sources.

All input is at a low level, either the Features, Interests or School Subjects levels. JOBBES is analagous to signal understanding systems such as Hearsay II [ERM80] which take only low level input and output a high level solution. The personality blackboard solves the personality problem which is a sub-task of the occupation problem.

The control blackboard is modelled on the ideas presented by Hayes-Roth for OPM [HR84a] and BB1 [HR84b,85]. This will be explained in greater detail in section 5.

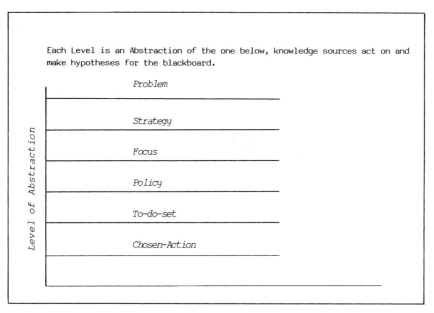

Figure 2. Control Blackboard levels in JOBBES

2.2 Knowledge Sources

Knowledge Sources are named groups of production rules deemed to belong together. In JOBBES domain knowledge sources exist to perform certain groups of tasks. For example there is a knowledge source which attempts to establish hypotheses on the ABILITIES level of the OCCUPATION blackboard, some of these KS's are illustrated in figure together with their stimulus and response frames.

3.0 Learning Environment

        The domain expert (the 'expert') is presumed to have no knowledge of the programs structure. Specifically no knowledge of the blackboard levels or any of the existing rules or knowledge sources is assumed. A learning program is under construction with which the expert communicates his reasoning processes. Each time the expert asks a question he gives a reason for the question (RFQ).

        The expert is limited to a restricted syntax and vocabulary, internally the learning program uses the following blackboard notation:-

B_{ij} = Blackboard i level j, where:

        $Blackboard_1$ = occupation

        $Blackboard_2$ = personality

        $Blackboard_3$ = control

Levels are numbered bottom to top.

P_{ij} = Primitives allowed within hypotheses on level j of blackboard i.

        P_{11} = [english, maths, french....]

        Lists of level primitives are given in the appendix.

        The blackboard levels and primitives are immutable.

Production Rules in the database have a left and a right hand side, representing the pre-condition and action respectively.

LR_iP = Primitives on LHS of Rule i

RR_iP = Primitives on RHS of Rule i

QP = Primitives in an experts question.

AP = Primitives in an experts answer (RFQ)

4.0 Domain Knowledge Acquisition

        Domain knowledge is acquired by watching the expert in action and comparing his performance with the system rules. The domain expert tells the learning program the first question he asks and what is hoped to be gained from the question (RFQ). These two elements correspond to the left and right hand side of a production rule. The Learning Program then tries to match the data obtained from the expert with JOBBES rules contained within knowledge sources. Data concerning the blackboard structure and primitives as well as the JOBBES rules is available to the learning program, the JOBBES system is not directly involved (see Figure 3).

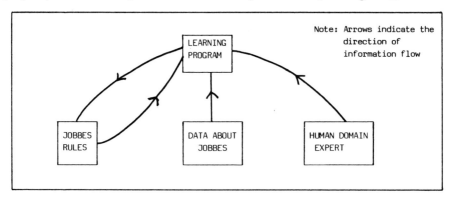

Figure 3. Structure of Domain Knowledge Learning Environment

After each cycle of inputting a question and RFQ training takes place. Five possible events may result:

a) Restriction : The experts opinion may be a restriction of the programs rule e.g. Does person take maths and physics ? is a restriction of Does person take maths ?.
b) Extension   : The inverse of a).
c) Different   : There may be no common primitives in any rule.
d) Contradictory : Existing rule is removed (both LHS/RHS) are required to prove contradiction.
e.) Same   : No action taken

Figure 4 is an action matrix showing what is done after examining the question and RFQ.

	Equal	Restriction	Extension	Contradiction	Different
Eq	Do Nothing	Replace RHS	Replace RHS	Quiz User/Replace	Add RHS
Re	Replace LHS	Replace LHS/RHS	Replace LHS/RHS	QUiz User/Replace	Replace LHS Add RHS
Ex	Replace LHS	Replace LHS/RHS	Replace LHS/RHS	Quiz User/Replace	Replace LHS Add RHS
Co	Quiz User	Quiz User	Quiz User	-	-
Di	Add LHS	Replace/Add	Replace/Add	-	Add new Rule

Figure 4. Action Matrix for Domain Knowledge Acquisition

4.1 An Example

This example shows how the action matrix can be applied. Only questions of the form: "Does the person take/have/" [primitive] are allowed. Only positive instances of the RFQ are used. The blackboard and rules described in the appendix are used and should be referred to while reading this section.

Let Q = Expert question
    QP = Primitives in Expert Question.

The experts statements are italicised, Primitives are underlined.

Q: Does the person take maths ?
    QP = maths
    LR_1P = maths, computing, chemistry
    LR_2P = maths, climbing
    LR_3P = scientific
    LR_4P = scientific
    LR_5P = woodwork, metalwork LR_6P = technical
    QP $\in LR_1$ only (since $QP_1 = LR_1P_1$)

RFQ: Person should take a scientific job
    AP = scientific
    RR_1P = scientific
    RR_4P = outdoor, scientific
    RR_3P = computer-programmer
    RR_4P = computer-operator
    RR_5P = technical
    RR_6P = welder, carpenter

    AP = RR_1

using the action matrix we can add a new rule trigger. In the next question/RFQ pair all the rules are not listed, they are the same as above.

Q: Does the person take English and French ?

    QP = English, French
    QP $\in LR_iP$ [i = 1..6]

RFQ: Person should go into teaching

    AP = Teaching
    AP $\in RR_iP$ [i = 1..6]

The action matrix says that a complete new domain rule needs to be added since neither the LHS or RHS were known.

5.0 Control Knowledge Acquistion

The previous section detailed how the systems domain knowledge could be learned. A more complex method has been devised for acquiring high level control knowledge by observation. This takes advantage of the hierarchical blackboard structure. In jobbes control knowledge exists on several levels, these are summarised as follows:

```
PROBLEM          : The actual problem to be solved
STRATEGY         : Sequential Problem solving strategy.
FOCUS            : Level or group of levels being concentrated on.
POLICY           : Specific decision on which attribute of  a  certain
                   level to work on.
TO-DO-SET        : Set of eligible knowledge sources.
CHOSEN-ACTION    : Knowledge Source scheduled for execution
```

Strategy rules of the type "Establish academic ability before job-type" can be learned by observing the experts low level actions.   High level control knowledge is of particular interest because of the difficulty in learning as reported by Hayes-Roth [HR84,HR85].   Only the Strategy, Focus and Chosen-Action levels are required.

5.1 Overview of the Strategy Learning Process

A record is made of each action taken by the domain expert in the form of a control vector which has the following attributes:

(lhs/rhs, cycle_number, action-primitives, action-levels, score)

These actions are noted in a database and inferences about control knowledge can be asserted. Only the essential data of the experts activities is remembered in the control vector, this is in terms of the various levels and primitives that exist in the blackboard. The expert activities are made up of a question and reason for question (RFQ).

The question : Does the person like maths and climbing ? on cycle 1 would be recorded in the following manner:

(LHS,1,(explicit primitive climbing) (implicit level interests))

(LHS,1,(explicit primitive maths)   (implicit level school-subjects))

Inferences about the control rules of the database can be made by taking advantage of the hierarchy, for example:

Chosen Action Level

      CHOSEN-ACTION is : go for rules with climbing as a pre-condition.

      CHOSEN-ACTION is : go for rules with maths as a pre-condition.

Focus Level

      FOCUS is : go for rules with pre-conditions on the interests level.

      FOCUS is : go for rules with pre-conditions on the school subjects level.

Strategy Level

      STRATEGY is Concentrate on domain rules with low level pre-conditions.

Each control level inference is an abstraction of the one beneath it. A single statement allows inferences to be made about the experts control knowledge at all three levels. Intuitively this method is reliable at the lower level, i.e. CHOSEN-ACTION and less reliable at the strategy level, since there has not yet been enough information to build a picture of the overall problem solving strategy. The more data that reaches the database then the more reliable inferences can be at the higher levels.

Note that the low levels are the most volatile, the chosen-action changes every cycle or so, whereas the strategy may remain the same during the whole problem solving process. This makes it easier to infer higher level control concepts because the domain experts high level goals remain constant for a large amount of time enabling information to be built up over this period.

The relative volatility of different levels of control knowledge is illustrated in Figure 5. An experts strategy changes rarely, his focus and chosen action alter more frequently.   New control rules may be created which the expert was unable to articulate during the conventional knowledge acquisition stage of system building. The expert might not even be consciously aware of rules uncovered by the program. Wherever possible the program attempts to match the systems inherent control knowledge with that being determined.

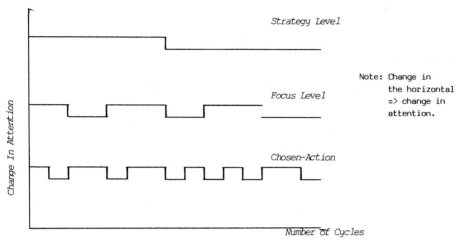

Figure 5. Volatility of Control Knowledge Hierarchy

5.2 Control Rule Combination

Control knowledge is acquired during a training cycle which is the candidates problem solving process. The <u>control state</u> iteratively evolves being modified by the <u>control vector</u> after each cycle. The following formula represents the learning cycle:-

$$S_n = CV_n * S_{n-1}$$

Where '*' is the combination operator. S_n is the control state after cycle n. CV_n is the control vector for cycle n. Both S_n and CV_n are stored in terms of the triple (S,F,C) where S = Strategy rule etc. Combination is defined in Table 1.

(i)	X * Y = X	if X=Y for S
(ii)	X * Y = ∅	if X <> Y for C
(iii)	X * Y = Z	if (X,Y) ∈ Z for F
(iv)	X * Y = X	if X<>Y and (X,Y) ∉ Z for F
(v)	X * Y = XY	if X<>Y and (X,Y) ∉ Z for S
(vi)	X * Y = Y	if X = ∅ for S

Table 1. Combination rules for Control Knowledge

Where : X,Y $\in$ (S,F,C)

Z = set of elements in (S,C,F) for example, low levels = school-subjects and interests.

CHOSEN-ACTION rules usually change after each cycle. FOCUS rules tend to last longer since an actual level or group of levels are being operated on. Pre-determined information about level groupings are known to the system. STRATEGY rules are modified whenever the focus changes.

5.3 Sample rule creation session

This section shows how control knowledge is created by observing a domain expert at work. The example is kept as small because of the complexity of the system.

The blackboard levels and rules described in appendix 1. are used for this example. For simplicity only the RFQ will be used for control inferences. The RFQ is more valuable than the pre-condition because it is goal oriented. Comparison with existing control and domain rules is also ignored, learning/comparison of domain knowledge and would have been as in section 4. Italics denote domain expert conversation:

Initially: $S_0 = \emptyset$

Q1 : Does the person like climbing ?
RFQ1 : If true then the person might like an outdoor job.

CV_1 = (RHS,1,(explicit primitive outdoor) (implicit level job-types))
        translated into the (S,F,C) triple :-
    = CHOSEN-ACTION is : go for rules with outdoor as an action
      FOCUS is : go for rules which act on the job-types level.
      STRATEGY is : go for rules which act on the job-types level.

$(S,F,P)_1 = CV_1 * (S,F,P)_0$
          $= CV_1$

Q2: Is the person good at mathematics and computing ?
RFQ2 : If true then the person might like a scientific job

CV_2 = (RHS,2,(explicit primitive scientific) (implicit level job-types))

   = CHOSEN-ACTION is : go for rules with scientific as an action.
     FOCUS is : go for rules which act on the job-types level.
     STRATEGY : go for rules which act on the job-types level

Combining the information from RFQl and RFQ2 ($CV_2 * S_1$) we have S_2 :-

  CHOSEN-ACTION is Ø
  FOCUS is : go for rules which act on the job types level
  STRATEGY is : go for rules which act on the job types level.

Q3: Does the person like <u>outdoor</u> work and can he do a <u>scientific</u> job ?

RFQ3 : If true then the person could be an <u>engineer</u>.

CV_3 = (RHS,3, (explicit primitive engineer) (implicit level specific-jobs))

   = CHOSEN-ACTION is : go for rules with engineer as an action.
     FOCUS is : go for rules acting on the specific-jobs level
     STRATEGY : go for rules acting on the specific jobs level.

There is change in all three levels, chosen-action is expected to change from cycle to cycle. Strategy changes gradually, for it to change a <u>turning point</u> in the state of the blackboard must have occurred. Combining the combined results from RFQ2 and RFQ3 we get S_3:-

  CHOSEN-ACTION is : Ø
  FOCUS is   : go for rules acting on the specific-jobs level
  STRATEGY   : FOCUS on rules which act on the job-types level then
                  FOCUS on rules acting on the specific-jobs level.

The STRATEGY rule can be strengthened noting that the job-types level was focused upon for two successful (successful=> ANS = yes) cycles, i.e. -

STRATEGY : FOCUS on rules which act on the job-types level for two successful cycles THEN FOCUS on rules acting on the specific-jobs level.

Data for a new high level strategy rule has been learned, it can be made more specific but the detail may have to be altered with further training. The degree of specificity allowed is currently being investigated.

Other new rules can be implemented hierarchically. The first part of the strategy, "focus on job-types level" creates a corresponding focus rule which can itself create new chosen-action rules. The further down the control hierarchy we are then the more specific the rules and are inherently less reliable.

5.4 Weaknesses

Weaknesses with the learning by observation method of control knowledge include :-

a) Changes in focus form <u>turning points</u> in Strategy limit the variety of knowledge that can be learned

b) Limited Acceptable Grammar for Expert Question and RFQ.

c) 'Bad' strategies may be acquired, if the expert follows a long and inefficient line of reasoning then this will still be learned.

d) Insufficient data is contained within the control state to create a full rule - i.e. there is no English explanation of the rationale or goals of the rule which the system could present if asked to explain its reasoning.

e) A significant amount of time is still required for communication between the system and expert.

6.0 Conclusion

The JOBBES system operates in a careers advice domain and acts as a platform for a learning system. The learning program uses techniques not previously applied to blackboard systems and takes advantage of the inherent hierarchical structure. Work is currently in progress to improve the methods given.

References

[BOYLE85] C.D.B. Boyle, An Introduction to the Jobbes system, Dept. of Computer
           Science, Queen Mary College, 1985

[ERM80]   : L.D. Erman, V. Lesser, D.R. Reddy, F. Hayes-Roth "The Hearsay II
            Speech Understanding System: Integrating Knowledge to resolve
            uncertainty", Computing Surveys, p.214-253, 1980.

[HR84a]   : Barbara Hayes-Roth, "A blackboard model of control" HPP-83-38,
            Stanford, August 1984

[HR84b]   : Barbara Hayes-Roth "BB1: An architecture for blackboard systems that
            control explain and learn about their own behaviour", HPP-84-16,
            Stanford, December 1984

[HR85]   : Barbara Hayes-Roth, M. Hewett, "Learning Control Heuristics in BB1",
            HPP-85-2, Stanford, 1985

[MILL84] : Ruth Miller and Anna Alstion "Equal Opportunities a careers guide",
            Penguin Books, 1984

[NII80]   : H. Penny Nii, "An introduction to the Blackboard Model, Knowledge
            Engineering and Age": HPP-80-29, Stanford, March 1980

[WILK84] : D.C. Wilkins, B.G. Buchanan, W.J. Clancey, "Inferring an experts
            reasoning by Watching", HPP-84-29, Stanford, June 1984

APPENDIX

Occupation Blackboard Levels:-

specific-jobs   level 5 (top level)

job-types   level 4

abilities   level 3

interests   level 2

school-subjects   level 1

Personality Blackboard Levels:-

relationship   level 3

character   level 2

feature   level 1

Assume a 'standard' control blackboard with the following levels:

problem   level 6 (top level)

strategy   level 5

focus   level 4

policy   level 3

to do set   level 2

chosen action   level 1

Domain Rules known to the unrefined Jobbes System

R1: IF (school-subjects = [MATHS, COMPUTING, CHEMISTRY])
    THEN job-type is SCIENTIFIC with score average of school-subjects scores.

R2: IF (good at maths) and (likes climbing)
    THEn JOB-TYPE =(OUTDOOR, SCIENTIFIC)

R3: IF (job-type = SCIENTIFIC) AND (score > 60)
    THEN SPECIFIC-JOB = computer-programmer

R4: IF (job-type = SCIENTIFIC) AND (score < 60)
    THEN SPECIFIC-JOB = computer-operator

R5: IF (school-subjects = [WOODWORK, METALWORK]
    THEN job-type = TECHNICAL

R6: IF job-type = TECHNICAL
    THEN specific-job =(welder, carpenter)

NOTE: Where figures are not specifically used as in domain rule 2 'good' and 'likes'
are taken to mean a score greater than 0.6. Allowing this helps with operationalising
the information obtained from the expert.

Example Domain Primitives

P_{11} = maths, computing, chemistry, english maths, french, metalwork, woodwork

P_{12} = climbing, computing, football.
P_{13} = scientific, manual, administrative, outdoor
P_{14} = computer-programmer, computer-operator, plumber, engineer, carpenter, welder,
secretary.

P_{21} = calm, aggressive, shy, nervous, rude, tidy, quiet, friendly
P_{22} = comprensible, rational, unpredicatable
P_{23} = independent, co-operative, leader, communicative, unreliable

ALTERING THE DESCRIPTION SPACE FOR FOCUSSING

J. Wielemaker
University of Amsterdam, Weesperplein 8, 1018 XA Amsterdam, Holland

A. Bundy
University of Edinburgh, Hope Park square, Edinburgh EH9 8NW, Scotland

ABSTRACT

This paper discusses improvements on the heuristic rule and concept learning technique, called focussing. Central to this technique is the description space. It is a set of trees, representing knowledge about the domain in which the concepts (or rules) to be learned are described (see figure 2-1 for an example). The heuristic information is kept in the hierarchy of these trees. Unfortunately focussing cannot learn a concept or rule with just any hierarchy. A technique called *tree hacking* is introduced to repair this flaw.
We also discuss a way to build description spaces for focussing, given the properties that are relevant and their possible values. The hierarchy is constructed by looking at a (large) set of concepts that share (parts of) their description space.

Acknowledgements

I (Jan Wielemaker) would like the thank Jim Howe, Alan Bundy and Bob Wielinga for their work done to let me visit the AI department in Edinburgh. I also would like to thank Bernard Silver for his advise, and all the others who made this visit interesting.
This research was supported by SERC grant GR/C/20826.

keywords: concept learning, rule learning, focussing, tree hacking, description space

1. INTRODUCTION

Focussing is a heuristic technique to learn concepts or rules from examples and counter examples (called *specimen*). Because there is no difference between learning rules and learning concepts only learning concepts is mentioned from now on. Focussing uses a set of trees (called *description space*), to represent its knowledge about the domain in which the concepts (or rules) to be learned are described. Each tree describes an aspect and its possible values. For example a tree might describe *tense*, with values *past*, *present* and *future* (see figure 3-1). The structure of the tree represents the heuristics for the learning process. Markers on the trees represent the state of the learning process. Focussing is discussed in more detail in section 2.

Focussing does not need to store all the specimens presented in the past. Together with its heuristic nature these are the main advantages of the technique. Unfortunately focussing also has a some serious flaws. One of them is that the hierarchy of the trees in the description space might not be suitable for learning a specific concept. In this case focussing will eventually find a contradiction in the learning process.

(Bundy 1982) and (Bundy e.a. 1984) describe a technique, called tree hacking to change the hierarchy of the trees when focussing faces a contradiction. Section 3 describes refinements on this technique and its implementation. Section 4 introduces another technique, not only to enable focussing to cope with ill structured trees, but also to build trees by examining a *set* of concepts. Suggestions for further research are presented.

2. FOCUSSING

2.1 A description of focussing

Focussing is a heuristic technique to learn concepts from specimen. It uses the *description space* to represent its heuristics and (possibly incomplete) description of the concept. This description space consists of trees representing all important aspects to decide whether a specimen is an example or a counter-example. For example the trees used to learn the concept of an arch are: *shape* tree, *support* tree, *touch-relation* tree and *orientation* tree. The state of the learning program is represented by two markers on each tree: the *upper marker* and the *lower marker*. See figure 2-1.

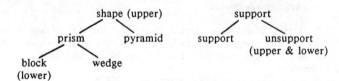

figure 2-1: Two of the trees used to learn the arch concept.

Definitions

The *current marker* in a tree is defined to be the node corresponding to the value of the property described by that tree of the specimen we are studying. A node is *under* a marker if that node belongs to the subtree whose root the marker marks (the node can be the root itself), a node is *above* a marker if it is not below that marker (note that this implies block to be above wedge, but also wedge to be above block in fig. 2-1). A specimen can be classified in three ways (Note that all specimen are uniquely classified this way):

- As an example (*yes*): All current markers are below the lower markers.
- As being out of the concept (*no*). One or more of the current markers is (are) above the upper marker.

- Undecided (*grey*). All the current markers are below the upper marker and at least one current marker is above the lower marker (otherwise it would be classified *yes*).

2.2 Learning a concept

To learn a concept we should start by presenting an example of this concept. On each tree the program puts the lower marker on the current marker and the upper marker on the root. The lower markers determine the part of the universe expected to be in the concept (the most specific view), the upper markers determine the most general view: all except what is *expected* to be out of the concept.

We now present the program a set of examples and counter examples and adjust our markers as follows:

- In case of an example:
  * If the classification is *yes*: do nothing (correctly classified).
  * If the classification is *grey*: raise the lower marker on all the trees where the current marker is above the lower marker (*grey* trees). The lower markers should be placed on the root of the smallest subtree containing the old lower marker and the current marker.
  * If the classification is *no*: contradiction, see discussion below.
- In case of a counter example:
  * If classification is *yes*: contradiction, see discussion below.
  * If classification is *grey*: On a non-empty subset of the grey trees we should lower the upper marker until it is below the current marker (classification should become *no*). If there is *one* grey tree we call the situation a *near miss*. If there are more of these grey trees we call it a *far miss*. If the counter example is a near miss the grey tree should be used to discriminate upon. Otherwise we encountered a choice point. See the discussion below for more details.
  * If classification is *no* there is nothing to be done.

Termination

The learning process is terminated if, on each tree, the upper and lower markers are in the same position (This is only true if the hierarchy of the trees is right).

2.3 Problems with focussing

- If a far miss is encountered the program cannot decide which subset of the grey trees to use to discriminate upon. Possibilities to handle this are discussed in (Bundy e.a. 1984). Under them are: setting up a search space, using a teacher, neglecting and avoiding (= adapting the training instances).
- The concept described by the markers is conjunctive. Focussing cannot cope with disjunctive concepts (Bundy e.a. 1984).
- Focussing cannot deal with noisy data.
- It is possible that the description space is not suitable for learning the concept we want to learn. There are three possible flaws:
  * A tree is not detailed enough. For example it might be necessary to refine the shape tree of figure 2-1 by splitting the concept pyramid in pyramid_4 and pyramid_3 (a pyramid with a square c.q. a triangle at the bottom).

*   The hierarchy of one or more of the description trees is wrong. (see section 3.1 for an example). In theory there are two ways to handle this situation: change the hierarchy or split the concept into a disjunction.

3. TREE HACKING

3.4 The purpose of tree hacking

Tree hacking is an extension on focussing. As stated focussing relies on a suitable set of description trees. Otherwise it will over-generalise and/or over-discriminate. See -for example- the following tree:

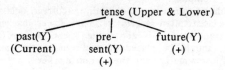

figure 3-1: The status of the tree after two positive training
instances.

Because of the two positive training instances on present(Y) and future(Y) the lower mark is lifted one level. If, at this moment, we present the program with a negative training instance with the current marker for this tree on *past* and also for all other trees below the lower marker a conflict is detected. Note that if, on another tree, the current marker is above the lower marker focussing will discriminate on that tree. This is a far miss situation that cannot be detected by the focussing algorithm.

On the other hand if the program discriminates on a tree the upper marker is lowered until an as small as possible subtree is eliminated. Nevertheless it is possible that this part is too large.

These are the two typical situations where a wrong hierarchy of one of the trees in the description space leads to a contradiction in the learning process. Tree hacking now changes the hierarchy of the tree so it becomes consistent again with the old data and the specimen that made the inconsistency visible. To do so it needs information about the status of each node with respect to the past training instances. Tree hacking splits the original tree in consistent subtrees and constructs a new tree.

3.5 When to use tree hacking

Basically the tree hacking algorithm should be called when focussing meets a contradiction, but before invoking tree hacking we need to verify that a faulty hierarchy is the cause of the contradiction. This implies we should *know* that the concept is conjunctive, there is no noise in the data and the description space is complete.

3.6 Information needed by the algorithm

To be able to hack the tree into an -for this state of the learning process-acceptable hierarchy we have to know the status of each tip-node with respect to the previous training instances. We distinguish between four classes of tip-nodes:

- *Positive* marked tip-nodes.
- *Negative* marked tip-nodes.
- *Visited* marked tip-nodes.
- Not marked tip-nodes.

During learning the process described in table 3-1 is used to mark the nodes.

specimen	classification	action
example	*yes/grey/no*	Mark all current nodes *positive*.
counter-example	*yes*	Mark current node in the tree you are going to hack *negative*.
counter-example	*grey*	Mark current node in the tree you are going to use for discrimination *negative*.
counter-example	*no*	If only one of the current nodes is above the upper marker: mark it *negative*. If there are more of these nodes mark the not marked nodes *visited*.

table 3-1: Marking of nodes to obtain necessary information for tree hacking.

The visited marks are necessary to make sure that, once correctly classified, a specimen will always be correctly classified. The only difference compared to a negative mark is that there is only an *indication* that this node should be above the upper marker, while a negative mark is a *proof* of this (provided the only flaw in the description space are unsuitable hierarchies). This implies there is no problem bringing a visited marked node below the lower marker. This is not allowed with negative marked nodes.

3.7 The algorithm

Fortunately, the hacking algorithm for the two cases in which tree hacking is useful are identical. The cases differ only in the part that detects which tree should be hacked:

Example presented, but classification gives *no*:

- Hack all trees with the current mark above the upper mark. It is advisable not to hack the whole tree, but the smallest subtree containing both the current mark and the upper mark (and thus the lower mark). This is the smallest subtree to restore consistency in the whole tree. Therefore as little as possible of the heuristics kept in the hierarchy is destroyed.

Counter-example presented, but classification gives *yes*:

- Find those trees for which the the current marker is on a not earlier marked tip-node. If there exist more of these trees then we have to deal with an analogous problem to the far miss problem during focussing: we have to choose which tree to hack. At this moment the program just takes one of these trees.
- Hack the selected tree. The smallest possible tree to hack is the subtree with as root the lower mark. In spite of this it is not advisable to hack just that subtree because the upper mark will be lowered by the hacking program to somewhere in the changed subtree, excluding the whole grey area that existed. Therefore it is better to hack the subtree with as root the upper marker.

The hack algorithm

There are many ways to hack a tree into a consistent tree. The algorithm below describes one that destroys as little as possible from the original hierarchy and grey area (e.i. conserves as much as possible from the original heuristics).

- Split the tree into the following three sets of subtrees:
  * A set of *consistent positive* subtrees. A consistent positive subtree is an as large as possible subtree of the original tree, only containing positive marked tip-nodes and not marked tip-nodes, with at least one positive marked tip-node.
  * A set of *consistent negative* subtrees. A consistent negative subtree is an as large as possible subtree, only containing negative, visited and not marked tip-nodes.
  * A set of *consistent undefined* subtrees. A consistent undefined subtree is an as large as possible subtree, only containing not marked tip-nodes.
- Rearrange the subtrees to the tree showed in figure 3-2:

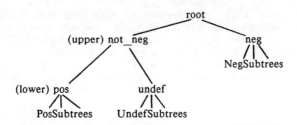

figure 3-2: Structure of the new tree

One may wonder what the purpose of the visited markers are. Their role is to make sure that a negative training instance that was once classified correct will still be classified correct after tree hacking. Without using the visited markers it is possible that a negative training instance that was once specified correct because it encountered an undefined marked tip-node above the upper marker will be classified wrong after the hacking process because the tip-node is included in the unmarked subtrees.

3.8 An example

This example is derived from Winston's arch program. I will discuss the focussing on the tree, that describes the lintel of the arch. Suppose this tree starts with a structure as in figure 3-3:

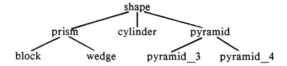

figure 3-3: Shape tree as used for testing the tree hacking algorithm.

The table below shows the given specimen, and the actions that the learning program performs (We just consider what happens to the lintel, it is assumed that the other parameters don't lead to far misses).

specimen	in concept	action.
block	yes	Put upper mark on shape, lower on block.
pyramid_4	yes	Lower mark is raised to shape.
pyramid_3	no	A contradiction is detected, the whole tree is hacked into the shape shown below.

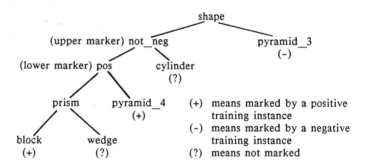

table 3-2: A worked example of the extended focussing program.

3.9 Conclusions

Tree hacking is a sufficient algorithm to enable focussing learning a concept with ill structured trees in the description space, but it does not change the existing heuristics in an optimal way.

It is likely that, if a tree is wrong shaped and used for various concepts, it will get different hierarchies in most occurrences (the *shape* tree occurs three times in the description space of *arch*). The final hierarchy also depends on the order in which the specimen are provided. We believe that it is preferable to check whether it is possible to hack the tree so that it satisfies as many occurrences as possible. This idea is discussed in more detail in the next section.

Above we briefly explained the traditional focussing algorithm. The various problems with this algorithm are pointed out and tree hacking was proposed to repair one of them. We introduced the following extensions to the existing theory.

- A new category of tip-nodes is introduced -the *visited* nodes- to ensure that once correctly classified specimen will always be correctly classified.
- Our algorithm does not destroy all of the existing grey area in a tree that has to be hacked.
- We discussed ways to preserve as much as possible of the original hierarchy.
- The possibilities, but also the limitations of tree hacking are made explicit.

4. BUILDING A DESCRIPTION SPACE

When using focussing to learn a concept there are a lot of possible ways to build and alter the hierarchy of the trees which constitute the description space. In this section we present a way to build and maintain the description trees. A tree that describes a certain property can be used to learn properties of various objects or relations in a concept and for many concepts. I will call these occurrences of the tree.

A suitable tree

If a certain concept is completely learned the upper and lower markers on each tree are on the same node (see *termination*). This divides the set of tip-nodes of each tree into two fully defined subsets (those below, and those above both markers). This division is determined *only* by the concept we are learning, and therefore it is only possible to learn a specific concept if each tree has a node that establishes the right partition. Apart from this it is unimportant (It only affects the effectiveness of the heuristics) what the structure of the subtree below this node is and how the rest of the tree is structured.

An ideal tree

An ideal tree is a tree whose hierarchy is most likely to be suitable for learning the concept we want to learn. One thing is sure: you cannot build the ideal shaped tree by looking at just one occurrence of the tree. The reason for this is that all suitable trees (see above) are as ideal as each other as long as you are just concerned with this one occurrence. This means that you should a) have more information about the properties used in the tree and/or b) use information from other (earlier) learned concepts.

Here the second possibility is examined. An obvious solution is to build a tree that satisfies an as large as possible subset of the occurrences. We will call this tree the *consensus* tree. If the set of occurrences is representative for the universe of occurrences of this tree it is most likely to be suitable for learning an *arbitrary* concept. This does not mean it is ideal for a particular concept, but without additional information we cannot do better.

4.10 Computing the consensus tree

The main problem in this approach is computing the tree that fits for as many as possible occurrences. The formalisation of this problem is given below:

given:

- A set of properties F.
- A set of occurrences C. Each occurrence $C(i)$ has two sets connected to them: $Cmax(i)$ (the disjunction of the positive and undefined marked properties), and $Cmin(i)$ (the positive properties).

For example take the tree of table 3-2. Here F would be {block, wedge, pyramid_4, cylinder, pyramid-3, Cmin would be {block, pyramid_4} and Cmax {block, wedge, pyramid_4, cylinder}.

to compute: a tree T that satisfies the condition below.

- For as many as possible occurrences $C(i)$ there exits a subtree S. The set of tip-nodes of S is a superset of $Cmin(i)$, and a subset of $Cmax(i)$.

Of course this algorithm should have an acceptable order: generating all tree and selecting the best is not a solution in a practical sense of view.

A heuristic approach

While learning the concepts the sets $Cmax(i) \backslash Cmin(i)$ (the grey area) will gradually disappear. This means that if we can solve the problem stated below we have a heuristic solution, that will get closer to the ideal solution as the grey areas get smaller.

To compute in a reasonable order a tree T that satisfies the condition below.

- For as many as possible concepts $C(i)$ there exist a subtree S. The set of tip-nodes of S is $Cmin(i)$. After constructing this tree try (in a heuristic way) to include the remaining concepts by using the grey areas.

The first part of the problem is well defined and solvable in order N cubed (N is the number of occurrences involved). Adapting the construction if only one subset $Cmin(i)$ changes can be even more efficient. So far no attention has been paid to the heuristic part of this algorithm but it should be possible to write an acceptable and fast algorithm for this.

4.11 A criterion for the existence of one consensus tree

Lemma 1

Given a set of property-sets Cmin. There is a tree, so that for every $Cmin(i)$ there is a subtree with a set of properties equal to $Cmin(i)$ if and only if for every $Cmin(i)$, $Cmin(j)$ one of the following statements is true:

- Cmin(i) and Cmin(j) are disjoint.
- Cmin(i) is a subset of Cmin(j).
- Cmin(j) is a subset of Cmin(i).

Proof:

If this criterion is met it is possible to build the tree with the algorithm given below. This proves existence.

If this criterion is not met there exist two sets Cmin(i) and Cmin(j) with a nonempty intersection $I(i,j)$. The elements of $I(i,j)$ have to be in two subtrees: the subtree with root $S(i)$ for Cmin(i) and the subtree with root $S(j)$ for Cmin(j). The subtree with root $S(i)$ has a tip-node set Cmin(i). The elements of $Cmin(j)\backslash I(i,j)$ should be outside this subtree, but in the subtree of $S(j)$. Thus $S(j)$ is not a node in the subtree of $S(i)$. In the same way $S(i)$ is not a node in the subtree of $S(j)$. Because $S(i)$ and $S(j)$ are both in the tree there must be a loop (root - $S(i)$ - "element of $I(i,j)$" - $S(j)$ - root). Contradiction.

4.12 The algorithm

Given the set of properties F and a set of Cmin sets of which we know they satisfy lemma 1, we can compute the consensus tree using the algorithm below.

Let the tree be represented as:

    tree ::= tree(<node name>,
               [list of properties in the subtree of the node],
               [list of subtrees])

- Initialise the tree as tree(<root>,F,[]).

Now we start building the tree by concerning the Cmin sets one at a time.

- If Cmin = F we are finished as such a subtree already exists. Note that F cannot be a subset of Cmin.

To fit a Cmin into a tree we concern the relation between Cmin and the property sets Ps(i) of the subtrees directly connected to the root.

- If there is an i, so that Cmin is a subset of Ps(i) (Because of Lemma 1 there is at most one such i) call the fit_in algorithm recursively with Cmin and the subtree belonging to Ps(i).
- Whenever we reach this points there are two classes of Ps(i)'s: one class that are subsets of Cmin, and on that are disjoint to Cmin. Therefore we construct a new node with property set Cmin, and attach those subtrees with Ps(i) being a subset of Cmin to it. Now we attach our new node together with the subtrees with Ps(i) being disjoint to Cmin to the root.

4.13 Splitting the occurrences

To use the algorithm above we should first determine the maximum set of Cmin's that can be together in one tree.

- Build a graph. The vertices are the Cmin sets. If two sets do not meet lemma 1 they should be connected by an arc.
- Do until there are no arcs left in the graph:
    * Eliminate the vertex with most arcs connected to it. If there are two or more vertices with an equal number of arcs remove an arbitrary member of this set.

The remaining set of vertices is the largest non conflicting set of Cmin sets.

4.14 Experiment

On the basis of this theory a Prolog program was build to learn simultaneously a set of concepts. As mentioned no attention has been paid to the heuristic part of constructing the trees so far.

The program handles incoming specimen using focussing. If a contradiction is detected in the focussing process the program looks for trees to be altered in the same way as the tree hacking extension described in section 3. Then all occurrences of this tree are considered and a new set of trees is created. There are many other ways to use this description space building algorithm in focussing. For a further discussion see section 4.7.

Because of limited time no real life testing environment, but a set of nine abstract concepts, sharing a description tree with ten properties was used to test the idea. The concepts where designed to need three different trees.

The program was tested by presenting it 90 specimens in a random order, but so that for a specific concept the first one always is an example (necessary for focussing). To reconstruct the three trees from one tree in which all properties were directly attached to the root it needed to change the description space 17 times.

4.15 Further research

We discussed an algorithm that uses information of other occurrences of the same tree to build a hierarchy for description trees. The presented algorithm needs further research on the following aspects:

- What is the optimal heuristic algorithm to maximise the number of occurrences of the tree for which one common hierarchy fits? Solving this problem will especially improve the behaviour of the algorithm on partially learned concepts.
- How should the tree changing algorithm interact with the focussing program. Some possibilities are:
    * Change all occurrences of the tree after every specimen.
    * Change all occurrences of the tree if a contradiction occurs in the focusing process (the solution I choose).
    * If a contradiction in the learning process occurs look to see if it is possible to use another tree of this set. If not then change all occurrences.

* Change part of the occurrences in one of the above situations.
- In what sense can the information stored from other concepts help to provide heuristics for choice points in the learning process (far misses, choosing between one of the alternative options described above etc.)

5. SUMMARY

We presented a technique -called tree hacking- to enable focussing learning concepts while the hierarchy of one or more of the description trees is wrong. Ways to select those trees whose hierarchies should be changed are discussed.   An algorithm that restores the consistency of the tree but changes as little as possible of its hierarchy is presented.

Section 5 starts a discussion about how to build an optimal hierarchy for description trees.   The basic idea of this section is that the optimal hierarchy is the hierarchy that is most likely to be suitable to learn a new -arbitrary- concept. If other occurrences of the same tree is the only information available this tree is the tree that is suitable for as many as possible of these other occurrences.   An outline of a concept learning program based on this idea is presented, together with suggestions for further research.

6. REFERENCES

Bundy, A. (1982).   *Changing a description space by tree hacking*, D.A.I. Note 106, 26 march 1982
Bundy, A. & Silver, B. & Plummer, D. (1984).   *An analytical comparison of some rule learning programs*, D.A.I Research Paper No. 215.
Mitchell, T.M. (1978). *Version Spaces: An approach to concept learning*. PhD thesis, Stanford University, 1978.
Winston, P. (1975).   *Learning structural descriptions from examples*, in Winston P.H. (editor), The psychology of computer vision, McGraw Hill.

DEEP KNOWLEDGE REPRESENTATION TECHNIQUES

Anthony G Cohn
Department of Computer Science
University of Warwick
Coventry CV4 7AL
UK
Net address: agc%warwick.uucp

Abstract. It has been recognised that most of todays expert
systems, successful though they may be, are based on "shallow
knowledge". They do not possess any "deep knowledge" of their
domain which would allow them to reason from first principles.
Such an ability would provide many advantages such as greater
flexibility in their problem solving ability and the
possibility of better explanations. This paper briefly
discusses some of the issues and problems in representing and
using deep knowledge and describes some techniques to help
overcome some of the problems. In particular an introduction
to many sorted logic is given and its advantages in this
respect explained.

Introduction

It has been recognised that most of todays expert systems,
successful though they may be, are based on "shallow knowledge". They do
not possess any "deep knowledge" of their domain which would allow them to
reason from first principles. Such an ability would provide many
advantages such as greater flexibility in their problem solving ability
and the possibility of better explanations.

This paper discusses some of the issues and problems in
representing and using deep knowledge and describes some techniques to
help overcome some of the problems. In particular an introduction to many
sorted logic is given and its advantages briefly explained. This paper is
an expanded version of a position paper given at a recent Alvey workshop
on deep knowledge.

The structure of the rest of the paper is as follows. First we
discuss what we mean by deep knowledge and outline some problems with
building and using deep knowledge based systems. Then follows an
introduction to many sorted logic. Finally the ways in which many sorted
logic can help with the problems discussed in the first section are
described. The paper is deliberately informal; precise definitions of the
logics discussed can be found in the references.

What is Deep Knowledge?

An obvious question is what exactly do we mean by a deep
knowledge based system? It is not the purpose of this paper to discuss
this point at length. Indeed a panel discussion at an Alvey workshop on
the subject failed to reach a unanimous definition of the term. We will
content ourselves here with indicating the sort of systems with which we
are concerned in fairly general terms.

Although systems such as Mycin, (Buchanan & Shortliffe 1984), display a highly competent problem solving behaviour, the knowledge with which they operate, although extensive, is surface knowledge in the sense that the rules tend to be heuristic problem solving rules of thumb which take observed data such as patient symptoms and lab tests as input and infer results such as diagnoses without any real (or deep) understanding of the physiological or other causal mechanisms which support the conclusions. Such a lack of understanding not only limits explanations to be either canned text or traces of the firing sequence of shallow rules, but also tends to limit the range and nature of problems the system is able to solve. For example the Mycin knowledge base was found to be totally inadequate for use as a tutoring system (Clancey & Letsinger 1981). An extended example of a problem which would not be solvable by a shallow knowledge expert system is discussed in (Davis 1982). Davis argues for explicit causal models which represent the structure and function of the domain objects and processes which will thus render the underlying knowledge accessible and open to a variety of uses.

Research which might be viewed as tackling some aspect of deep knowledge includes the work on envisioning (de Kleer & Brown 1982) on qualitative process theory (Forbus 1983), on naive physics (Hayes 1979, 1983), and on causal reasoning in medical expert systems (Gotts & Hunter 1985).

Deep Knowledge Representation: Some Problems

In this section we discuss some of the problems of building and using deep knowledge based systems. Perhaps the biggest problem is what might be described as the conceptualisation problem. Given a domain, in what terms should it be described? For some domains (electrical circuits might be an example) the appropriate ontology might already exist in textbooks but this is not always the case, particularly for those domains whose experts seem to practice "black magic" and indeed for most "common sense" type reasoning. Many domains require a deep representation for notions such as space and time and although there has been some progress, eg (McDermott 1980, 1982; Marr & Nishihara 1975; Allen 1981), fully adequate conceptualisations seem to be *very* difficult to produce. This is perhaps the hardest problem of those we shall mention and one to which we do not offer a solution. The only work which really begins to address this problem with an attempt at automation are the concept discovery systems of Lenat (Davis & Lenat 1982; Lenat 1982).

A second problem is one discussed by Hayes in his Naive Physics Manifesto (Hayes 1979), namely that of trying to ensure a "high fidelity" axiomatisation. The problem is that a given formalisation may have a much simpler model than that intended. (Incidentally, this also shows how important it is for a representation language to have a proper semantics as is argued by Hayes (1977) and McDermott (1978) since we cannot even talk about the simplest model of a description unless the representation language has a well defined semantics). Hayes (1977) and McDermott (1976) point out that just because a concept has been given an appropriate name does not mean that its meaning has been captured by axioms in the formalisation. The fidelity of an axiomatisation might be measured by the closeness of its simplest model to the intended interpretation. He points out that a high fidelity axiomatisation is likely to be dense in the sense that the ratio of facts to concepts will be high in order that the concepts are "tied down". (For those who feel more at home with frames, this is equivalent to saying that frames should have a lot of slots). Although not a sufficient condition to guarantee a "high fidelity" axiomatisation, he suggests that ensuring that the representation language has certain features and that these are used will help in this respect. One such feature is that representation language should have special facilities for handling taxonomic knowledge. At the very least this means the presence of an isa-hierarchy but considerably more power can be derived if the arguments to predicates (slots in a frame, arcs in a semantic network) and functions symbols are tied into the type hierarchy. A logic with such features is known as a many sorted logic and will be discussed further below.

A third and related problem is that of ensuring a consistent knowledge base. It can be a non trivial problem to determine that a given set of axioms has a model at all, particularly in the case of very large knowledge bases. The problem is especially hard since any system with the expressive power of first order predicate calculus (and surely we need at least this amount of expressiveness) is only semi-decidable: there is no decision procedure to compute whether an axiomatisation is satisfiable. The problem is closely related to ensuring data base integrity. Within the AI paradigm there has been relatively little work specifically addressed to this issue. Davis (1982) built Teiresias to help with the maintenance of large rule based programs by using notions such as rule models and type checking to check new rules for sensibleness. The work on reason maintenance (eg Doyle (1979)) is clearly also of help in this context.

A final problem we will mention here is the problem of actually "running" a deep knowledge based system. If a system is reasoning from first principles this is likely to result in very long inference chains compared to a shallow knowledge system. The search space is thus likely to be very large indeed which is likely to cause considerable problems. In his naive physics work, Hayes does not even wish to consider the implementation issues, though he admits that this problem will exist and will clearly require sophisticated meta level control information to constrain the operation of the deduction engine to useful lines of inference.

These problems are all real as is evidenced by many articles in the literature. For example, Cunningham (1985) reports his experiences in building naive physics axiomatisations and found it very difficult to know what models if any his axioms had. He tried to alleviate these problems by building a model finding program.

An Introduction to Many Sorted Logic

In a many sorted logic the individuals in the intended universe of discourse are divided into different sorts and the sorts of the arguments of all the non-logical symbols in the language and the sorts of the results of function symbols are specified. Inference rules can be devised for such a logic so that many inferences which are obviously 'pointless' (to the human observer) can easily be detected to be such by the system because functions or predicates are being applied to arguments of inappropriate sorts. From the semantics view point the descriptions of the sortal behaviour of the non logical symbols restrict their possible interpretations. Sortal information can thus be viewed as a form of meta-knowledge.

Many sorted logics thus provide an simple syntactic way of specifying semantic information. Several mechanised many sorted logics have been proposed or built: eg (Reiter 1981; McSkimin & Minker 1977;

Walther 1983; Weyhrauch 1978; de Champeaux 1978; and Frisch et al 1982).
Unfortunately most of these lack a sound theoretical foundation -
Walther's logic is an exception.
    A fairly simple, conventional many sorted logic such as
Walther's can be described (informally) as follows. A set of sorts S must
be specified and can be partially ordered according to the subset
relationship of the subsets of the universe they are intended to denote. A
sort always denotes a non empty set, so not every monadic predicate is
necessarily a sort. An n-tuple of sorts is associated with every n place
predicate symbol describing the allowable sorts of its arguments (eg
<HUMAN,HUMAN> might be associated with the predicate PARENT) and a n+1-
tuple is associated with every n place function symbol to describe the
sorts of its arguments and its result (eg <NATURALNUMBER,HUMAN> might be
associated with the function symbol ageof). Constant symbols obviously
have a single sort associated with them.
    A well sorted formula is one where the sort of every term
matches the sort of its argument position. Matches usually means "is a
subsort of" (this includes the identity case). Some mechanism for
associating a sort with variables must also exist, typically either by
global type declarations for each variable or some naming convention or by
subscripting each quantifier. Thus nonsense formulae such as
PARENT[fred,42] and PARENT[fred,ageof[fred]] and other much more
complicated examples can be easily detected since they are not well
sorted.
    Many varieties of many sorted logic are possible. Perhaps the
simplest is a variety of logic known simply as restricted quantification
which differs from a standard logic only in that a sort structure is given
and quantifiers are subscripted with the sort over which they quantify.
However even this simple machinery can give computational benefits as is
shown in Frisch (1985).
    Sorts in a logic are rather akin to types in conventional
programming languages and problems often found in strongly typed
programming languages may also occur in many sorted logics. In particular
the typing/sorting mechanism often reduces the expressive power of the
language: it is not long before a Pascal programmer becomes frustrated by
the impossibility of writing general purpose library procedures because
procedures may not be polymorphic.
    If we are building large and sophisticated axiomatisations
such as to be found in Hayes (1978) it is clearly important that the
knowledge representation language does not arbitrarily restrict the
expressive power available to the knowledge engineer.
    The many sorted logic LLAMA (Cohn 1983a, 1983b) is a
particularly expressive many sorted logic. It is an extension of the logic
sketched in (Hayes 1971) and used in (Hayes 1978). It is possible to
specify very detailed sortal information about the non-logical symbols
which can then be used by the inference rules to reduce the search space.
By "particularly expressive" we do not mean that there are new concepts
expressible which were not expressible before (as would be the case when
we say that predicate calculus is more expressive than the propositional
calculus) but that it is easier to express (some) concepts (as is the case
when we say that a high level language is more expressive than machine
code and full first order predicate calculus is more expressive than
clausal form). It is worth noting that there appears to be a
expressiveness / efficiency tradeoff in mechanised inference systems. As
the language becomes more restricted (full first order logic, clausal
form, Horn clauses) so inference becomes more efficient. The success of
Prolog (Clocksin & Mellish 1981) may owe much to having found a useful

point in this tradeoff scale. (A problem with Prolog is that it is not
complete; as Cohen (1980) points out, completeness is not just of
theoretical interest, since very simple theorems are often not provable if
a system is not complete. A further problem is that most implementations
are not sound either since they omit the `occurs in' check during
unification).

LLAMA is unusual in that the quantifiers are unsorted; the
restriction on the range of a quantified variable derives from the
argument positions of the function and predicate symbols that it occupies;
associated with every non-logical symbol is a sorting function which
describes how its sort varies with the sorts of its inputs; polymorphic
functions and predicates are thus easily expressible and statements
usually requiring several assertions may be compactly expressed by a
single assertion. The sort structure may be an arbitrary lattice.
Increased expressiveness is obtained by allowing the sort of a term to be
a more general sort than the sort of the argument position it occupies.
Furthermore, by allowing three boolean sorts (representing `true', `false'
and `either true or false'), it is sometimes possible to detect that a
formula is contradictory or tautologous without resort to general
inference rules. Inference rules for a resolution based system have been
developed which are both sound and complete.

LLAMA allows axiomatisations to be much smaller than even a
conventional many sorted logic as is shown in (Cohn 1985). The table
below summarises the results of axiomatising a particular problem in three
different logics.

	Unsorted logic	Walther's logic	LLAMA
No. of clauses initially	27	12	3
No. of literals initially	65	16	9
No. of possible inferences initially	102	12	7
Length of proof	33	10	5

Some statistics concerning the axiomatisation
of Schubert's Steamroller in various logics.

As can be seen the LLAMA axiomatisation is not only smaller in terms of
the number of axioms and their size but also results in a shorter proof
and a smaller search space. The complexity of the proof system is of
course increased as are the run time overheads of maintaining the sort
information but these costs are polynomial in the number of sorts (which
is fixed) and the maximum size of a formula, whereas additional axioms
incur a greater overhead since the search space is typically exponential
in the number of axioms. The LLAMA axiomatisation is smaller because of
its polymorphism and because of the use it makes of the three boolean
sorts which allow it to determine the truth value of some formulae or
subformulae without resort to normal inference. For example the statement
"birds like to eat caterpillars but not snails" can be expressed using

sorting functions rather than axioms and subsequently statements such as
E[tweety,crawly] and E[tweety,slowcoach] can be evaluated directly as
being true and false respectively without resort to normal inference. (E
is intended to represent the "likes to eat" relation and tweety, crawly
and slowcoach are constants of sort bird, caterpillar and snail
respectively).

Many Sorted Logic as a Deep Knowledge Representation Language

What use is a many sorted logic as a representation language
for "deep knowledge" bases? The benefits are several. Firstly the search
space of a problem formulated in many sorted logic is likely to be much
smaller than otherwise it would be. There are two main reasons for this.
(a) no further inference will be done on ill sorted formulae, (b)
axiomatisations will be smaller either because fewer axioms are required
or because axioms themselves are smaller. Axioms may be smaller because
sortal preconditions do not need to be explicitly stated. Fewer axioms
may be required because the axioms which describe the sort structure and
which describe the sortal behaviour of the non logical symbols are
absorbed into the inference machinery and thus not needed. (The situation
may be compared to special purpose inference rules for equality such as
paramodulation which dispense with the need for axioms defining equality).
Since reasoning from first principles is likely to involve long inference
chains and huge search spaces, any help in this respect is clearly very
welcome. Of course many sorted logic is no total solution to this problem,
the search space problem will still exist in a non trivial form for any
sizeable problem but the boundary of difficulty will be pushed back.
        Of course if the problem has little or no sortal structure
then the benefits will be negligible; for example a standard theorem
proving problem in group theory may well gain little from an
axiomatisation in many sorted logic and will still have a large search
space. However "real world" problems are typically very structured, there
are many different kinds (sorts) of objects in the world and most
predicates only make sense of a few of them.
        Secondly, the well sortedness check, and in the case of LLAMA,
the ability to assign a formula in to one of four categories (ill sorted,
definitely true, definitely false, either true or false) can be used as an
integrity checking mechanism for formulae as they are added to a knowledge
base. Any ground atom which is inconsistent purely by virtue of sortal
information can be detected as such by the well sortedness calculation.
This is clearly a valuable aid in maintaining the consistency of a
knowledge base although of course it does not guarantee it.
        Thirdly, many sorted logic is a convenient notational tool
since sortal preconditions can be omitted. Many researchers use many
sorted logics for this reason, for example Hayes in his naive physics
axiomatisations (Hayes 1978), McDermott in his temporal logic (McDermott
1982) and Forbus in his work on Qualitative Process Theory (Forbus 1983).
        Using a many sorted logic is also, like using a typed
programming language, good mental hygene: it forces one to think about the
problem being axiomatised and its structure more deeply than perhaps
otherwise one might.
        The use of a many sorted logic will help with the fidelity
problem discussed earlier because of the structure it imposes on the
axiomatisation and the restrictions imposed on the interpretations of the
non-logical symbols reduces the number of possible models. Of course a
similar effect might have been achieved by adding additional axioms and

literals to an unsorted logic but at the very least a many sorted logic should explicitly encourage such information to be given.

Final Remarks

We have concentrated on logic as a knowledge representation language here for reasons of personal preference of the author. However many of the notions of many sorted logic will clearly translate into other formalisms.

Many knowledge representation schemes recognise the value of factoring out taxonomic reasoning and representation and dealing with it specially for reasons of economy. Much of the work in semantic nets and special purpose reasoning methods in frame systems is concerned with this sort of inference. However many of these languages are less expressive than logic, particularly in respect of the quantificational apparatus and thus the translation from many sorted logic is not always easy or possible. For example polymorphism does not easily carry across to a typical frame system.

This paper is intended to provide a brief informal introduction to many sorted logic and some of its advantages particularly in respect of building, maintaining and using sophisticated and complicated knowledge bases. Of course these tasks are still difficult even if many sorted logic is to be used, but a little less so.

Acknowledgements
This research reported here was partly supported by an SRC studentship and partly by an SERC grant (GR/C/65148).
I am particularly indebted to Pat Hayes for many helpful conversations. I would also like to acknowledge the useful discussions I have had with many colleagues including Jon Cunningham, Alan Frisch, Christoph Walther and Bob Welham.

References

J F Allen, `A General Model of Action and Time,' TR 97, University of Rochester (1981).

B Buchanan and E Shortliffe, Rule Based Expert Systems, Addison Wesley (1984).

D de Champeaux, `A Theorem Prover Dating a Semantic Network,' in Proc AISB/GI Conf on AI, Hamburg (1978).

W J Clancey and R Letsinger, `Neomycin: Reconfiguring a Rule Based Expert System for Application to Teaching,' IJCAI 7, (1981).

W Clocksin and C Mellish, Programming in Prolog, Springer Verlag (1981).

D Cohen, `Knowledge Based Theorem Proving and Learning,' CS-80-115 Thesis, CMU (1980).

A G Cohn, `Mechanising a Particularly Expressive Many Sorted Logic,' PhD Thesis, University of Essex (1983).

A G Cohn, `Improving the Expressiveness of Many Sorted Logic,' in Proc AAAI, Washington DC (1983).

A G Cohn, `On the Solution of Schubert's Steamroller in Many Sorted Logic,' Proc IJCAI 9, (1985).

J Cunningham, Phd Thesis, University of Essex (1985).

R Davis and D Lenat, Knowledge Based Systems in Artificial Intelligence,
          McGraw Hill (1982).
R Davis, `Expert Systems: where are we? and where do we go from here?,'
          AI Memo No. 665, MIT (1982).
J Doyle, `A Truth maintenance system,' Artificial Intelligence Vol.
          12 pp. 231-272 (1979).
K Forbus, `Qualitative Process Theory,' in Qualitative Reasoning about
          Physical Systems, ed. D Bobrow, North Holland (1984).
A Frisch, J F Allen, and M Giuliano, An Overview of the HORNE Logic
          Programming System, University of Rochester (1982).
A Frisch, `Parsing with Restricted Quantification,' Proc AISB, (1985).
N M Gotts and J R W Hunter, knowledge in Medical Artificial Intelligence""
          `Using "Deep" knowledge in Medical Artificial Intelligence,'
          Proc Alvey Workshop on Deep knowledge, (1985).
P J Hayes, `A Logic of Actions,' in Machine Intelligence 6, Edinburgh
          University Press (1971).
P J Hayes, `In Defence of Logic,' in Proc. IJCAI 5,   (1977).
P J Hayes, Ontology of liquids, University of Essex (1978).
P J Hayes, `The naive physics manifesto,' in Expert Systems in the Micro
          Electronic Age, ed. D Michie, Edinburgh University Press
          (1979).
P J Hayes, `The second naive physics manifesto,' Cognitive Science
          technical report URCS-10, University of Rochester (1983).
J de Kleer and J S Brown, `Foundations of Envisioning,' in Proc. AAAI,
          (1982).
D B Lenat, `Heuretics: Theoretical and Experimental Study of Heuristic
          Rules,' in Proc. AAAI,   (1982).
D Marr and H K Nishihara, `Spatial disposition of axes in a generalised
          cylinder representation of objects that do not encompass the
          viewer,' memo 341, MIT (Dec 1975).
D McDermott, `Artificial Intelligence Meets Natural Stupidity,' SIGART
          Vol. 57(1976).
D McDermott, `Tarskian semantics, or no notation without denotation,'
          Cognitive science Vol. 2(1978).
D McDermott, `A Theory of Metric Spatial Inference,' in Proc. AAAI,
          (1980).
D McDermott, `A Temporal Logic for Reasoning about Processes and Plans,'
          Cognitive Science Vol. 6(1982).
J R McSkimin and J Minker, `The Use of a Semantic Network in a Deductive
          Question Answering System,' in Proc IJCAI 5, Cambridge
          (1977).
R Reiter, `On the Integrity of Typed First Order Data Bases,' in
          Advances in Data Base Theory, Volume 1, ed. H Gallaire,
          J Minker, J M Nicolas, Plenum Press (1981).
C Walther, `A Many Sorted Calculus Based on Resolution and
          Paramodulation,' in IJCAI 8, Karlsruhe (1983).
R Weyhrauch, Lecture Notes for a Summer-School, Istituto di Elaborazione
          dell'Informazione, Pisa (1978).

AN APPLICATION OF KNOWLEDGE BASED TECHNIQUES TO VLSI DESIGN

Hilary J. Kahn
Dept. of Computer Science
University of Manchester, Manchester, M13 9PL, England

N. P. Filer
Dept. of Computer Science
University of Manchester, Manchester, M13 9PL, England

ABSTRACT

The complexity of the task facing designers of Very Large Scale Integrated (VLSI) systems is universally accepted. Current Computer Aided Design (CAD) tools, however, are unable to provide the degree of assistance and assurance that such designers require. This paper describes a knowledge based approach to CAD system design which it is hoped will be one way of providing the urgently required improvements in CAD software. The work described includes an expert system shell which, although written in Prolog, permits access to procedural applications software and wider system functions. This shell has been used to produce an expert system exemplar which, even in its prototype form, shows promising results.

INTRODUCTION

It is now universally accepted that sophisticated Computer Aided Design (CAD) systems are of central importance in assisting hardware and system designers to meet the challenges offered by the complexity of VLSI chips. This paper describes a knowledge based approach being adopted to help meet these challenges.

Previous CAD systems produced within the Department of Computer Science have been used by engineers involved in producing large computer systems implemented using printed circuit boards (PCBs), wirewrap and gate arrays. These systems were produced by very small teams and the experience gained has significantly influenced the approach outlined here. In particular, systems such as the GUARDSMAN system [Kahn & Loyns 1984] were structured around well-defined data sources such as a Component Library which held all the component information needed by the application programs and a Design Model which stored the designs as defined by the engineers. Some of the software was data-driven so that developing a program to handle a new technology was mainly a process of redefining configuration and technology data. In other cases, significant software modification or development was necessary.

One of the well-known problems with CAD systems is that they rarely perform at a level comparable with that of an experienced human designer. The result is that automatic design processes are usually supplemented by interactive processes which permit the designer to complete the current task manually. While this approach has proved acceptable in an era of medium and large scale integration, the complexity of VLSI designs is such that it is quite unrealistic to contemplate manual design completion in the future. An important trend, therefore, in current CAD research is to explore the applicability of knowledge based techniques to hardware system design so that some human expertise in solving design problems may be encapsulated within CAD systems.

One of the main aims of the current system under development is to further formalise the separation of application procedures from technology control rules and design semantics. The intention is to produce a CAD system which will be adaptable over a wide range of technologies and will contain the design semantics necessary to support a full range of application processes using hardware accelerators, standard procedural approaches and knowledge based techniques as appropriate. Figure 1 illustrates the general structure of the system.

Figure 1: General Structure of the CAD System

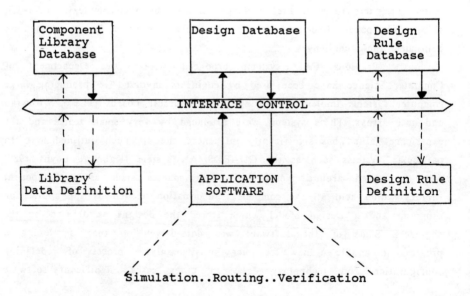

Simulation..Routing..Verification

There are three main data stores, the Library, the Design database and the Technology Design Rule database. A formal interface structure is defined between application processes and these data stores to ensure system flexibility and extensibility. The result is a system fully integrated at the task level. The intention is that, where appropriate, application processes should be formal expert systems able either to guide the designer or to act on his behalf in performing the particular design task. In order to investigate the viability of this approach and to assist in identifying the classes of semantic data needed within the system, one of these expert application assistants has been designed and implemented; the application area concerns the interconnection of devices on a board or chip.

EXPERT SYSTEMS AND CAD

There are several examples of knowledge based systems used as aids in computer design. The EL system [Sussman & Steele 1977] reasons about circuit parameters by symbolically propagating known electrical constraints through a circuit. The SOPHIE system [Brown et al 1974] aids in fault diagnosis by experimenting with a simulated model of a circuit. The R1 system [McDermott 1980 a,b] now known as XCON, is used to configure VAX computers.

WEAVER [Joobani & Siewiorek 1985] is a knowledge based routing system for VLSI circuits. It consists of a number of cooperating experts using a blackboard structure to control sharing of information. This blackboard structure is based on that used in HEARSAY II [Erman et al 1980] and HEARSAY III [Balzer et al 1980]. Another proposed system concerned with device interconnection is BLOREC [Joseph 1985] which attempts blockage recovery when one connection is blocked by another. Fujita and Goto [1983] describe a system to aid in the manual completion of an uncommitted logic array layout; this system appears to reduce design completion time satisfactorily. Antognetti et al [1984] describe a chip layout assembler which is under development as part of an expert chip planning system.

CHOICE OF AREA TO EXAMINE

The problem area concerning the interconnection (routing) of devices was selected for the work described here because it is an area which current CAD systems deal with either by relying on manual completion by the designer or achieve automatically only by imposing significant constraints on the design. It is a particularly interesting area to consider because there are numerous factors which affect the success of the routing process. Note that the term <u>board</u> is used in the following discussion to mean both PCB and semi- and full-custom chip.

Relevant factors affecting the success of routing include the type of the routing algorithm being used, the order in which sets of points (nets) are interconnected and the ordering of the points within each net, the density of the layout at the time each net is considered, the positioning of devices relative to each other and hence the implied functionality of areas of the board, the board structure, etc. These are factors which the experienced human designer seems to balance successfully using, *inter alia,* a combination of his awareness of the functionality and semantics of the design, the topologies of routing patterns which are applicable under differing circumstances and his visual skills in identifying areas of actual or potential blockage. This ability is most noticeable when observing a designer manually completing a layout which automatic CAD software has failed to route in full.

ROUTING AND ROUTING ALGORITHMS

Devices to be interconnected lie on a plane and may be interconnected using one or more routing *layers*. Where inter-layer connections are required, *vias* (plated through holes on PCBs or contact cuts on chips) must be used. Vias tend to be expensive in their use of board or chip area and may have other electrical effects which affect the performance of the design. When routing chips, 100% completion of the interconnections is obviously essential; however, even when handling PCBs, completion of routing is important as handwires are expensive both to put on and to maintain.

There are a large number of different procedures for routing. These differ in the types of interconnection that they can achieve, the information they hold about the board topology and in the methods they use. Lee's Algorithm [Lee 1961] and its many derivatives is essentially a maze-running technique which, in its purest form, guarantees to find a path between two points if such a path exists. It is usually slow and expensive in its use of store and its use tends to be ill-advised in the early stages of routing a design. Line routers [Aramaki 1971; Heyns <u>et al</u> 1980] search for an interconnection using relatively simple horizontal/vertical line segments.

Channel routers do a two-stage routing; initially routes are tentatively assigned to routing channels, subsequently detailed route assignment within the channels is performed. These routers tend to be most useful where the layout is highly regular, as on gate arrays. Other routers are suited to the interconnection of particular types of structure. River routers, for example, are used for the interconnection of bus structures or other single-layer connections. Interconnection on full-custom chips is ideally achieved without any routing at all; where possible devices (cells) are abutted. If the cell geometries do not align, it is often worthwhile to stretch one or both of the cells to achieve abutment. This obviously affects the characteristics of the cells and may therefore not be possible if the design functionality is to be maintained.

SUPPORT FOR A KNOWLEDGE BASED APPLICATION

As stated earlier, the complete CAD system being developed (Figure 1) has three major sources of design and technology data, the Library, the Design database and the Design Rule database all of which are accessed via a common interface. Applications may be procedural or may make use of expert knowledge. This expert knowledge is specific to the application but information may be shared between tasks via the data stores. These data stores and the common interface therefore provide the same functionality as the blackboard structure of WEAVER and HEARSAY in addition to providing facilities for more orthodox applications.

In its current form the Design database holds minimal semantic information about the design, but its structure permits the inclusion of such data as the requirements for semantic information become better understood. It supports multiple views of the design data so as to present specialist applications with a well-structured definition of a design.

The Library holds information about all aspects of the components or cells used in a design. This information encompasses logical, structural, schematic, behavioural, functional and physical component details and multiple representations may be included where necessary.

The Design Rule database provides the technology adaptability within the system as it is used by other processes to configure themselves to suit a particular technology. The support software for the Design Rule database is largely written in Prolog and the subsystem allows designers to specify technology rules in a structured and readable manner. Technology data will be passed to applications either in the form of numeric or string data and formulae or, where a knowledge based application is being used, in the form of rules.

There is no intention in this system to abandon completely the use of procedural applications where appropriate; on the contrary, it is felt that software written in Pascal or other procedural languages or even hardware accelerators are a vital part of the system. These application processes must, however, be accessible from a knowledge based environment. An expert system shell, written in Prolog, has therefore been developed to support the knowledge based subsystems. This shell has facilities for communicating between separate tasks and also permits expert rules to include calls to algorithms written in Prolog or Pascal and other procedural languages.

The design task involves searching a very large search space. This problem is solved in R1 by using a set of expert modules which are applied sequentially with no feedback between modules. This forwards progression without feedback allows R1 to limit the possibilities it considers to those options selected by the preceding module. Backtracking within a module is permitted to allow the best possible answer to be derived at each stage. In the system described here, limited feedback between modules is permitted to support re-design when satisfactory results are not obtained initially. The use of feedback is controlled by the designer under guidance from the knowledge based systems. Using feedback requires that the system store alternative solutions, reasons for making decisions and reasons for electing to follow a feedback loop.

SUMMARY OF SHELL FEATURES

Rules within the expert system shell may be encoded in pseudo-English (using a convention suggested by Steele [1981]), Prolog or as functional routines in other languages such as Pascal or Fortran. Because system commands and the compilers for languages are themselves functional routines, these too can be used directly by rules. This facility is particularly well supported on the current host machine MU6G [Edwards et al 1980] running under the MUSS [Theaker & Frank 1979] operating system but will also be incorporated in the version of the CAD software currently being transferred to a UNIX environment.

The shell uses initial data to select an hypothesis to prove using a forward-chaining or data-driven method. Having selected an hypothesis, it tries to prove its validity using backwards chaining. In order to control focus of attention and task ordering, each rule has an associated context within which it is applicable. Rules about the applicability and ordering of contexts may be stated and these ordering rules are used to control the staging of tasks to be analysed. The flexibility of this method allows knowledge to be shared between tasks as needed and can be used to offer the designer considerable overall system control if required. This feature is particularly useful during prototype system development.

Reasoning with uncertain information is supported using redundancy, default values and inference. Probability values are used to specify how true or false the system believes each assertion to be. The use of these probability values and their manipulation is based on the approach used in MYCIN [Shortliffe 1976].

User application processes are controlled using inter-process message passing which is well supported on MUSS. Currently, these processes are all software (eg a router and a net editor both written in Pascal), but linking to hardware accelerators can be achieved in the same way.

Relatively simple user interface handling is supported at present. The system can give HOW and WHY explanations by outputting rules in which variables are replaced by data values. It is intended to add the ability to give WHY NOT, WHAT IF and WHEN explanations as well.

EXAMPLE SYSTEM - NET ORDER PROCESSOR (NOP)

The example system NOP takes as input a design which is ready to be routed i.e a design that is functionally complete, and assists the designer by carrying out the following tasks:

Net ordering: Both before routing and during routing it is necessary to order the nets to be routed. Prior to routing, this ordering will consider factors such as the likely interference between nets; during routing, additional factors must be considered to take account of routing space currently used, the board density and the types of route being handled.

Point Ordering: The order in which points within each net are connected is a significant factor in determining the type of net topology created. The point ordering also affects the number of connections successfully completed. Technology design rules may affect point ordering as certain net topologies are electrically unsatisfactory for particular technologies.

Router selection: The system selects the type of router to use, applying criteria such as the generality of the router, the types of topology that it can support and its speed and controllability.

Result Monitoring: After routing, it is necessary to determine whether each connection was completed. This information is used to update the system's knowledge about the track density in various regions of the board and whether the required net topology has been created within the design rule constraints. NOP can then reorder other nets and points within nets to take account of this information.

Route Failure Diagnosis: If the selected router fails to complete a connection, it is necessary to analyse why this happened. NOP can suggest reasons for not routing a connection and may indicate how the connection can be completed.

Knowledge needed by NOP

In order to perform these tasks NOP needs knowledge about the design and its environment. The information of this type required is summarised in Figure 2. Much of the data is available from the design database, the library and the design rule database; router details are held in an application-specific knowledge base. In addition, net ordering rules are enhanced with knowledge acquired in discussion with designers, from experience with applying routers to real design problems and by analysis of design sessions.

Figure 2: Examples of types of knowledge required

Board Details   - size, layer count and usage,
                  board type (PCB, CMOS chip,etc)

Layout Details - Region usage, routing space,
                 component slots, edge connector
                 space

Design details - Component types, nets and their
                 current completion state

Technology   - Design rules, manufacturing
                 method

Router details - Type, facilities, algorithm

NOP uses meta-rules to select the type of information required for processing a particular design. These meta-rules are additional to the focus of attention control method and specify which subjects should be examined.

Subjects currently examined

Currently NOP examines the following topics in order:

Board and technology characteristics: This information, held mainly by the design system, is queried for each fact required. If the information is not available in the design system, the user is consulted.

Figure 3: Classes of routing tree

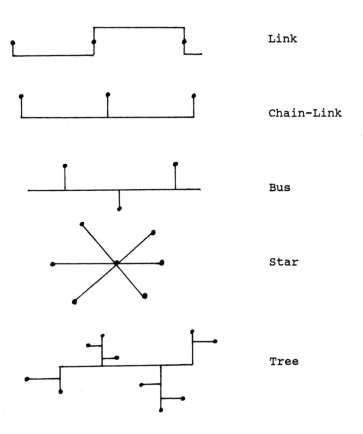

Link

Chain-Link

Bus

Star

Tree

Topology class selection: The net topology class specifies the type of tree that is to be created for the current net under consideration. Figure 3 illustrates the classes of tree supported.

   Link: This allows simple point-to-point connection without any
             sharing of track with other connections using the same points.
   Chain-link: Point-to-point connections with limited track sharing.
   Bus: Two selected points are routed; intermediate points are then
             connected to the main route.
   Star: A source point is connected to each termination point in turn
             with no track sharing.
   Tree: Any generalised tree is permitted.

Point Identification: A set of connection points for each net is derived. This may involve considering the facilities of the router to be used to make the connection. For most topologies start and finish points for a net are selected using criteria such as:

   (i) Is the point a driver point?
   (ii) Is the point a termination point?
   (iii) Is the point an edge connector point?
   (iv) Is the point a long way from others in the net?

Once start and finish points have been identified, the points are ordered according to the selected topology.

Point Ordering: An initial connection ordering is derived for each net. The main criterion used is the estimated degree of interference between point-to-point connections. For example, long connections, connections in the centre of the board and connections which form part of a large net tend to have high interference values. Interference values are obtained using heuristic methods. Initially, connections with low interference values are routed early and those with medium levels of estimated interference are routed later; connections with high interference factors are stored separately and are explicitly considered before regions they use become too densely packed.

Router selection and routing: Router selection is based on suitability of the router to achieve the required connection. NOP controls access to the router and activates the selected routing process as required.

Knowledge updating: After routing, NOP notes whether the connection was successfully achieved and records how many track segments and vias were used, whether the connection conforms to technology design rules and what effect there is on routing space in affected regions of the board. This information is then used to re-order the connections, if necessary, to connect those points likely to become blocked if not processed soon. It is in this monitoring section that decisions are taken about when it is necessary to go back to modify previously completed tasks. Typically, a small adjustment to component positioning is made or the nets may be re-processed.

Route failure diagnosis: This task is activated when NOP fails to complete a connection. Its purpose is to try to discover why the failure occurred and to attempt to specify how NOP can have its performance improved so that this type of connection does not fail in the future.

Examples of NOP rules

As stated earlier, the majority of the rules within NOP use a pseudo-English convention. The form of the knowledge base rules is illustrated in Figure 4. Names beginning with an upper case letter are variables given values at run time, names beginning with lower case letters are either predicates (relations) or atoms (values).

The 'if' form is used for representing rules; the left hand part of the 'if' is the hypothesis, the right hand part is a set of conditions which, if proved, cause the hypothesis itself to be proved. The 'is-fact' form is used to state

Figure 4: NOP Rule Formats

```
X if Y and Z
X if Y or Z
X is-fact
X is askable-when Y
X expect Y
X item-of Y
```

that a piece of knowledge is known to the system. NOP only asks questions of the CAD system data stores or the user if the knowledge base states explicitly that it can ask the question; the 'is-askable-when' is used to state that the knowledge of the left hand side is obtainable by asking if the right hand side conditions (if any) are met. The 'expect' form is used to tell the system the type and range of values to expect on asking a question. The 'item-of' form is used to control the system when asking for a number of facts. Examples of some of these rule forms are given in Figure 5 and in the topology selection example which follows.

Figure 5: NOP rule examples

```
net X termination-points N is-askable when not-variable X.
net X termination-points TP expect
        number (0, obtain(N, total-points N)).
net X total-points 3 is-fact
net X termination-point P item-of net X termination-
        points TP
```

Topology selection example

This example illustrates some of the rules for determining the topology type to be used when routing a particular net. The cut at the end of the first and last rules indicates that if either of these rules fires, then there are no alternative topologies which may be used for the net in question.

In each topology rule, the variable X is the name of the net; this is checked using the 'not-variable' predicate on X to ensure that the name has been given a value. A stub is a 'side branch' of a net which involves the introduction of a new track junction other than one of the original points; the stub length is the length of the side branch. In certain technologies, the stub length must be severely constrained to avoid undesirable electrical effects in the net. Termination points are net points of a particular type, often resistors of some kind, and driver points are signal source points such as the outputs of logic gates.

Rule ordering is simply a matter of taking each rule in turn until no more rules are available; the last rule is therefore a 'catch all' case. The topology types represented by each of these rules are shown in Figure 3.

```
net X topology link if
        not-variable X and
            net X total-points 2 and cut
```

```
net X topology link if
    not-variable X and
        net X termination-points T and
        T less-than 2 and
            net X max-stub-length 0

net X topology chain-link if
    not-variable X and
        net X max-stub-length L and
        L greater-than 0 and
            net X termination-points 1

net X topology bus if
    not-variable X and
        net X max-stub-length L and
        L greater-than 0 and
            net X termination-points 2 and
            net X driver-points DP and
            DP greater-than 1

net X topology star if
    not-variable X and
        net X termination-points T and
        T greater-than 1 and
        net X driver-points 1

net X topology tree if
    not-variable X and cut
```

CONCLUSIONS

In its present state, the expert system shell is operational and has permitted the development of the Net Ordering example. Links to procedural modules are proving very successful and are used to permit access to a standard router written in Pascal. In addition, the human-computer interface aspects of the NOP system have been improved by the ability to call GKS as a functional module from within NOP. This has meant that the results of attempting to route a connection can, optionally, be displayed to the designer.

The NOP system itself performs net topology selection, point ordering within a net and controls a router. Currently only one router is available, so router selection is not yet implemented. Monitoring of router results and route failure diagnosis within the system are currently being investigated. Implementation on MU6G uses a very inefficient version of Prolog, so development and run times are unacceptably slow; transfer of the system to a UNIX environment including a more efficient Prolog is expected to improve performance considerably. Despite its incomplete state, the NOP system is producing satisfactory results when tested on example designs and it has been used experimentally to improve the routing of both a gate array and a PCB.

The knowledge based software is being developed in parallel with the CAD system itself and is proving to be a useful source of information about the kinds of semantic data that the data stores of the CAD system must support. Much work obviously remains to be done on completing NOP and developing further knowledge based applications within the framework of the CAD system; in particular, attention must be paid to improving the user interface of the system both in permitting the user to 'converse' with the expert assistant and in taking advantage of the sophisticated interactive techniques designers expect to use with workstations.

REFERENCES

Antognetti, P., de Gloria, A., Repetto, L. and Allena, F. (1984) "An Expert Chip Planning Tool" IEE Conf. on Electronic Design Automation (EDA84) 174-178

Aramaki, I. (1971) "Automation of Etching Pattern Layout" CACM 14 no. 11 720-730

Balzer, R., Erman, L.D., London, P. and Williams, C. (1980) "HEARSAY-III: A Domain-independent Framework for Expert Systems "Proc. 1st Conf. American Association for Artificial Intelligence 108-110

Brown, J.S., Burton, R.R. and Bell, A.G. (1974) "SOPHIE: A Sophisticated Instructional Environment for Teaching Electronics Troubleshooting" BBN Report 2790 Bolt, Beranek and Newman, Cambridge, Mass.

Edwards, D.B.G., Knowles, A.E. and Woods, J.V. (1980) "MU6G: A New Design to achieve Mainframe Performance from a Mini-sized Computer" Proc. 7th Annual Symp. on Computer Architecture 161-167

Erman, L.D., Hayes-Roth, F., Lesser, V. and Reddy, D. (1980) "HEARSAY-II: Speech Understanding System:Integrating Knowledge to Resolve Uncertainty" Computing Surveys 12 no.2 213-253

Fujita, T and Goto S. (1983) "A Rule-based Routing System" Proc. Int. Conf. on Computer Design: VLSI in Computers 451-454

Heyns, W., Sansen, W. and Beke, H. (1980) "A Line-expansion Algorithm for the General Routing Problem with a Guaranteed Solution" Proc. 17th ACM/IEEE Design Automation Conf. 243-249

Joobani, R. and Siewiorek, D.P. (1985) "WEAVER: A Knowledge-Based Routing Expert" Proc. 22nd ACM/IEEE Design Automation Conf. 266-272

Joseph, R.L. (1985) "An Expert Systems Approach to Completing Partially Routed Printed Circuit Boards" Proc. 22nd ACM/IEEE Design Automation Conf. 523-528

Kahn, H.J. and Loyns, A. (1984) "A Step towards Technology Independence in CAD Software" Proc. IEE Colloquium on Design Software

Lee, C.Y. (1961) "An Algorithm for Path Connection and its Applications" Trans. Elec. Comp. Vol. EC-10 346-365

McDermott, J. (1980a) "R1: A Rule Based Configurer of Computer Systems"
Tech. Report CMU-CS-80-119 Dept. of Computer Science,
Carnegie - Mellon University, Pittsburgh, Pa.

McDermott, J. (1980b) "R1: An Expert in the Computer Systems Domain"
Proc. 1st Conf. American Association for Artificial Intelligence
269-271

Shortliffe, E.H. (1976) "Computer Based Medical Consultation: MYCIN"
New York: American Elsevier

Steele, B.D. (1981) "EXPERT-The Implementation of data-independent Expert
Systems with Quasi-Natural Language Information Input"
M.Sc. Thesis, London; Dept. of Computing, Imperial College

Sussman, G.J. and Steele Jr., G.L. (1977) "Electrical design: A Problem for
Artificial Intelligence Research" Proc. 5th International
Joint Conference on Artificial Intelligence 894-900

Theaker, C.J. and Frank, G.R. (1979) "MUSS- A Portable Operating System"
Software Practice and Experience 9 633-643

WHERE'S THE EXPERTISE?: EXPERT SYSTEMS AS A MEDIUM OF KNOWLEDGE TRANSFER.*

H.M.Collins
Science Studies Centre

R.H.Green
School of Management

R.C.Draper
School of Physics

University of Bath, Bath BA2 7AY, Avon, England

Abstract: Expert systems can be looked upon as a medium for transferring knowledge between an expert and a naive end-user; by consulting an expert system an end user ought to be able to accomplish new tasks. One of the most important features of expert systems might be that they can transfer more than media such as the written word or the diagram. Some knowledge engineers approach the design of expert systems as though they could compete with face-to-face communication as a means of transferring skills. This, however, is not the case.

Three existing models of skill transfer are examined and the role of 'tacit' or cultural knowledge is explained. The importance of tacit knowledge is frequently overlooked. It is shown how this concept helps to explain the developmental potential of expert systems. Finally, the importance of the concept of tacit knowledge for knowledge elicitation is explained, drawing on experience of an expert system for crystal growers built at Bath. Participation in the relevant skill is important if knowledge engineers are to avoid mistakes.

INTRODUCTION

At the university of Bath we have built a small expert system for growing semi-conductor crystals. This is written in micro-prolog and APES. The system is to be used in the physics department, but part of the purpose of building it was to explore wider questions to do with the potential of expert systems as replacements for skilled persons. In particular, we wanted to look at the extent to which expert systems could capture those aspects of skill frequently referred to as 'tacit knowledge'. This paper explains some of the social science ideas which underlie the project and illustrates them through our crystal

*Research supported by ESRC grant No. CO8 25 0002

growing and other experience. The paper argues that the concept of tacit knowledge makes it possible to see where the development of expert systems is going and how it will get there. Also, it demonstrates one of the implications of tacit knowledge for knowledge elicitation.

The purpose of an expert system is to enable an 'unskilled' end-user to do things that previously only an expert could do. The expert system stands between the expert and the end-user; it is a vessel into which the expert pours knowledge and from which the end user takes knowledge. To get straight into the metaphors, this knowledge is like chicken soup with dumplings, and the expert system is like a collander; with all known expert systems, the dumplings get transferred but the soup is lost. The dumplings are the readily explicable facets of knowledge such as factual information and articulateable heuristics, whereas the soup is the context/meaning of the facts and the non-articulated but 'taken for granted' practices and 'ways of going on' in practical and theoretical settings. I will refer to the soup as 'tacit knowledge'.

Most expert system designers are worried about the size of the holes in the collander. One might describe a lot of current research as being directed toward making the holes ever smaller so that eventually the whole broth can be transferred without loss. But social scientists know that nearly all interaction between human beings involves the recipient of knowledge supplying most of the soup. That is why current expert systems, and other instances of human-machine interaction, work. The collanders are full of enormous holes, but the end users provide so much soup that the dumplings are all that are needed to complete the meal.

Completely closing the holes in the collander is a distant, and hardly foreseeable goal. It is a matter of research in the wider field of AI, in philosophy and in many aspects of different sciences; it is not a matter of a bit more knowledge engineering. But knowledge engineers do not need to worry about the defects in their systems in terms of this distant goal. They can continue to build systems with equanimity accepting that the end users will provide much of what the system cannot. Once we are clear about the way these things work we will know better how to use the fifth and subsequent generations of knowledgeable machines, and there will be fewer surprises, less disillusion, and not so many still-born and oversold projects. My aim in the rest of this paper is firstly to describe how humans provide the soup, and secondly, to explain the consequences of this for aspects of the problem of knowledge elicitation.

SUPPLYING TACIT KNOWLEDGE: THREE MODELS

In the 1960's Harold Garfinkel (1967), a Professor at UCLA, provided students with an experimental counselling service. The service was free, but questions had to be asked of the counsellor in such a way that simple Yes/No answers would be adequate. The students presented the questions and received the replies without actually seeing the counsellor. Many of the students were able to make sense of the question and answer sessions, and felt that they had recieved some counselling. The counsellor could have been a rudimentary expert system with a poor output repertoire but as a matter of fact, the counsellor comprised a list of random numbers keyed to the yes/no answers (see also Oldman and Ducker,1985). In this case the end users provided the whole meal, not only all the chicken soup, but also the [imaginary] dumplings.

Humans are so good at providing interpretation and meaning to data that we can even make sense of information that isn't there! In the light of Garfinkel's experiment the 'successes' of Weizenbaum's Eliza are hardly surprising, nor is the interactive sufficiency of other simple computer programmes. Humans are so accustomed to constructing what counts as sense out of the rudimentary signals that comprise conversation with other humans in a familiar cultural context, that they can easily construct sense out of the output of a machine. It is not always the same sense as was intended by the conversational partner, or programmer (Suchman, 1985), but that is another story.

In the 'counsellor' example we saw the end user inserting not only the interpretation, but also making up some imaginary information to fit it. Suppose the counsellor is thought of as an expert system. Then, if one pictures the expert system situated between expert and end user thus,

EXPERT ---- EXPERT SYSTEM ---- END USER

one might say that all the knowledge was inserted at the right hand end.

This, of course is rather an extreme model of knowledge 'transfer' and exaggerates the role that the end user plays. The opposite case is represented in the following study where end users were able to provide so little 'soup', that they were unable to make any use of even copious quantities of information.

In the early 1970's Collins (1974, 1985) found that scientists who wanted to build Transversely Excited Atmospheric pressure lasers (TEA-lasers) did not succeed if they used only written sources of information even when the authors tried their best to make certain that the documents contained every relevant fact and heuristic. What is more, these scientists were unable to build the laser even after they had engaged in prolonged conversation with 'middlemen' who knew a great deal about the devices, but had not yet built one themselves. Even where a scientist had prolonged contact with a successful laser builder this would not guarantee success; such prolonged contact was a necessary but not a sufficient condition for knowledge transfer. One might say of this case that it was impossible to find a collander with small enough holes to transfer the knowledge. The end user, if he [they were all men] was to succeed in building a laser from a set of instructions, had first to become a full blown expert himself. This he could only do by serving something close to an apprenticeship with an existing expert. Those who did not possess the skills themselves could not act as satisfactory masters to apprentices.

In this example of knowledge transfer, all the knowledge was inserted in at the left hand end, and since we have no collanders without holes, it could not be transferred by any kind of intermediate vessel including unpractised human beings.

The model of communication which arises out of this study of laser builders is again an extreme. It occurs because the skill in question is very new. This means that end users, try as they might, have insufficient experience to provide the interpretations of the information that would allow it to make sense. Fortunatly, the areas of expertise which knowledge engineers are trying to model are not like this. They are much more familiar, and therefore we can rely on the end user providing far more. A third, in-between, model of knowledge transfer, which represents this state of affairs is well known. (Though it has probably not often been analysed in terms of the extent to which the end user inserts knowledge.)

The third model occurs when we do manage to use a written list of instructions in order to accomplish some task that we were otherwise incapable of doing. The use of a recipe is a good example. I have a recipe for Port Wine Souffle. Since I have no face to face communication with the author of the cookery book I cannot learn skills from her after the manner of an apprentice, nevertheless, at the end of the day, the recipe will enable me to make the souffle. This is because of what I, as an end user, bring to the interaction.

For example, the recipe contains the following instruction: 'Beat the egg whites until stiff and then fold in.' To manage this I have first to contribute my knowledge of what all the words mean and this includes knowing that 'a white' is not white but is transparent – at least until it is beaten when it becomes white. I must know how to get the white from the egg by cracking it and seperating it from the yolk and the other bits which may well be white – (the membrane inside the shell and perhaps the shell itself). I must then know how to beat the egg and with what to beat it. If I am not an experienced cook I probably won't succeed in making the whites 'stiff' since unless you know what to expect one might appear to beat for an awfully long time without making much appreciable difference. When one starts to beat eggs it seems most unlikely that they will ever be so stiff that the bowl can be turned upside down without them falling out, but that is what stiff means. Then I have to know the special meaning of 'fold' in the context of cooking. In short, I will have to be a fairly accomplished cook at the outset to be able to make use of this instruction. How did I become so accomplished? The answer is 'through apprenticeship'. The tacit knowledge involved in cooking a souffle has not been transferred via the written recipe but via face to face contact – in this case, with my mother.

In the first model of knowledge 'transfer' the expert tranferred nothing to the end user, so no intermediate vessel was involved (even though the end user did not realise that this was the case.) In the second model of knowledge transfer, the expert and the end user shared little or nothing and that is why no medium of knowledge transfer could work. (The only medium that could work, would be the elusive 'collander without holes'.) Fortunatly, it is the third model which represents the typical situation for the knowledge engineer. Once the nature this typical relationship is grasped, the relative difficulty involved in building expert systems to fulfil various tasks is easily understood. It becomes clear, that systems largely filled with information should be easy to build provided they are used by end users who know how to interpret the information. It is also clear, that the more expert the end user, the easier it will be to build a system that will be useful. Thus, the immediate value of expert systems, and of AI in general, is not to replace skilled persons – there is no immediate prospect of this – but to act as aids to increase the productivity of skilled persons, and perhaps replace the relatively unskilled. But, in making use of this prediction, the word 'skilled' has to be interpreted in a very exact way. Skilled means just that – it does not mean knowledgeable. The plumber is in less danger than the accountant; the general practitioner is in less danger that the medical specialist.

TACIT KNOWLEDGE AND KNOWLEDGE ELICITATION

Failure to understand the nature of the soup of tacit knowledge can lead to a mistake about that part of the knowledge engineer's job known as knowledge elicitation. The mistake is to think that if knowledge elicitation tools and techniques are sufficiently refined, and if enough time and diligence are dedicated to the task, the whole of an expert's knowledge can be elicited. This is untrue; one cannot elicit that which no-one knows that they know – that which they cannot articulate.

For example, in the laser case it eventually became clear that one of the reasons unskilled laser builders were unable to make their 1972 models of the TEA-laser work was because the leads running from their capacitors to the electrodes were too long. These leads, it turned out, had to be to less than eight inches in length. At the time nobody knew this – or more properly, nobody knew that they knew this. Successful laser builders happened to make their lasers that way – without knowing why –, but novice builders, working from circuit diagrams, would have no idea of the importance of lead length. Now, novice builders who learned their craft from an accomplished master would be likely to make the leads the appropriate length because they would be likely to copy many of the 'irrelevant' features of their master's craft; they would thus build a device with similarly short leads without giving the matter any conscious thought. Neither expert nor successful apprentice need consciously know anything about the importance of the length of the leads in order to pass on the skill and neither would, or indeed could, report this feature of the device to even the most persistent knowledge engineer. One might say that this feature was known only tacitly to the laser builders; it comprised part of their non-articulateable laser building skill. Such features of the background 'soup', of course, may eventually turn into 'dumplings' of information as the science develops - as it did in this case.

There are three morals to be drawn from this story. The first of these is that the crucial division in knowledge is not the seperation between information and heuristics, as most work on knowledge elicitation has stressed (Welbank, 1983, Buchanan et al, 1983, Breuker and Weilinga, 1983/4) but between the articulateable and the tacit. It is this division that ensures that knowledge engineers must rely on end users' abilities, not on refinements in knowledge elicitation techniques. The second point which follows directly, is that one should not set about building an expert system without a clear model of the end user for whom it is intended. A lot of time and uneccesary effort will be wasted if every knowledge engineering project takes its aim to be the encapsulation of 'all' the expertise pertaining to an area. The third point is that it is far easier to prepare a system for a skilled user than for an unskilled user. As the art develops we may expect to see successive 'generations' of expert systems catering for wider bands of users with less specialised skills. The machines built now should be designed as 'end user dependent', and future generations will be less end user dependent. However, the pace of these developments depends not only upon advances in knowledge engineering and generalised AI (natural language interfaces, pattern recognition and so forth) but also upon the state of the sciences upon which the skills in question are founded. The laser example makes this clear: a putative expert system built in 1972 as a laser builder's aid could not possibly have contained information about lead length however clever the knowledge engineering, however persistent the knowledge elicitation and however advanced the state of AI. This development awaited the advance of the underlying science. The consolation is that not all inadequacies in expert systems can be blamed on inadequacies in knowledge engineering.

THE FORMAL KNOWLEDGE ILLUSION

A less general *caveat* for knowledge engineers arises out of the fact that we are rarely generally aware of the extent to which our knowledge is tacit and skill-laden. Even though tacit knowledge itself is widely distributed, the model of knowledge that is almost universally believed is a formal text-book model. This makes the 'seam' between formal, theoretical, information and accomplished skills hard to see, and even where an expert knows that the skills he has are essentially practical he will tend to think of this as a *defect* rather than an accomplishment. Where a source of, what is taken to be, 'equivalent' book knowledge is available it may be presented by the expert as a more 'perfect' representation of the area in question. This can lead experts, quite unwittingly, to offer formal book-knowledge in the same way as, or instead of, their practical accomplishments, thus misleading the knowledge engineer.

The problem arose in our crystal growing project. This was deliberatly set up so that the knowledge engineer (second author) would have no first hand knowledge of crystal growing; he had never set foot in the laboratory, but he had read a thick book on crystal growing techniques. The first author was undergoing an apprenticeship in crystal growing at the same time as observing and recording the knowledge engineer's interaction with the expert (third author). What soon became clear was that the knowledge engineer's questioning of the expert, *and the experts replies* were for the most part cast in terms of the systematic framework for crystal growing presented in the text book; the many text book techniques and variations, laid out in an abstract schema, were giving shape to the outline plan for the completed system.

After a number of sessions of this type, it was pointed out that the actual experience available to the expert was of just two or three very simple and inexpensive techniques that were regularly used in the physics department of the university whereas nearly all the interaction that had taken place to date amounted to the expert telling the knowledge engineer his own interpretation of the the same book that the knowledge engineer was already reading. This was done in all innocence; the expert was simply unaware that his book knowledge was of a qualitatively different type to his practical experience. Without some first hand experience of the limited range of techniques available in the physics laboratory it would have been impossible to know when real experience ended and when the schematic outline of idealised practice took over; this applied to knowledge engineer and expert alike. The possibilities and dangers of knowledge engineers writing systems based on knowledge that is not experientially based are evident. Anyone but the most experienced end users would be likely to find systems prepared in this way both disappointing and misleading.

One final illustration reaffirms the same point: In one of the the well understood methods in regular use in the Bath physics laboratory, a crystal is grown in a sealed ampoule made of glass or quartz. The constituent elements of the crystal are heated in the ampoule until they melt and then the whole assembly is cooled gradually over a period of, perhaps, two weeks. One crucial variable, included within the expert system we have built, is the pressure of the reactants as they reach melting point; this determines the suitability of the method and the required strength of the ampoule. Our expert would decide on the pressure by referring to the 'vapour pressure' of each constituent element. All the first versions of our system contained, therefore, some rule relating these vapour pressures to ampoule strength - itself a function of size and wall thickness. In early versions, which contained no data base, the system was interactive and asked the user 'what is the vapour pressure of the reaction involving "CRYSTAL X" ?'.

All of this seemed reasonable both to us and to the expert and one version impressed everyone by relating the answer to the question concerning pressure to ampoule burst-strength using exact figures from a table supplied by the glass manufacturers. In interaction with this prototype system, users, when asked the pressure question, explained that they did not know the answer exactly but they would take a guess at it. The guess would be entered, and the system would eventually produce its impressively exact answer for ampoule size and wall thickness.

Only after substantial thought about the experience of crystal growing did we realise that the whole issue of vapour pressure was erroneous. In fact, the crucial variable is not the vapour pressure of the elemental constituents but the actual pressure, in grams per unit area, within the ampoule. This depends only partly on the vapour pressure of the elements. It depends also on the ratio of the size of the ampoule to the quantities of the different elements and on the rate at which the mixture is heated and on the way it is heated. For instance, if a very small amount of volatile element is included in the mixture it will make little contribution to the net pressure inside the ampoule. What is more, if the mixture is heated very slowly, so that the volatile elements have chance to combine into less volatile compounds before they are fully vapourised, then the maximum pressure reached need not be excessive. Finally, one experimenter in the laboratory had invented a technique where part of the ampoule was kept cool to allow volatile elements to condense while the less volatile were melted. Again this allowed the volatile elements to combine gradually without reaching their full pressure potential. The complexity of the combination of factors which determine the maximum pressure within an ampoule means that the actual pressure reached in any crystal-growing run is simply never known. It was not that experts had approximate, or probabilistic, knowledge but that the pressure was variable from run to run; it was simply not useful to think about pressure in quantitative terms. Nevertheless, when discussing the method of growing crystals in ampoules, and when interacting with the expert system, the experts were unaware of the innapropriateness of this quantitative information.

In fact, a high vapour pressure in an element indicates little more than that care must be taken, and this translates in practice into using a pretty thick walled small ampoule and heating things slowly. If the ampoule still explodes after those precautions have been taken, then some other method such as keeping part of the ampoule cool, or using solution growth (in which the volatile elements are dissolved rather than melted) must be used. Successful choice of container was a matter of 'having a feel for the materials' and making a good guess at the size of ampoule required.

The moral of this story is that not even the experts were consciously aware of the fact that they could not use quantitative data. Though they knew that they did not in fact use it, they thought of this as an inadequacy on their part. They did not use the 'glass blowers rules' for the strength of ampoules (which had been laboriously encoded into the system) but they felt that they could have used them if they were less lazy and if the rules had not already 'entered the folklore of the department'. Their conscious model of their own activity was, in other words, an approximation to the text book model and since that part of the expert system dealing with pressure and strength seemed to come closer to the text book model than their own practice, they felt it to be an improvement rather than a mistake – at least, at first sight. Thus, the knowledge engineer would not be likely to obtain criticism of this system even from the expert, and naive end users would experience the problem as an inadequacy in their quantitative knowledge; this could lead them in the wrong direction. The only way for the knowledge engineer to spot the discrepancy between the model and practice, would be for the engineer to spend a period of apprenticeship on the task himself.

CONCLUSION

So long as human knowledge is thought of as being fully exhausted by information and heuristics many of the general features of the development of expert systems, and some particular features of the process of knowledge elicitation, will remain puzzling. The promise and development of expert systems can be much better understood once it is realised that limits are set by the fact that substantial components of knowledge are not articulateable; humans have ways of using components of knowledge without knowing how they use them or even *that* they use them. Advance in expert systems, then, is tied to the pace of advances in the foundational sciences that underpin the skills in question, and it is tied to much more general work in AI, philosophy, psychology and modern sociology of knowledge.

Tacit knowledge also has implications for knowledge elicitation within the current state of the art. One implication arises out of the invisibity of the 'seam' between formal knowledge and skilled accomplishments, our lack of awareness of our own skills, and our frequently misplaced respect for theory-like representations of what we believe we know. The only solution to the problem demands that the knowledge engineer must do more than tap the knowledge of the expert at one remove but must undertake at least a short apprenticeship – a period of participant observation – as part of the elicitation process.

REFERENCES CITED

Breuker J. and Wielinga B. (1983,4) 'Analysis Techniques for Knowledge
    Based Systems and Techniques for Knowledge Elicitation and
    Analysis' Reports on Esprit Project 12 on 'The Acquisition
    of Expertise' University of Amsterdam.
Buchanan, B. et al (1983) 'Constructing an Expert System' Chapter 5 in
    Building Expert Systems, Hayes-Roth, F., Waterman D. and
    Lenat,D. Reading, Mass:Addison-Wesley
Collins H.M. (1974) 'The TEA-Set: Tacit Knowledge and Scientific
    Networks', *Science Studies*, 4, 165–86
Collins H.M. (1985) *Changing Order: Replication and Induction in
    Scientific Practice*, Sage:Beverley Hills and London
Garfinkel H. (1967) *Studies in Ethnomethodology* Prentice Hall:New Jersey
Oldman D. and Ducker C. (1985) 'The Non-reproducibility of Ethno-
    Methods', in Gilbert G.N. and Heath C. (eds.) *Social Action
    and Artificial Intelligence*, Aldershot:Gower Press.
Suchman L. (1985) 'Plans and Situated Actions: The problem of human-
    machine communication', Thesis, Xerox PARC, Corporate
    Accession P85-00005.
Welbank M. (1983) 'A Review of Knowledge Acquisition Techniques for
    Expert Systems' Martlesham Consultancy Services, Ipswich.